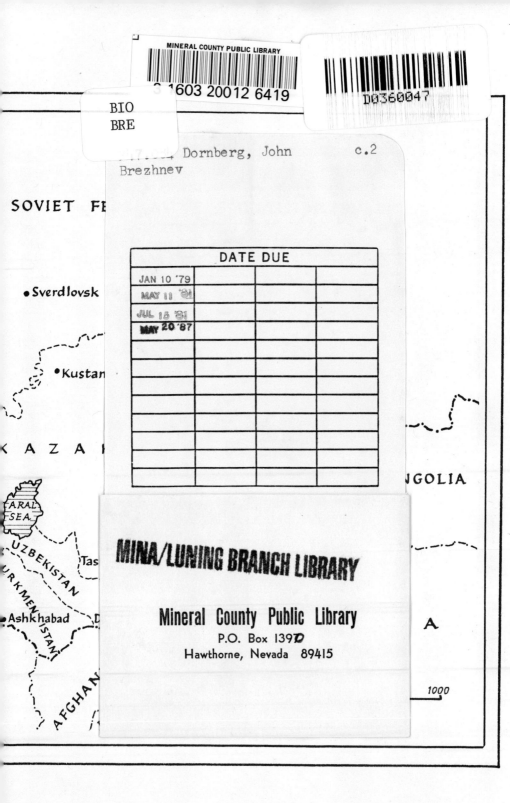

Dornberg, John   c.2
Brezhnev

SOVIET FE

• Sverdlovsk

• Kustan

K A Z A

ARAL
SEA

UZBEKISTAN
Tas
URKMEN
Ashkhabad D
STAN
AFGHAN

NGOLIA

A

1000

BREZHNEV

BREZHNEV

The Masks of Power

JOHN DORNBERG

Basic Books, Inc., Publishers

NEW YORK

Contents

6 CONTENTS

PART FIVE   POWER IN THE KREMLIN

PART SIX   OF CULTS AND PERSONALITIES

Illustrations

7

Preface

The dilemma one faces in writing a book such as this has been so eloquently stated by Mark Frankland in the preface to his excellent biography of Nikita Khrushchev, that I can do no better than repeat it here.

"A biography of a living, if not actually still ruling statesman must necessarily be a tentative affair. But when the biography is of a living Soviet figure, then it must be very tentative indeed. This is mainly so because most of the material that biographies are usually based on is simply unavailable."

More than that, the available materials are of such scantiness and of such dubious veracity and reliability that one often despairs of using them at all. Moreover, the information they contain is frequently contradictory.

Thus, some Soviet reference works state that Leonid Brezhnev served in the Soviet Army, after graduating from Kamenskoye's metallurgical institute. Other, more recent Soviet sources omit this and assert that he went right to work in the local steel mill. Why? The biographer is inclined to suspect that there is something to hide. That is a suspicion that recurred frequently as I studied the Soviet materials on which much of this book is based.

The biographer of Khrushchev has at least one advantage. Khrushchev was by nature garrulous and spoke frequently about his past. Perhaps he prevaricated, perhaps he exaggerated, perhaps he embellished the facts with descriptive color. But he did talk and he did tell the world something about his youth and early career.

Leonid Brezhnev, except for his lengthy, formal speeches is a silent man. To update Churchill: he remains largely a riddle wrapped in a mystery inside a clam. To date he has given but two interviews about his personal life: to *L'Humanité*, the official organ of the French Communist Party, and to West Germany's *Der Stern*. It is even impossible, for example, to determine with certainty when he married or when his children were born.

9

I state this not so much in apology but to underscore the equivocation and the qualifications that are so often expressed by me in the narrative itself. Of necessity one must frequently conjecture.

That is why I am particularly indebted to those many sources and institutes who gave so willingly of their time and provided so much information, without which this book could never have been written.

I am especially grateful to Mr Nathan Kruglak of Milwaukee, Wisconsin and his brother Professor Haym Kruglak of Kalamazoo, Michigan for their descriptions of early Kamenskoye; to Mr Christian Duevel of Munich for his constant advice and kremlinological observations; to Professor Oleg Pidhainy of Auburn University, Professor Emanuel Turczynski of Bochum University; and Professor Nicholas Nagy-Talavera of California State University at Chico for their helpful hints in locating additional sources and materials. I would like to thank my predecessor in Moscow, Mr Robert Korengold, and my successor, Mr Jay Axelbank, for the information they provided and for kindly letting me use some of their materials. My gratitude goes, also, to those informants in the United States, Canada and Western Europe who asked specifically that they not be identified for personal or professional reasons. I owe a special measure of thanks to the staff members of the Radio Liberty Research Library and the Osteuropa Institute in Munich for their kind patience and assistance in the use of their materials and facilities. Finally I would like to express my deep appreciation to my wife who helped so immensely in the research work.

J.D.

Munich, June 1973

Part One

FIRST AMONG EQUALS

Once there was a Russian peasant who was traveling on foot to an isolated village. He knew the direction but not the distance. As he passed through a birch forest he chanced upon a wizened old woodsman whom he asked how far away the village was. The old man shrugged and said: "I do not know." The peasant sighed, shifted his bundle from one shoulder to the other and strode on. Suddenly the woodsman shouted out: "Fifteen minutes down the road." Perplexed, the peasant wheeled around and asked: "Why didn't you say so at once?" The old man replied calmly: "First I had to see what size steps you take."

Leonid Brezhnev to
Richard Nixon, May 1972

CHAPTER I

Profile in Power

It was in his vacation villa at Sochi, a Black Sea resort, that Nikita Sergeyevich Khrushchev engaged in his last public act as head of the Soviet Government and chief of its Communist Party. At 9 a.m. on 13 October 1964, a balmy, autumn day, he met with Gaston Palewski, the French science and space minister. Their talk lasted only thirty minutes. Then Khrushchev excused himself, saying that he had to leave on a "trip".

Two days later his name disappeared from the newspapers and his portrait from Moscow streets where it had hung as part of the celebrations for the USSR's three newest cosmonauts. The tough-minded peasant who had ruled the Soviet Union for a decade was abruptly relegated to political oblivion.

The rest of the world responded to the coup apprehensively, regarding with scepticism the faceless coalition that had assumed power. In contrast to Khrushchev's worldwide notoriety, Aleksei Nikolayevich Kosygin, the new prime minister, and Leonid Ilyich Brezhnev, the new first secretary of the Communist Party of the Soviet Union, were virtually unknown. But from what little the world did know, they lacked both dynamism and stature.

Moreover, kremlinologists prophesied, no collegiate leadership could rule long under the Soviet system. It would be only a matter of time before intrigue or force, or both, would again concentrate power in the hands of one man. The arguments sounded plausible and familiar.

Nine years have passed since Khrushchev's fall, but by no means all the prognoses have proved accurate. The team that toppled Khrushchev has set a record for durability that many Western governments would envy. One reason may well be that they are a different breed from the men who had previously ruled the Soviet Union. "Unlike the early Bolshe-viks," as the late Charles Thayer, a diplomat and writer, pointed out, "these men are not ex-outlaws with nothing to lose. They are respected leaders of a stable state, personally affluent and custodians of a huge industrial complex."

Their solidarity, compared with the purges that typified the Stalin and Khrushchev eras, is astounding. Of the twenty-one men who either were members of the Politburo on the day of Khrushchev's fall or have joined that august assemblage since October 1964, sixteen belong to it to this day. Of the five who were ousted, three either died or retired honorably. Only two were expelled in a genuine purge, and that not until April 1973.

But for all the veneer of continuity and collectivity, relative weight and power within the ruling circle *has* shifted – at first gradually, then quickly and dramatically – to benefit one man: Leonid Ilyich Brezhnev. He has emerged as almost the un-challenged chieftain of the Soviet political jungle, fourth in the elitist line of rulers after Lenin, Stalin and Khrushchev.

Shortly after Khrushchev was deposed a new joke began circulating in Moscow. At a party meeting, so the story went, a propaganda lecturer was asked whether, in view of recent developments, the *kult lichnosti* – the personality cult – had finally been abolished in the USSR. "Of course," the propa-gandist replied. "How can there be a personality cult if there is no personality?" When Brezhnev heard that joke at a Krem-lin reception he roared with laughter. But he said nothing. The joke has long been forgotten in Moscow and the assessment of Brezhnev has been drastically revised.

"We just didn't give him enough credit from the beginning," a Western diplomat in Moscow once confided. "Everybody wrote him off as a party hack, as a colorless *apparatchik*, as a compromise candidate."

In the shadow of his ebullient, effervescent patron and master, Brezhnev was all those things, indeed. And considering the murkiness of Kremlin waters, no one can really be blamed for misreading the signs. But there had been signs.

From 1956 to 1960 Brezhnev was one of the powerful secretaries of the Central Committee of the Communist Party of the Soviet Union and a member of its Presidium, as the Politburo was then called. In 1960 he was "promoted" to the chairmanship of the Presidium of the Supreme Soviet, that is, to the "presidency" of the USSR, a largely honorary post. But he retained his seat on the Politburo. When Frol Kozlov, the man whom Khrushchev had once called "my successor", suffered an incapacitating stroke in 1963, Brezhnev returned to the Central Committee Secretariat as Khrushchev's new heir apparent.

In those years a Western diplomat called him a "Soviet-style manager-politician-executive, the efficient organization man, a Communist in a gray flannel suit."

By consensus it was the best-cut gray flannel in the Kremlin. In fact, if anything distinguished Brezhnev from the coterie of baggy-suited *apparatchiki* around Khrushchev, it was his sartorial trimness. Foy D. Kohler, a former US ambassador to the Soviet Union, used to say that Brezhnev "must have the best tailor in Moscow".

When the hierarchy, in a compact little group, trailed behind Khrushchev into a Kremlin reception hall, Brezhnev's ruggedly handsome face and his military bearing contrasted agreeably with the humorless appearance of most of the other leaders. He looked a little less forbidding than most, exuding the forced heartiness of a professional hail-fellow-well-met. Occasionally he would display some of the back-slapping, hand-pumping traits associated with American politicians. By Soviet standards he was even somewhat of a charmer with the ladies and could turn it on, when needed, for visiting dignitaries. But in contrast to Nikita Khrushchev he remained two-dimensional and bland.

He was Ambassador Kohler's table neighbor at occasional dinners and exchanged pleasantries with him at many receptions. Brezhnev was, as Kohler noted (in his book *Understanding the Russians*) "always superficially affable, but never had anything to say that sent me flying back to the embassy to cable Washington or, indeed, that I had not already read in my morning *Pravda*."

Yet, even in those years, Soviet sources were hinting that Brezhnev bore watching. "Don't underestimate him," a Soviet official told Michael Page, a British correspondent in 1962. When the newsman suggested that "people with real power" do not become president in the USSR, the Russian replied:

"Just wait a while. I know your diplomats have written him off, but they are making a big mistake."

By 1963 Soviet sources were even more insistent about Brezhnev's future role. "For us," one official told Harry Hamm, a German journalist, "there is no doubt about his present position and future career. He is the coming man: intelligent, able, modest and very popular in the Party."

That remark explains succinctly why Brezhnev was selected to fill the more important of Khrushchev's two posts: the party leadership, traditionally the font of supreme power in the USSR. Whether Brezhnev was one of the active conspirators against Khrushchev or merely acquiesced in a *fait accompli* is a question which may never be resolved. The record shows that during the crucial week, while the plot was crystallizing, Brezhnev was absent from Moscow – on a formal visit to East Germany. He did not return until two days before Khrushchev's recall from Sochi. But Brezhnev was the logical candidate to replace him. Although he was Khrushchev's newest chosen heir and had risen to the top of the Soviet hierarchy on his patron's coat tails, he was, oddly enough, also the most acceptable man to Khrushchev's opponents. For decades he had sublimated all manifestations of personal ambition and acquired a reputation for quiet, sensible, efficient execution of party decisions. He had deliberately maintained a low profile and avoided taking tell-tale stands for this or against that faction. Whatever firm and strong views he had had, he had apparently not broadcast them. He was the man on whom all the interest and pressure groups, all the warring and rival "lobbies" which comprise the Soviet establishment, could agree. He had few, if any, known enemies. Above all, he was demonstrably the most capable.

None had Brezhnev's breadth of experience in all the fields of which the Party's first secretary is required to be a master. He had formal training in both agriculture and industry with practical exposure to both. His service in uniform had provided him with extensive high-level military connections and first-hand knowledge of defense matters. The party had been his primary field of action, but he also knew the government. He had traveled more than any of his political peers and had learned how to behave among foreign emissaries and dignitaries.

He is undeniably a politician of considerable brilliance, toughness and guile. He knows precisely when to slap which back, shake which hand, promote which supporter and demote which adversary. One American Senator likened him to Chicago's Mayor Richard Daley and no less accomplished a politician than President Nixon called him, admiringly: "the best politician in the room".

In the limelight – on stage or on television – he is an image-builder's nightmare. Although his voice is deep and resonant, his delivery is deadly. Ponderous and heavy, encumbered by a Ukrainian inflection that leaves some people wondering whether he is drunk, others thinking he has a speech impediment, Brezhnev is an oratorical failure. In less formal situations, however – especially at the receptions which usually follow such performances – he is easy-going, heavy-drinking and totally relaxed. He is an entertaining *raconteur* with a stock of good anecdotes and jokes, quite a few of which are at the expense of Communism.

To West German Chancellor Willy Brandt he related the story of a party official who lectured on the great achievements of Communism at a village propaganda meeting. "You now have enough to eat," Brezhnev quoted the agitprop speaker. "You all have roofs over your heads, material for clothing and enough money to buy new shoes each year." Then, switching to a falsetto, Brezhnev imitated a wizened little grandmother who called out from the back of the room: "Right you are, comrade, just like under the tsars."

Brezhnev can weep unashamedly at the biers of dead cosmonauts and political cronies. He can gently pat the heads of Young Pioneers who present him with flowers. He is always at least a few paces ahead of his political entourage. At public rallies he bounds up the stage two steps at a time to display his sprightliness and virility. Newsmen and officials trying, breathlessly, to keep pace with him on his visit to Bonn in May 1973 kept mumbling in admiration: "a ball of pent-up energy, that's what he is." He bear hugs and embraces visitors or his hosts with rib-crushing enthusiasm and usually kisses them, male or female, squarely on the mouth. In fact, no one in the Politburo kisses quite the way Brezhnev does.

He has rarely been seen agitated or out of control and

appears to abhor demagogic escapades and agitation. He is every inch a successful engineer who has a predilection for the technical details. When visiting a mosque in Iran he was less interested in its history, artistic significance or its religious background than in how it had been constructed. While in Marseilles it was not the city's architecture or ambience that captivated his imagination but the plans for its future subway. Flying low over the red and pink rim of Arizona's spectacular Grand Canyon during his US trip in 1973, Brezhnev nodded in agreement with Nixon: "It's certainly very beautiful, Mr President, very beautiful indeed." Then Brezhnev, always the pragmatist added: "But another thought comes to mind – it's a pity that it's so barren . . . Are there any inhabited areas?"

Publicly he is a moralizer who exhorts people to ever greater achievements with finger-wagging monotony and orthodox Communist clichés. Behind the scenes he loves the good life: expensive clothes; gadgets; fast and ostentatious cars; thoroughbred horses; stiff drinks; spicy foods (he reportedly is an excellent cook who often prepares meals for friends); beautiful girls; loge seats at Moscow's Dynamo or Lenin stadiums where he can watch his favorite soccer team; boar hunting; duck shooting and yachting – in other words, the perquisites of belonging to the upper classless of Soviet society. While I was in Moscow other members of the Politburo rode in Soviet-made ZILs and Chaikas, but Brezhnev flashed about in his Rolls-Royce. Subsequently he was seen in the Cadillac which Nixon gave him in 1972 and presumably he now drives about in the Lincoln Continental he got from the President in 1973 or the steel-blue Mercedes 450-SCL he received from Willy Brandt.

He is also vain. He preens himself before any mirror he passes, combing and smoothing down his wavy hair, brushing any dust or lint from the lapels of his expensive suits. He has the facial lines erased from his official portraits and does not like being photographed with his rimless reading glasses. Once, when Egypt's President Anwer Sadat was in Moscow, Brezhnev posed enthusiastically for the cameramen and said: "They are always taking pictures of me but never give me any. Why don't you give me some of the photos?"

But no matter how charming he tries to be, his eyes often betray him. Blue and pale, they can laugh disarmingly or seem to observe with cool detachment. But when Brezhnev's guard is down, when he is not consciously attempting to impress, they are hard and icy.

Above all, Brezhnev is a veteran of more than forty years of Soviet-style political infighting. Never a revolutionary but a child of the Revolution, he waited to join the Communist Party until 1931, when he was almost twenty-five years old. By then Stalin was the Party's and the country's sole ruler, and Brezhnev became a product of the Stalin era, a paragon of the political shrewdness, ruthlessness and instinct for self-preservation nurtured by that epoch. Like Khrushchev, from whom he learned the political ropes, he is a master of the art of patronage and influence peddling. But whereas Khrushchev made many mistakes that eventually contributed to his fall, Brezhnev has made few, if any.

He is conservative, prudent and cautious. He has suffered several serious set-backs to his career and has learned to turn them to advantage. Those lessons which he learned on the way up the political ladder serve him well at the top today.

Like Lenin, Stalin and Khrushchev before him, he is a manipulator of men and skilled at tuning the party instrument so that it hums to his score. Unlike his predecessors, however, he is unusually circumspect in his manipulations. Lenin, a genius, out-thought, out-talked and out-maneuvered his opponents and subordinates. Stalin liquidated them physically or coerced and terrorieed them into total submission. Khrushchev out-shouted, intimidated and publicly embarrassed them, leaving them resentful and anxious for revenge. Brezhnev -- with a few notable exceptions such as his treatment of Alexander Dubcek after the invasion of Czechoslovakia – has preferred conciliation and arbitration to achieve his aims.

He has been called the Kremlin's "great compromiser", always prepared to take one step backward when he believes or hopes that it will lead to two forward. He makes few moves without first fully protecting his flanks and his rear. His authority rests on the maintenance of a fine balance of forces in the Politburo and on winning consensus in the Central Committee and the Communist party apparatus, the Soviet version of "public opinion". Although he has reaffirmed a basic rule of Soviet politics that ultimately collective rule at the top gravitates to one man, Brezhnev has demonstrated that it is a form of monocracy which depends on the consent of the collective. He behaves like a "chairman of the board", albeit a chairman whose power is virtually unlimited.

Brezhnev did not wait long after Khrushchev's fall to gather the strings of power in his own hands. Adroitly he moved his main rivals, Nikolai Podgorny and Alexander Shelepin, either up- or downstairs – away from directly threatening positions. He has neutralized most of the others by purging their chief supporters, transferring them laterally, gerrymandering the districts from which they drew their strength and has packed the collective with men who are loyal to and dependent on him. He has turned the Politburo into something closer to a Western-style cabinet than it has ever been in Soviet history.

Although a Russian, his political roots are in the Ukraine, along the Dnieper River, where he spent all but twelve of the first forty-four years of his life. Born, raised and educated in Kamenskoye, now called Dneprodzerzhinsk, he moved up the political ladder in nearby Yekaterinoslav, now called Dnepro-petrovsk, and Aleksandrovsk, now named Zaporozhe. It was not until 1950 that Brezhnev left his home base, the indus-trialized Dnieper Bend area, for party assignments elsewhere.

Today his team in Moscow is appropriately called the Dnieper Mafia. It is a clique of powerful politicians, *appara-tchiki*, aides, advisers and friends who started in politics, government and industry with and under Brezhnev in Dnepro-dzerzhinsk, Dnepropetrovsk and Zaporozhe in the 1930s and 1940s.

Today these men and other protégés and clients whom Brezhnev recruited along the path to supreme power provide the foundation for his might. They are men who have sworn allegiance or owe their political careers to him, just as he once owed his to Nikita Khrushchev. They assure him his working majority in the Politburo, give him his strength in the Central Committee, fill key positions on his personal staff, influence his views and policies, serve as his watchdogs in the government administration, control the police, the KGB and the party apparatus. It is a formidable list of the most important men in the Soviet Union.

Some of them are not only his closest friends but also his

neighbors. Brezhnev has lived in a tightly-guarded government apartment house at 24 Kutuzovski Prospekt in Moscow since the early 1950s. Today Nikolai Shchelokov, the Soviet minister of the interior and chief of its uniformed police, a member of the Dnieper Mafia, lives one floor below him and Yuri Andropov, the chief of the KGB, the secret police, one floor above. Not even Stalin in all his paranoia lived in such proximity to his top policemen.

Even more important, perhaps, than the Dnieper Mafia is Brezhnev's solid power base in the Soviet military establishment.

How far back do these military roots go? That remains one of the unanswerable questions which contribute to the patchwork of conjecture, supposition and fragmentary information surrounding Brezhnev.

Notwithstanding his growing power and rising profile, Brezhnev's life and biography remain veiled in secrecy. Official information is scanty and appears to change periodically depending upon the Kremlin's mood or intention.

One of the contradictions concerns his early military career. According to some biographical entries, such as the one in the 1965 Yearbook of the *Large Soviet Encyclopedia*, Brezhnev served in the Red Army in 1935 and 1936 after graduating with an engineering degree from the metallurgical institute in Kamenskoye. More recent sources, such as the new edition of the *Large Soviet Encyclopedia*, make no mention of this and assert that he went to work as an engineer in Kamenskoye's F. E. Dzerzhinsky steel plant right after graduation. The omission of military service from the record would be unusual for any politician anywhere. In the case of Brezhnev, whose wartime exploits have come to play an increasing role in his image build-up, it is baffling.

Whatever the truth about that early spell in the Red Army, there is no doubt about Brezhnev's subsequent military experiences. During World War Two he was a political commissar who rose to the rank of major general by the time he was thirty-eight years old. Highly decorated – he holds two orders of the Red Banner and one order of the Red Star (comparable to two Distinguished Service Crosses and one Silver Star) – Brezhnev was among the elite chosen to march before Stalin on Red Square in the 24 June 1945 victory parade.

Among the men with whom he forged lasting links and friendships during the war are some of the Soviet Union's most powerful generals and admirals, including Marshal Andrei Grechko, the present defense minister.

The war, however, was not to be Brezhnev's last spell in uniform. Another and perhaps politically even more significant period came in 1953, after Stalin's death, when Brezhnev suffered a major set-back in his political career and was named chief political commissar of the Soviet Navy and first deputy chief of the political administration of the defense ministry. He held that post, as a lieutenant general, a scant eleven months – just long enough to reforge the political alliances with the Soviet military establishment which provide a crucial pillar of his power structure today.

Undoubtedly the influence of the marshals and admirals has grown under Brezhnev's rule and Grechko's promotion to membership of the Politburo in April 1973 is ample proof of it. But as a member of the military old-boy network himself, Brezhnev has won a greater freedom of action than other potential successors to Khrushchev would have enjoyed. It seems doubtful that any other man could have met with Nixon for a Moscow summit conference only a few weeks after that same American President had ordered the mining of North Vietnam's harbors and directly challenged Soviet military might.

Besides the immense power he already enjoys, Brezhnev clearly seeks more power. For some time had his sights set on Aleksei Kosygin's job – the prime ministership – as well. It is axiomatic among many kremlinologists that he made an abortive bid for it in 1970. Whether and when he will make another remains to be seen.

If he cannot become head of the government *and* the Party, as Khrushchev, Stalin and Lenin were before him, then Brezhnev may seek to become head of state as well as the Party. It seems doubtful that he aspires to the same Soviet "presidency" which he held from 1960 to 1964. Instead, Brezhnev appears to be banking on a constitutional change which would create a "state council" – a collective presidency patterned after those in East Germany and Romania – with himself as the council's chairman as well as leader of the Party. In November 1971

Moscow and other East European capitals crackled with rumors that such a change was impending. Then, at the last minute, it seems, Brezhnev's gambit was thwarted. "Tipsters" – invariably agents of the KGB's Department of Disinformation – were telling newsmen in Moscow that reports of such a constitutional amendment were premature. How premature? That also remains to be seen.

Whether Brezhnev really needs a title is debatable. The absence of one dissuaded neither Nixon nor Pompidou nor Brandt from dealing with him as the *de facto* head of the Party and the Government and the State.

His signature next to Nixon's on the strategic-arms limitation (SALT) treaty set a precedent in international law: it was the first time that an agreement between two nations had been signed by one man in his capacity as party leader. In fact Nixon's counterpart on that document should have been either Podgorny, the Soviet chief-of-state, or Kosygin.

For many days afterwards Soviet officials attempted to explain this unique departure from protocol. They told foreign newsmen and diplomats that the Supreme Soviet, the USSR's parliament, had delegated this duty to Brezhnev. In reality, Brezhnev's signature on the treaty merely underlines what has become apparent in recent years. He is the new tsar in the Kremlin, title or no title.

The build-up began early in 1970. In March of that year, unaccompanied by other Politburo members or senior government officials except for Defense Minister Grechko, Brezhnev journeyed to Minsk to review the Soviet Army's spring maneuvers, an act that cast him in the role of supreme commander.

In June he set a noteworthy precedent by attending a meeting of the Council of Ministers, of which he is not even a member but whose chairman is Kosygin, and delivering what *Pravda* called a "major speech" that presumably dealt with the new five-year plan and the state of the economy. *Pravda*'s reports of the meeting created the impression that it had been held under Brezhnev's *de facto* chairmanship, which it probably had.

In February 1971, when the draft of the current five-year plan was published, the Central Committee decree approving it was signed by Brezhnev alone. Not since Stalin's death had a

Central Committee decree been issued with only the personal
signature of the Party's senior secretary.

The most persuasive evidence of Brezhnev's real power was
provided by the XXIVth Party Congress in April 1971. He
spoke for six hours – a marathon address approaching the
records set by Khrushchev and Stalin – and every minute of
it was telecast live to the nation. In contrast only excerpts from
Kosygin's speech were televised – as video-tape material. In
fact, at the very moment Kosygin began to speak in the Kremlin's cavernous Palace of Congresses, Soviet television started
re-broadcasting Brezhnev's report in its entirety. The conclave
was a closed-door meeting. But observers who watched the TV
film portion of the Kosygin talk later, noticed that as the
premier spoke Brezhnev was blatantly reading some correspondence; Pyotr Shelest, then a member of the Politburo and
party chief of the Ukraine, was engrossed in a magazine and
Mstislav Keldysh, the president of the Soviet Academy
of Sciences, sucked his thumb with an expression of total
boredom.

Since that Congress there has been little stopping Brezhnev,
especially as he began encroaching on what for years had been
Kosygin's special preserve: foreign policy. The dour face of
Kosygin, once familiar to televiewers and newspaper readers
around the world, has been virtually eclipsed.

At that Party Congress it was Brezhnev who presented the
Kremlin's six-point peace proposal and in succeeding months
Soviet officials and diplomats pointedly referred to the
"Brezhnev peace plan".

In September 1971 he invited Willy Brandt for a meeting to
the Crimea. Kosygin, nominally and constitutionally responsible for foreign policy, was nowhere in sight. Later that month
Brezhnev traveled to Yugoslavia for a summit meeting with
President Josip Broz Tito. In October, unaccompanied by
either Kosygin or Podgorny, he went to France where President
Pompidou welcomed him with a 101-gun salute, suites in the
Grand Trianon Palace at Versailles and the protocol normally
extended to a reigning monarch.

Compared with the mid-1950s when Khrushchev, at that
time, like Brezhnev today, merely head of the Party, used
Premier Bulganin as a diplomatic and protocolic cover during

his trips abroad, these were portentous and extraordinary performances. Even more surprising was the manner in which Brezhnev conducted himself.

As recently as his 1963 visit to Teheran it was a minor sensation when he spontaneously ad-libbed a toast "to freedom – long live freedom". But in September 1971, waiting for Brandt's plane to land at Simferopol, he seemed transformed.

As Nikolai Kirichenko, party chief of the Crimean region, began reeling off boring statistics about local production and the tourist trade for the benefit of the assembled West German newsmen and diplomats, Brezhnev tugged at Kirichenko's sleeve and said: "We know all that. Let's go over and talk to the *people* and see what *they* think. *That's* important."

Then, shrugging off two bodyguards, Brezhnev advanced towards a throng of Soviet vacationers at the airport and began pumping hands all around. "We can't see you, Leonid Ilyich," shouted a man from the rear. With the agility he frequently displays, Brezhnev hoisted himself up on a low fence. "Can you see me now?" he asked. It was a symbolic leap, for Brezhnev has gone to great efforts since early 1970 to raise his political profile for everybody to see.

The hand-shaking with his own countrymen over, Brezhnev turned to the knot of West German reporters standing nearby – the first time he had ever spoken to non-Communist correspondents – and exchanged small talk, even using a few words of German.

The conference with Brandt itself was a virtuoso display of Brezhnev's skill as a gracious host and a seasoned politician and statesman.

The treatment began as the chancellor stepped off the plane. "*Dobro pozholovat* – welcome," boomed Brezhnev. After asking perfunctorily whether Brandt had had a good flight, he took him by the arm and steered him towards the administration building's VIP lounge where, as Brezhnev phrased it, "our Ukrainian comrades would like to greet you with a few refreshments." The "few refreshments" turned out to be a three-hour feast with mountains of Russian delicacies, rivers of vodka, Crimean wine and champagne.

That set the tone for the next two days: a kaleidoscope of Black Sea bathing, boat trips, negotiations, picture-taking ordeals, private talks during which Brezhnev spoke freely of his youth and war experiences, banter with correspondents and banqueting – all against the backdrop of some of the most beautiful scenery in the Soviet Union.

Through it all Leonid Brezhnev, the *apparatchik*-turned-statesman, behaved toward Brandt like a long-lost friend. Once as Brandt stood alone at the balustrade of the Soviet government compound, looking out at the sea, Brezhnev rushed up from behind, thumped the unsuspecting German chancellor heftily on the shoulder, wiped the perspiration from his massive brow and said: "Excuse me for keeping you waiting, but your countrymen held me up so long with questions."

In Yugoslavia a few weeks later he dropped the last vestiges of his legendary aversion to the press. He ambled over to an American reporter, whom he apparently mistook for a Yugoslav, draped his arm around his shoulder and gave him a few breezy generalities about the talks with Tito.

On his visit to Paris in October 1971 Brezhnev grinned wherever he went, told little anecdotes, waved cheerfully and hugged his hosts. Nothing seemed to ruffle him, not even an elevator door in the Louvre that suddenly shut him off from all his bodyguards. The security agents rushed panting up the stairs to find Brezhnev strolling out of the lift quite unconcerned.

On several occasions during that hectic week Brezhnev was late for appointments without apparent cause. As a French official remarked: "He seemed to want to be late, to show he was master of his own time."

French newsmen who traveled with him expressed baffled admiration. "A new Brezhnev," they wrote, "a new style. He does not ramble, he's concise. He does not read from prepared texts but ad-libs. He's friendly and he does not applaud himself in the usual Russian style."

An even "newer" Brezhnev turned up in Bonn in May 1973. From the minute he bounded down the steps from his Ilyushin-62 airliner until his departure five days later, Brezhnev played to the press and the hidden television audience of Germany. Waving, smiling, his craggy face a study in constantly shifting emotions and reactions, willing to pose for hundreds of pictures and ready to give numerous impromptu interviews, he took the West German capital by storm. "Just like Khrushchev," said

one Bonn observer, not quite sure whether he had paid
Brezhnev a compliment or not.

Whatever "two-dimensional" stiffness Brezhnev may still
have displayed on occasions in the somewhat reserved German
atmosphere of Bonn, he dropped it dramatically on arrival in
the United States. During the week he spent with Nixon in
Washington, Camp David and the "Western White House" in
San Clemente, California, Brezhnev flaunted a deliberate
disdain for formality.

After a White House welcome that looked – despite the
formal twenty-one-gun-salute – more like the half-time ceremony at a college football game, Brezhnev bounded into the
small crowd of tourists that had been allowed onto the grounds
and began shaking hands enthusiastically in typical political
campaign fashion. When he spotted a familiar face among
newsmen at one reception he bellowed heartily: "I remember
you from Moscow." At one meeting with Congressmen he
button-holed a tobacco-state representative and complained
that Camels aren't as good as they used to be. Repeatedly he
tried out his smattering of English in whispered conversations
with the somewhat puzzled President.

Brezhnev joked and clowned, constantly playing up to the
vast American audience that, just as in Germany the month
before, was largely hidden and invisible behind the television
screens for security reasons.

During the signing of the agreement to prevent nuclear war,
Brezhnev jokingly raced Nixon to see who could complete his
signature first. Following another treaty-signing ceremony he
spilled some of his champagne and shamefully hid his face from
the TV cameras with a cocktail napkin. On one occasion he
playfully put his hands to his hips and the white cowboy belt he
had been given and pointed them as if drawing two six shooters.
On the flight from the East Coast to California in Nixon's jet,
Brezhnev and the President engaged in table-wrestling for the
benefit of delighted photographers. And there was no holding
him whatsoever when he met Chuck Connors, a popular
TV-Western star. Spotting Connors in the crowd once more
just as he was about to leave San Clemente, Brezhnev broke
protocol and rushed up to him and hugged him goodbye.
Connors, a Herculean man and at least a head-and-a-half

taller than Brezhnev, grabbed the Soviet party chief under the arms and lifted him bodily. Brezhnev howled with delight.

Brezhnev impresses diplomats, world leaders, big business-men and newsmen alike. He approaches people with spontan-eous empathy. He knows how to create a warm atmosphere, to build trust. In the United States he was seen putting his arm so reassuringly around the shoulders of Nixon, beleaguered by the Watergate scandal, that some observers wondered who was host and who was guest.

He appears to be in complete control of himself, confident in his role as the leader of 250 million people, surprisingly urbane, but very clearly convinced of his political beliefs and principles.

He is also a salesman. In talks with German industrial magnates he drew enticing pictures of limitless possibilities of investment in the USSR that bordered on the adventurous. He spoke of cooperative agreements to exploit Soviet resources that could extend over thirty, forty – "and why not fifty years?" With a broad smile he told some of them: "We could do it this way. I'll buy from Krupp and sell to Patolichev (the Soviet minister of foreign trade) with a 10 percent mark-up. Patolichev can sell it somewhere else with another 10 percent mark-up. That way we'll all make money." He exhorted the German industrialists: "Don't wait, don't hesitate to do business with us. Get in on the ground floor with us now."

Although he won high marks as "an effective politician" from American Congressmen and Senators – one of whom even remarked in June 1973 that "we have now spent more time with Mr Brezhnev than any of us have ever spent with Mr Nixon" – Brezhnev has shown some obvious gaps in his knowledge of foreign affairs. His exuberant admiration of Western technology seems to overestimate the capabilities of capitalist industry.

The Germans, for example, were baffled when Brezhnev, speaking about interest rates for long-term credits, said: "We really shouldn't let one percent more or less become a stumbling block." Some of the industrialists to whom Brezhnev talked of long-term mammoth projects in Siberia urged on him the wisdom of Soviet cooperation with smaller Western consortia. "That's OK by me," he replied, "but only two or three firms. I won't have the whole world coming in."

The gaps may be attributable to the many filters through which information reaches him. As a man raised and trained in a dictatorship which gives orders to state-owned industrial corporations and banks, he has little appreciation of how a capitalist economy works. Just why the German banks would want a commercial long-term rate of around 9 percent to finance his Siberian projects against the 6 percent he was willing to pay, was quite beyond him. As Bertold Beitz, the general manager of Krupp industries, put it: Brezhnev and the people in the USSR "just cannot grasp that we industrialists are not the employees of Chancellor Brandt and Foreign Minister Scheel."

Yet those world leaders with whom he has dealt never fail to register their admiration.

US Presidential adviser Henry Kissinger expressed surprise that Brezhnev was much smarter, more intelligent and better informed than he had expected. Kissinger was struck by the way Brezhnev spurned instructions and briefings from aides or subordinates and that he always knew what was at issue.

Chancellor Brandt, in an interview with Munich's *Sueddeutsche Zeitung* said: "He's a man of great experience and great determination. But in addition to his experience, which naturally focuses primarily on the Soviet Union and its problems, there is great curiosity. It is the curiosity of a man, no longer young, for the problems and leaders of a country, a part of the world, to which he has had little previous exposure."

It is on the German question, in fact, that Brezhnev has concentrated most of his newly acquired interest in foreign affairs. The *rapprochement* with West Germany was described to my successor in Moscow, Jay Axelbank, by a prominent Soviet editor as "Brezhnev's doing". Brezhnev himself pushed the German negotiations because "he hopes to go down in the history books as the man who made peace with Germany."

But Brezhnev also appears to be a man with few illusions. "I don't expect that your German people will suddenly begin to love me or the Russian people," he said on one occasion, "but at least we must see that a solid friendship grows up between us."

It is this kind of candidness, mixed with a desire to show the world he can be trusted as no Soviet leader has been trusted before, that has typified Brezhnev's behavior since entering the stage of world diplomacy in 1971.

Meeting charges in Washington that Moscow might renege on its promise to relax emigration policies for Soviet Jews once the USSR had been granted "most favored nation" treatment in trade, Brezhnev shot back: "I have heard it said that the Soviets would change their minds and cheat. That is not true. Once we give our word, we keep it." In Germany he made the astonishingly frank revelation that "this opening to the West has not been easy for many of us in Russia." And just before departing Bonn in May 1973, he went into an airport huddle with Brandt's closest adviser, Egon Bahr, and told him: "Don't be suspicious. I promise you we'll stick to what we have said. But give us a little time to work it out."

Virtually every diplomat who has dealt with him has expressed relief and gratification that Brezhnev has taken the reins of foreign policy from Kosygin's hands.

"It's easier to talk with him," explained one European ambassador. "Kosygin is like a machine gun with a computerized mind." One senior Western ambassador in Moscow told an American correspondent: "Kosygin is the toughest negotiator of the whole damn bunch. When he has instructions from the Politburo he doesn't budge an inch. Don't misunderstand: Brezhnev is plenty tough, too. But he seems to have more give and more authority to give."

Most Western observers concur that Brezhnev has always had the authority. What has changed in the last few years are his style, his attitude, his way of doing things, his higher profile.

Powerful as Brezhnev may have been from the start of his stewardship as party leader, a rich stock of whispered political jokes in the 1960s suggested that he was anything but generally popular. According to one such tale, the only difference between Brezhnev and Stalin is that the mustache has risen over the eyebrows. In another story, an agitprop official, asked what genuine interest the Soviet Union could have in trying to put the first man on the moon, replied: "The first man in the USSR is Leonid Brezhnev."

Since 1970 few efforts have been spared to revise that image. A number of books and a series of magazine articles have sought to portray him as a courageous, heroic officer in the war whose only concern was for the welfare of his men. According to *Ogonyok*, a Soviet illustrated weekly, he was a man who knew the whole 18th Army from the commander to the private soldier. "He was their favorite, understood their moods and thoughts, and was able to kindle in them a thirst for victory. How many times did this man's resoluteness make the impossible possible? At the most critical moments of battle he would find stirring words which had a powerful effect. Repeatedly he showed personal bravery and iron coolness. His assured, calm voice rang out in the noise and roar of battle."

His speeches and photographs began to dominate the party press. Increasingly he traveled to the provinces to deliver major speeches which were frequently televised live.

The drive to humanize the Brezhnev image gained momentum with the Brandt visit. At Oreanda he was photographed with Brandt – without tie and wearing sunglasses. Tass, the official Soviet news agency, soon released an official picture of Brezhnev which made him appear like a movie star or yachtsman and ten to fifteen years younger than his age. Clad in blue windbreaker, T-shirt and suspenders, dark glasses and his wavy salt-and-pepper hair fetchingly windswept, he was shown with his arm resting nonchalantly on the railing of a motor launch. In more recent photos he can be seen as race-horse fancier, successful nimrod, gallant host and country squire.

Occasionally, the strictures of Soviet orthodoxy still intervene. One conference photo of Brezhnev, Brandt and Bahr, appeared in *Pravda* with heavy editorial retouching. A cigarette in Brezhnev's hand was air-brushed out of the Tass original. So were the bottles and glasses on the table. And the sleeve of Brezhnev's jacket was discreetly lengthened to cover the cuff of his shirt which stuck out too far for *Pravda*'s sartorial arbiters.

On New Year's Eve 1970–1 Brezhnev took the unprecedented step of delivering a 10-minute address to the nation in which he wished the Soviet people a happy holiday and exhorted them to set "new milestones in Communist construction".

At the XXIVth Congress he was eulogized and panegyrized by a succession of delegates who lauded his "tireless activity and constant concern for the welfare of the people" and proclaimed that his six-hour speech had brought "tears of joy and pride" to their eyes.

Soviet magazines and newspapers portray Brezhnev as a true son of the proletariat who grew up in a squat clay shack in a working-class slum. He is pictured as a hard-working, self-made man of whom people in his home town "always find the warmest, kindest words".

The world and many of his own countrymen tend to think of him as an international bully who invaded Czechoslovakia and crushed the frail flower of the "Prague Spring"; as a geopolitical thug who invented the infamous Brezhnev Doctrine of Moscow's right to interfere militarily in the affairs of other Communist countries; as the neo-Stalinist who uses concentration camps, psychiatric penitentiaries and the veiled threat of mass terror to suppress political dissent and ideological nonconformity. But Soviet image-makers are striving to present him as a man of peace, committed to creating a better life for his people, as a world leader and statesman respected by his peers: (a two-hour film of Brezhnev's trip to France continues to run in Soviet movie houses).

Apparently inspired by his three predecessors, Brezhnev also aspires to become a recognized exponent of Communist theory. In 1970 a two-volume collection of his speeches entitled *Following Lenin's Course* was published in an edition of 500,000 copies in the USSR. Although it proved to be considerably less than a best seller – stacks of the books can still be found in stores all over Moscow – a third volume was issued in the fall of 1972, and the critics have accorded it enthusiastic praise. The collection, understandably, includes no speeches delivered *before* Khrushchev's fall. In those days Brezhnev was full of adulation for his mentor, just as he had spared no accolades to Stalin before the dictator's death.

Serious students of Soviet affairs, moreover, will find the "Brezhnev collection" anything but an accurate record of his pronouncements. The texts, as comparison with the originals reveals, have been liberally edited to make them conform retroactively with shifts in party policy. Whole paragraphs alluding to unfulfilled political promises and to fallen Communist leaders such as Dubcek and Poland's Wladyslaw Gomulka have been artfully expunged.

Despite the steady build-up, the brakes on the Brezhnev cult are applied periodically. The refurbishing of his image appears to be carefully phased – perhaps even governed by some gentleman's agreement in the Politburo that if it approaches Stalinist or even Khrushchevian personality cult proportions the whistle may be blown.

It was obviously blown sharply and shrilly in mid-1970. Brezhnev, or some of his protégés, taking advantage of general confusion in the USSR over the thirteen-day discrepancy between the pre-revolutionary Julian and the new-style Gregorian calendar, attempted to update his birthday by thirteen days from 19 December 1906 to 1 January 1907 so that it would fall on New Year's Day, a major public holiday in the USSR. Publication, production and distribution of the Soviet Union's many different official and semi-official calendars, all of which must pass government censorship, starts as early as 11 months ahead of time. Thus, by mid-year, four of the 1971 calendars listing Brezhnev's "new" birthdate had already been distributed. Apparently other Politburo members intervened when they realized that Brezhnev's birthday had previously been updated, along with everyone else's in the Soviet Union, after the Revolution. The 1971 calendars passed for printing and distributed after the middle of the year list the 19 December date. It was a major setback to the growing *kult lichnosti* around Brezhnev. He has been far more prudent since then.

Brezhnev is a realist, a pragmatist, a conservative. Unlike his bucolic tutor, he takes few chances. He does not implement "wild schemes" to solve his problems. More often than not he postpones their solution. He does not like to rock the boat nor will he permit others to rock it. He does not go to the brink; instead, he seeks to defuse the international crises, such as the Middle East and Vietnam, that could lead to brinkmanship. Instead of expanding the empire he seems content to conserve and protect what his predecessors conquered.

In Moscow it is said that Brezhnev's hope is to become the Party's first leader to retire honorably. Whether he achieves that goal remains to be seen. He is alleged to have had at least one heart attack and a reported operation for an unspecified liver ailment in 1972 left him temporarily wan and shaky. The record shows a number of political set-backs as well. But he has vaulted back resiliently, more vigorous than ever, from both the physical and the political reversals.

Nevertheless, one should consider that rule in the Kremlin is analogous to that over an animal herd. Eventually the strongest gains supremacy. It is a predominance, however, which he must defend against a succession of new and younger challengers. Brezhnev has moved adroitly to neutralize the challenge by packing the collective with his supporters. But as Brezhnev, Nikita Khrushchev's protégé, has excellent reason to know, there is no guarantee that they will support him indefinitely.

The struggle to reach and to remain at the top is the story of Leonid Ilyich Brezhnev's life.

Part Two

APPARATCHIK IN THE MAKING

Soviet leaders still like to boast, especially to foreigners, of their mean beginnings.

"I started life as a pigherd until I was promoted to cowherd," Khrushchev told Averell Harriman at our meeting in 1959.

"My father was a destitute worker," Anastas Mikoyan hastened to add.

"And mine was a landless peasant," Frol Kozlov said, joining the chorus.

"Mine was a beggar," Gromyko chimed in from the foot of the table.

Those lacking pigherds, paupers or beggars in their family trees tend to invent them or to keep silent about their social origins.

Charles Thayer in April 1965

CHAPTER II

Child of the Revolution

The Dnieper River rises west of Moscow in the Valday Uplands of the Ukraine. For 1,430 miles it flows, first west, then sharply south to Kiev, from there southeast to Dnepropetrovsk, then south again for 60 miles to Zaporozhe, then once more southwest until it reaches its estuary, the *dneprovski liman* of the Black Sea.

It was on the Dnieper's banks at Kiev that the first Russian state was created in the ninth century and there, in its slowly churning waters, Saint Vladimir, the grand prince, baptized thousands of his reluctant subjects to Christianize the Slav domains and create a new empire.

Navigable for 1,300 miles, the Dnieper was part of the important trade route from Scandinavia to Constantinople during the Middle Ages. Flanked by rich deposits of ore and coal and some of the most fertile soil in Europe, it has for more than a millennium, been the fulcrum of strife, territorial expansion, raids, wars, treachery, terror and suffering: the Aceldama of a succession of dukes, princes, khans, tsars, kings, emperors, hetmans, warlords, bandits, anarchists, revolutionaries and dictators. The river has seen many rulers: Varangians, Slavs, Mongols, Lithuanians, Poles, Russians, Ukrainians, Austro-Hungarians and Germans.

For most of its course it flows serenely through the Ukrainian forests and black earth belt: except for the famous rapids between Dnepropetrovsk (formerly Yekaterinoslav) and Zaporozhe (formerly Aleksandrovsk). There, until the completion of Dneproges, the first big Soviet hydro-electric station, in 1932, the seemingly sleepy stream used to turn into a twisting, swirling hydra.

Just twenty-two miles west and upstream from Dnepropetrovsk, where the river makes a sharp bend, lies Kamenskoye, or

Dneprodzerzhinsk as it has been called since 1936. Today it is a thriving industrial city with more than 230,000 population. Two centuries ago it did not even exist.

The first mention of Kamenskoye can be found in church archives dating back to 1750. *Kamen* means "rock" or "stone" in Russian and the settlement took its name from the quarries which stretched along the river bank there.

For more than a hundred years, through the rule of Catherine the Great, the Pugachev Rebellion, the Napoleonic invasion, the Decembrist Uprising of 1825, the Crimean War and the freeing of the Serfs in 1861, Kamenskoye remained little more than a settlement of wood and clay huts inhabited by impoverished peasants and quarriers.

However, in the spring of 1887 – the same year in which Lenin's older brother Sasha was executed for attempting to assassinate Tsar Alexander III – the Southern Russian Company, a Franco-Belgian consortium, selected Kamenskoye as the site for what was to become the first metallurgical plant in the Ukraine. According to a Soviet guide book of the Dnieper valley: "The proximity of a good waterway, coal from the Donets Basin and ore from Krivoi Rog, but primarily the availability of cheap labor, held out the promise of great profits to the foreign owners of the plant." On 2 March 1889 the first of its two blast furnaces was blown.

Whatever promises the plant may have held out to its foreign owners, it also held out the prospect of employment and good wages for Yakov Brezhnev, an iron and steel maker from the area around Kursk, a city near the southern Russian border with the Ukraine. He arrived in Kamenskoye with his family, including his son Ilya, not long after the plant began production and went to work in its rolling mill. The son joined him in the plant as soon as he was old enough.

That period in Russian history was tempestuous and electrifying. The Trans-Siberian railway was being built. Tsar Nikolas II, the last of the Romanov rulers, took the throne. Russia's first labor law, limiting the factory working day to eleven-and-a-half hours, was enacted. Lenin was exiled to Siberia and later emigrated to Western Europe. The Russian Social Democratic Party held its first congress in Minsk. Leo Tolstoy, Maxim Gorky and Anton Chekhov dominated the literary scene with their novels and plays of social criticism. Russia went to war with Japan, suffering a defeat that touched off a year of demonstrations, mutinies, revolts and strikes – the Revolution of 1905 – which brought the regime of Tsar Nikolas to the brink of collapse.

In the shadow of these portentous developments young Ilya Brezhnev met and married a striking, dark-haired, eighteen-year-old girl named Natalya. On 19 December 1906 in their squat clay shack in a squalid working-class slum adjacent to the Kamenskoye steel and iron plant, their first son, Leonid Ilyich, was born. Another son, Yakov, and a daughter soon followed.

Not much is known about the Brezhnev family in those years between Leonid Ilyich's birth and the outbreak of World War One. A Soviet journalist who visited Dneprodzerzhinsk in 1972 claimed that people in the town, "always find the warmest and kindest words when speaking about the Brezhnevs . . . (they) . . . speak with great respect, not only about Leonid Ilyich, but also about his late father, younger brother, sister and mother who, just as in the old days, is called simply Auntie Natasha." From what little Brezhnev has told foreigners about his youth and childhood, his mother must have played the dominantly influential role. It was she, for example, who constantly admonished him to "be polite to the ladies, Lonya", a quality that endeared Brezhnev to the wife of French President, Georges Pompidou. Now eighty-six, "Auntie Natasha" lives with her famous and powerful son in his apartment on Moscow's Kutuzvoski Prospekt.

The Brezhnevs must have prospered in those prewar years, for it seems certain that they moved to a slightly better neighborhood, up on the hill, away from the plant itself. Kamenskoye prospered, too. By the end of 1913 it was a bustling town of about 22,000 people. More than half were Russians, like the Brezhnevs. The remainder were Poles, who constituted the plant's managerial and administrative staff and provided the majority of its engineers and skilled craftsmen, Germans, Czechs and Jews.

Native Ukrainians played an insignificant role. In fact, it was not until after the Revolution in 1917, in the wake of Lenin's attempt to win the loyalties of the Russian Empire's many nationalities, that the Ukrainian language and culture began to make any impression on Russified industrial towns such as Kamenskoye.

As a schoolmate of Brezhnev, Nathan Kruglak of Milwaukee, Wisconsin, has pointed out: "The Ukrainians were the *muzhiki*, the peasants, from the nearby villages such as Romankovo, who came to town to sell their farm products in the marketplace or their grain to wholesale dealers like my father. They were the barefoot, impoverished 'invisible' people who inhabited the clay shacks and *zemlyanki*, the dugouts, that dotted the *Livada* district and the *Peski*, the sands, down by the river: areas so notoriously rough and dangerous that kids from the upper sections of town dared not wander into them."

The *zavod*, or plant, was the Ukraine's largest in the output of iron, steel and rolled metal in that prewar era. In fact, iron production had reached the respectable figure of 499,000 tons by 1913, the last year of peacetime capitalist operations. It boasted 5 blast furnaces, 10 Marten ovens, Bessemer converters and a rolling mill. It produced rails, boilers, wire, a wide range of foundry items and bricks and cinder blocks from the waste products.

The plant dominated the life of the town. Smoke and fumes belched continuously from its furnaces and ovens and hung like a permanent, choking ochre-gray canopy over Kamenskoye. When steel was poured at night the sky was ablaze with orange and the roar of the furnaces was deafening.

Although Soviet sources now describe the Southern Russian Company as an avaricious, profit-seeking enterprise whose management "treated Russians intolerantly" and cruelly exploited the labor force, it appears to have been, however, even by today's criteria, a very socially conscious and paternalistic corporation which had turned Kamenskoye into a thriving company town. It maintained an orphanage, a polyclinic where workers received free medical care, and even a forty-piece string and woodwind orchestra, whose Czechoslovak and German musicians were on the company payroll. They gave free public concerts in the plant-sponsored auditorium or in the ornate wooden band-stand of Kamenskoye's *gorodskoi* (city) park.

Above all, the corporation provided low-cost housing for

many. On the hill above the plant, bordering on a tree- and shrub-lined promenade, was the *Verkhnaya Koloniya*, the Upper Colony, a walled-off enclave that encompassed the cliquish Engineers' Club, mansions, villas and brick apartment houses reserved for top-level executives, chief engineers and higher-ranking clerical employees. Below, near the plant entrance and not far from the river, was the *Nizhnaya Koloniya*, the Lower Colony, a compound of small cottages with individual garden plots for white-collar workers, foremen, skilled laborers, the orchestra musicians and hospital employees. Both these colonies were the only sections of town with paved streets, running water and electricity.

The rest of Kamenskoye, surrounded by a three-mile-long railway spur that extended from the *zavod* to Trituznaya Station and from there to the main Kiev-Yekaterinoslav line, was a maze of wooden houses and clay huts with here and there a two-or-three-story brick building: the police station and jail; the county hospital with its single doctor and two nurses; the high school for boys. The streets, including the main *Prospekt* and the central square, the *Ploshad*, were all unpaved. Glaciers of snow and ice in the winter, they turned into rivers of ankle-deep mud in the spring and deserts of dust and sand in summer. It was there, in a clay cottage on a street running parallel to the *Prospekt*, that Leonid Brezhnev must have lived in his early teens. Kruglak used to see him walk to school from that area quite often.

Kamenskoye was a typical Russian provincial town of that period. An Orthodox church with glittering cupolas dominated the center. There was also an Old Believers' and a Polish Roman Catholic church as well as the "small", the "large" and the "tailors'" synagogues.

Until a memorable conflagration burned down Mr Danilo-vich's *apteka* shortly before the start of World War One, there were two pharmacies. After the fire, which elderly residents still talk about, only one apothecary was left: Golosovker's. Leonid Brezhnev, like others who lived in Kamenskoye during that period, probably remembers the blaze: not just because the volunteer fire department proved so completely inept at quenching it but because a new "movie house" soon took the pharmacy's place.

Like the other two "cinemas" it was a ramshackle store-front affair whose unreliable dynamo, the only power source, gave out frequently, and invariably in the middle of a good silent film. The audience was left sitting in the dark while the proprietor tinkered with the generator in the light of a kerosene lamp. If he couldn't start it again, everyone went home.

As an occasional alternative to the cinema a middle-aged couple, Mr and Mrs Nyechay, used to stage amateur dramatic productions in the auditorium and until 1917 the Truchnaya Circus set up its tents in the main square for two months each summer. Wrestling was one of its main attractions and while a few professionals usually traveled with it, the majority of contestants were local volunteers.

Youngsters like Leonid Brezhnev had few other amusements, at least of the kind they could afford. Brezhnev, to this day an avid soccer fan, probably learned to play the game on the football field in the *gorodskoi* park. In the summer months they could swim in the Dnieper, if they were not afraid to brave the hazards of a walk through the *Livada* or *Peski* to the shore. Twice weekly passenger boats from Kiev and Yekaterinoslav docked down by the river and watching them or the freight barges plying up and down the river was also fun. Whoever had a kopek or two could buy sweet *buza*, a millet beverage, or *makovki*, sesame and poppyseed squares, from Kamenskoye's two Turkish candy shops. And then, of course, there was the only automobile: a fire-breathing, smoke-coughing contraption owned by the notary public which, when it ran at all, was always followed by a swarm of screeching, shouting kids. It must have made a lasting impression on Brezhnev.

Kamenskoye, true to its Russian traditions, was a hard-drinking town. Besides numerous taverns there were two government vodka stores, called *kazyonki*, which sold spirits in small pint and half-pint bottles. Nathan Kruglak still remembers the first strike in the *zavod* in 1916. Whatever it achieved has slipped his memory but he does recall hundreds of drunken workers milling about on the town square. "I can still see how one laborer hit another in the face with a metal rod, bending the cane and tearing the other man's cheek open. I left in a hurry."

There were four schools: a little two-year elementary school run by the plant; a Lutheran one for German and other foreign students operated by a man named Otto Meneksar; the *Zhenskaya Gymnaziya Moroza*, a girls' high school run by a Russian named Moroz, his wife and their daughter; and right next to it, on the main street, the all-boys' *klassicheskaya gymnaziya*, also subsidized by the plant, in which a "skinny, freckle-faced" Leonid Ilyich Brezhnev enrolled in the fall of 1915.

To send him there Brezhnev's father, Ilya, must have scrimped and saved, for despite the *zavod*'s support of the school, annual tuition represented about a month's wages to a steelmaker. In the class of forty Leonid was virtually the only poor millhand's son. He must have been determinedly ambitious for the "entrance exam" required that he be able to read and write, do basic arithmetic including multiplication, recite certain prescribed poetry and take a dictation text. To prepare for it the majority of boys had been taught at home by parents, relatives or private tutors. Whether this happened in Brezhnev's case or whether he had first attended the two-year elementary school, is uncertain.

Nathan Kruglak's initial recollection of the present secretary general of the Communist Party of the Soviet Union is that of a small, somewhat unruly boy jumping up and down on his seat on the first day in class. For the next six years, until both completed the school's abbreviated course*, Brezhnev was to sit three desks in front of Kruglak.

Until the Revolution and the subsequent civil war when the educational system and traditional society broke down, academic standards were high. Latin, German and French were compulsory subjects. So were Russian grammar and literature; ancient, modern and Russian history; biology, chemistry and physics; mathematics including algebra, geometry and trigonometry, geography and art. Classes began at 8 o'clock in the morning and lasted until 2 p.m. with a recess for lunch.

Standards of discipline were even higher. On matriculation each boy was given a booklet of the rules and these were rigorously enforced. When a teacher entered the classroom all had to rise and remain standing until the instructor gave

* GCE O-levels in the British system

permission to sit down. The pupils wore uniforms and when they met one of their teachers on the street they were required to doff their school caps and bow. The school had a janitor, Dyadya (Uncle) Yakob. Each morning he would put on a long, dark blue uniform coat and a visored cap, then ring the bell to start classes. All the boys were afraid of him. Any wrong move on their part, and he would report them to the vice principal, Inspector Zolotaryov. And he was a martinet who imposed punishments for the slightest infractions – a missing tunic button, dirty shoes or uncombed hair. He would twist the boy's arm behind his back, shake him roughly and shove him toward a large pendulum clock in the main hall where he had to stand at attention against the wall for one to three hours.

School each morning began with prayers, and every classroom had, until the Revolution, an icon corner and the portraits of Tsar Nikolas II and Empress Alexandra. On special occasions, when there were victories to celebrate or lost battles to mourn, Brezhnev and his school-mates had to attend religious services in the school's little auditorium. A local priest, Father Konstantin, officiated.

The roster of teachers over a period of a number of years is a long one. Most of them have been forgotten but some are unforgettable. A strikingly beautiful woman, Alexandra Petrovna, was Brezhnev's class teacher. Otto Meneksar, the director of the Lutheran school, came in to teach German. He spoke almost no Russian at all. One teacher of mathematics was a scrawny, nervous little man with a balding pate from which a thin tuft of reddish hair stood straight up. The kids called him Petushok, the Rooster. But the teacher who must have impressed Brezhnev the most – for his strictness, unchallenged brilliance and political vacillations – was Iosif Zakharovich Shtokalo.

A young man, only nine years older than Brezhnev himself, Shtokalo taught physics and all mathematical subjects. Rigid and precise, he was a strict disciplinarian. He permitted no whispering, no laughter, no smiles and demanded a ramrod posture of every boy at his desk. His standards of achievement could never be met and he prided himself on never giving anyone a grade higher than "в". In five minutes he could walk through a class of forty boys to check their homework and never fail to spot a wrong answer or a problem unworked.

Behind his back the boys nicknamed him "The Jesuit". The sobriquet alluded not only to his severity but to his religious devotion and his origins: he was born near Lvov in the Western Ukraine where the Orthodox Church, the Uniates, have recognized the authority of Rome and the primacy of the Pope since 1594. Shtokalo was devoutly religious until the Revolution when he suddenly became an ardent Bolshevik supporter and an atheist.

That was a wise change of course. When the school's management disappeared – Zolotaryov reputedly joined the White Army in 1919 – Shtokalo became the principal. He continued in that role until 1931, studying in his spare time at the University of Dnepropetrovsk, from which he graduated with a degree in mathematics. Shtokalo then moved on to teaching posts at various Ukrainian universities and technological institutes. Today he is professor of physico-mathematical sciences at the University of Kiev and a full member of the Ukrainian Academy of Sciences.

Little distinguished Brezhnev in those high school years. He was usually a bit aloof and alone, quiet and introspective. Nathan Kruglak has called him "sneaky, a kid who kept his thoughts to himself". He drew that conclusion from Brezhnev's attitude towards the eight Jewish boys in the class – scapegoats of constant hazing by teachers and fellow pupils. To protect themselves they staked out seats at the back of the classroom with their backs to the wall.

Although Brezhnev never participated in the harassment, Kruglak never felt easy about him. "We didn't trust him," he recalled. "We felt he was the kind who might do something behind your back." Once, in 1919, when Denikin's White Army drove into the lower Dnieper basin and local peasant partisan bands raged lawlessly around Kamenskoye, conducting murderous pogroms, most of the Jewish families fled to Yekaterinoslav where they thought they would be safer. After ten days, when the raiders left Kamenskoye, they returned. The following day the Jewish boys went to school again. The teacher read the roll call and when he came to the first Jewish name on the list, the class bully taunted them: "Oh, you came back." Then the entire class jeered. "Brezhnev turned around and had a sneaky smile on his face. He said nothing. He just smiled."

He was anything but an outstanding student: average in most subjects, poor in foreign languages, but good in Russian which was "hammered in every day, six days a week". Had it not been for the Revolution Leonid Brezhnev might have become little more than a skilled worker in the Kamenskoye *zavod*, perhaps a foreman with a cottage in the *Nizhnaya Koloniya*, at the most an engineer with an apartment in one of the brick buildings in the Upper Colony.

The Revolution changed Leonid Brezhnev's life along with the lives of other children of Russia's proletariat. It transfigured that of Kamenskoye and its *klassicheskaya gymnaziya* which was soon to be renamed the *Trudova Shkola*, literally the Labor School.

The winter of 1916–17 was filled with a sense of impending disaster. The war was going badly. Soldiers were deserting from the front in droves, discipline was crumbling and there was widespread discontent. In March 1917 Revolution burst on Russia like a storm, disrupting traditional life. Schools, factories, offices, shops, public institutions meant little beside the dramas of the snow-covered streets where demonstration followed upon demonstration and an endless procession of speakers outshouted other speakers. For eight months, while Alexander Kerensky's Provisional Government reigned, there was pandemonium mixed with uncertainty. Then Lenin and his Bolsheviks staged their *coup d'état*. What had been a storm in March became a typhoon in November. Russia plunged headlong into chaos.

The Ukraine presented the most chaotic picture of all. Power was contested by three factions – the Bolsheviks, the forces loyal to the Provisional Government, and the Ukrainian Nationalists who sought independence from Russia for the Ukraine. The Nationalists won. Thirteen days after the Revolution in Petrograd they declared an independent Ukrainian People's Republic with its capital in Kiev. The Ukraine became one of the rallying-points of opposition to Lenin's regime.

The next four years were harrowing and bloody: Whites

fought Reds; Social Revolutionaries struggled against Bolsheviks; Cossacks raided indiscriminately; peasant, partisan gangs massacred and plundered at will. Economic life came to a standstill almost overnight and famine, deprivation, death and disease reigned supreme.

The predominant feature of all the various regimes, Soviet and anti-Soviet, which ruled the Dnieper valley after 1917 was their instability. It was a time when any small band of determined men, regardless of their politics, could readily impose their will on large areas.

Kamenskoye's *zavod* shut down as its foreign executives and engineers fled. For all practical purposes it would remain closed until 1925 when Felix Dzerzhinsky, the chief of the Cheka, the dread secret police, was transformed into a "metallurgical specialist" and "quickly organized the plant's reconstruction". Until then there was virtually no coal or ore and the few skilled workers and foremen left on the scene could do little more than produce hand-crafted products of their own. Among these were iron stoves; several *bronepoyesdy* – armored trains – with which Leon Trotsky and his generals directed and won the Civil War, and an iron statue of Prometheus in honor of the plant's first Red Guard detachment. Prometheus – the local peasants called him Timofei – was set on a stone column in the city park where he stands to this day.

The infant Ukrainian government was forced to surrender Yekaterinoslav and Kamenskoye to the Bolsheviks by January 1918. The Reds, mostly illiterate and disorganized, pillaged and rampaged.

Meanwhile the representatives of the Ukrainian Republic concluded a separate peace treaty with Austria and Germany. In exchange for grain and other foodstuffs the Germans helped crush the Bolsheviks in the Ukraine. German troops entered Kiev on 2 March 1918. Two weeks later, after bitter fighting, Austro-Hungarian units occupied Kamenskoye.

The killing did not stop. In Yekaterinoslav and Kamenskoye scores of revolutionaries were executed and hundreds of roaming gypsies were massacred by the occupation forces.

Eight months later, when the Germans surrendered to the Allies on the western front, the Reds started driving back into the Ukraine. The Austrians and Germans fled. During their advance the Soviet forces were augmented by peasant bands. One of the most ruthless and effective of these was led by a bloodthirsty partisan named Grigoriev who had established his headquarters in Romankovo, the Ukrainian village three miles from Kamenskoye.

Grigoriev's love affair with the Bolsheviks was brief. When the Reds began requisitioning peasant livestock and grain he switched sides and joined forces with General Denikin's Whites. But regardless of whose side he fought on, Grigoriev left a trail of blood. His 16,000 followers, supported by sixty cannon and several armored trains, were hard-drinking, uncontrollable brigands. In all the towns they occupied they massacred Jews and Bolsheviks indiscriminately.

Grigoriev was finally killed by another partisan leader, Nestor Makhno, who, at the height of his power, headquartered in Yekaterinoslav. Makhno was an anarchist, an enemy of both Reds and Whites, and viewed any government as bad. But his methods were the same as everyone else's: death, destruction, brigandage and pillage, the focus of which was frequently Kamenskoye.

Sympathies of the Ukrainian *muzhiki* in the surrounding countryside were clearly for the nationalist cause and the Whites. But in town, among the metal workers, loyalty to the Bolsheviks was unquestionable. The workers did their part for the Revolution and once when Trotsky came to address them from his armored train at Trituznaya Station, he affectionately referred to them as *"nashi kamenskiye bosyaki* – our Kamenskoye bums".

At first, from the youngsters' viewpoint, the Revolution and the succeeding turmoil seemed a boon. Whenever the bells on the nearby Russian Orthodox church rang out their awesome tocsin, it meant that Reds, Whites, Nationalists, Germans or bandit gangs were marching on the town. But it also meant no more school, at least for a day or so.

The Revolution had, of course, sparked political activity in the school and some youths dropped out to join either the Red Guards or the White Army. A few used the opportunity for personal vendettas.

One boy, the son of a Kamenskoye barber named Pavlov, rode with Denikin's White Army cavalry. In July 1919 when his detachment stormed victoriously into town, he raced his horse to the school, arrested his former Russian literature teacher, marched him to the river bank and shot him. Another teenage killer, a dropout from the neighboring girls' school, was Syonka Mishuk who became an executioner for the Cheka. Primed with enough vodka she would shoot forty to fifty "enemies of the people" in a night. Among them, apparently, were her former principal, Moroz, his wife and their daughter. One day in 1919 Syonka rounded them up and killed them in the town square.

If Leonid Brezhnev had any political views in those turbulent times, he kept them to himself. He took no part in the ferment. But like everyone else he suffered. Being the poorest of his classmates, he probably suffered the most.

Hunger and misery were everywhere. By 1920 six continuous years of World War, Revolution and Civil War had torn Russia asunder. In the Ukraine alone 140,000 Reds and 400,000 anti-Bolsheviks had been killed in the fighting. Harvests were only a third of the prewar level, the livestock population had been decimated. Light industry was producing less than half of what it had in 1913. Heavy industry had virtually ceased to exist.

The winter of 1920–21 was the bleakest. Typhus was rampant. Nine out of ten in Brezhnev's class were stricken and he was among the first to come down with the disease. When he finally returned to school he was skinnier than ever.

As the situation deteriorated no one could pay the school fees. The teachers agreed to continue their work, however, if parents would remunerate them with food and clothing. Where they obtained the goods was their business.

Discipline disintegrated. The school had always emphasized appearance and protocol. But in the spring of 1921 when some families had only one remaining pair of shoes or boots to share among four or five people, the school ruled that students and teachers could come barefooted. Even the new principal, Shtokalo, strutted to school on bare feet. Academic standards fell by the way. There was no paper left to write on and no fuel with which to heat the classrooms. To keep from freezing in the winter of 1920–21 Brezhnev and his classmates stamped their feet during lessons.

For most youngsters the days started before 5 a.m. when they rushed to queue for bread rations, more often than not only to discover by the time they reached the front of the queues that supplies had run out. People lived by primitive barter and when they had nothing of value left to sell or trade with the peasants for food they faced starvation. In Kamenskoye hundreds died. Swollen or reduced to walking skeletons, their bellies bloated, their legs covered with festering sores, they dropped and died on the streets. Each day the corpses were gathered by the dozen, loaded on open horse carts and then taken for burial. In the Ukraine, according to some estimates, two million died of starvation by the spring of 1921.

In the summer of 1921 Brezhnev's class "graduated". The ceremony in the school's assembly hall was a dreary affair: a few speeches, and farewells in a room illuminated by a half dozen flickering candles. There was no kerosene. The boys' "treat" was the minuscule piece of sugar each had brought to sweeten a cup of hot water.

Official Soviet biographies of Brezhnev claim that his "working life began at age fifteen". If indeed it did, he was more fortunate than most of Kamenskoye's young men and women. There was no work in the town and except for occasional shipments of American Hoover Relief Administration food, virtually nothing to eat.

Young Brezhnev whiled away the months until in the spring of 1922 an unemployed engineer, Petrov, organized a "metallurgical vocational school" in the abandoned buildings of the Kamenskoye zavod. Brezhnev and five other high school classmates, including Nate Kruglak, enrolled as its first students. That was the beginning of the technical school which, according to some official Soviet sources, Brezhnev was to run briefly in 1937 and 1938. Classes were held in one of the offices of the plant's empty administration building. Petrov's instruction consisted mainly of showing the boys drawings and blueprints of the machinery and teaching them how iron and steel are smelt. The practical part of the course entailed crawling in and out of the cold blast furnaces and scrambling about the mill where the grass and weeds grew waist-high after five years of neglect.

Young Brezhnev persevered in Petrov's "polytechnicum"

for another year – until the summer of 1923. The New Economic Policy had been launched two years before and an uneasy peace mixed with a hint of economic stability had returned to the land. We may never know what persuaded him to drop steel-making that year and turn instead to agriculture. Perhaps it was the paucity of good prospects in Kamenskoye whose plant was not to reopen for another two years. Perhaps he was inspired by the promise of a new deal for Russia's peasants.

What we do know is that he joined the *Komsomol*, the Communist youth organization, that year and as a member of the new labor aristocracy had no difficulty matriculating in the Technicum for Land Utilization and Reclamation in Kursk, the Russian town near which his family origins lay.

In the summer of 1923 he left Kamenskoye to begin a four-year vocational course in Kursk. No doubt he felt that he was leaving his home town for a long time if not forever. He could not have known how soon he would be returning.

CHAPTER III

Admission to a New Elite

Vladimir Ilyich Lenin was gravely ill but still alive in 1923 when Leonid Ilyich Brezhnev left Kamenskoye. By the time Brezhnev returned to the city in 1931 Stalin had become the virtual master of the Party and the Soviet Union.

In the intervening years the USSR had embarked on a new and in many ways more sweeping revolution than the one which had brought the Bolsheviks to power: liquidation of the more affluent peasantry; forced collectivization of agriculture; suppression of dissent and opposition, and a campaign of rapid industrialization designed to reshape the country regardless of the costs.

Millions of people – many of them voluntarily but many under duress – were carried along by the force of events beyond their control which radically changed the course of their lives. For the most part they were ragged, hungry, cold and deprived of the comfort of hope and illusion.

Even the newly privileged lived frugally with but a minimum of basic amenities. Young party men like Nikita Khrushchev who attended the XIVth CPSU Congress in Moscow in 1925 were housed in "simple and crowded quarters". They "slept on plank beds and were all stacked together like logs".

The press and radio shrieked out the slogans of the new era. Liquidation of the Kulaks as a Class! Forward to Industrialization! Overtake the Capitalist Countries! The lives of young men like Brezhnev were a round of study, work, propaganda meetings, exhortations, harangues against foreign and internal enemies, and experiments no sooner begun than abandoned.

The record on Brezhnev in those eight years between Lenin's terminal illness and Stalin's consolidation of power is scanty and contradictory. From 1923–27 he studied at the Land Utilization and Reclamation Technicum in Kursk. It prepared him for a career as a surveyor and melioration technician.

His first assignment was as a surveyor in a district near Orsha in White Russia, 300 miles west of Moscow and almost 1,000 north of Kamenskoye. An ancient town, frequently fought over, once an eastern outpost of Catholicism, and an important Polish fortress until it became Russian in the eighteenth century, Orsha had one thing in common with Kamenskoye: it, too, is situated on the Dnieper. It is there that the river becomes navigable on its course to the south. According to some sources, it was in Orsha that Brezhnev first met his wife, Viktoria Petrovna, a nurse.

A brief period back in the Kursk area followed before he went east, 1,000 miles to the Urals, where he became chief of the Bisertsky district agricultural department in Sverdlovsk province. There he also took his first tentative step into politics, becoming deputy chairman of the executive committee of the district soviet, approximating that of a county councillor.

An important promotion followed quickly. In late 1929 or early 1930 Brezhnev was named deputy chief of the Sverdlovsk province department of agriculture, an agency responsible for farming, collectivization and land reclamation in an area covering 74,400 square miles.

When Brezhnev left Sverdlovsk, what he did before returning to Kamenskoye to work in the *zavod* and study engineering, why he changed careers again, this time from an obviously promising future in agriculture to metallurgy, we do not know. Official Soviet sources such as encyclopedias, yearbooks, biographical directories and calendars are either silent or provide conflicting answers. The suspicion of deliberate obfuscation is hard to dispel.

An official Tass biography of Brezhnev, released on the day he became first secretary of the Party in 1964, states cryptically:

"He worked for a short time in land surveying but this has not become his profession. When the Soviet Union set about the industrialization of the national economy, thousands of young people exerted their efforts precisely in this field. The thirst for knowledge, above all, technical engineering knowledge, attracted youths and girls . . . Leonid Brezhnev enrolled in the metallurgical institute of his native town."

According to the newest edition of the *Large Soviet Encyclopedia* this was in 1931. Earlier sources, such as the Yearbooks to the *Large Encyclopedia*, say it was in 1930. The *Small Soviet Encyclopedia* skirts the question entirely. The 1962 Encyclopedia Yearbook contains the most perplexing entry of all. It states that from 1930–31 Brezhnev studied at an agricultural institute in Moscow, presumably the prestigious Timiryazev Academy.

Soviet reference books are not to be taken lightly. The editors are known to make "political mistakes", sometimes with grave personal consequences. But factual errors – exclusive of deliberate distortions of history – are rare. Moreover, the texts are read and checked by a succession of high-level censors before being cleared for publication. When they concern a man of Brezhnev's stature and power, it is conceivable that he cleared the entry personally.

Did he really study in Moscow? If so, what happened there? Admission to the agricultural academy would have been an accomplishment for a minor provincial official, an open sesame to a successful career. Why did he leave so abruptly, change professions and opt for an education at a backwater industrial school? And why has this information been expunged from all subsequent reference works?

If this were a biography of any Western political leader, the discrepancies in the record would hardly be worth mentioning. In the Soviet context they are potentially of great significance. On the other hand, because we are dealing with the life of a Soviet official, the answers may never be forthcoming. We can merely speculate.

The least likely explanation is that Brezhnev made the switch of his own choosing. It was not a time when young men made such important decisions on their own. They were usually made for them.

One possibility is that a bureaucratic mix-up resulted in his transfer. It is also plausible that Brezhnev, just admitted to party membership, was sent to Kamenskoye on party orders because he was needed there. When he enrolled in it, the Dneprodzerzhinsk metallurgical institute hardly existed. A

Soviet journalist reported in 1972 that people in Dneprodzerzhinsk "remember how their now famous fellow citizen helped
to construct the local industrial institute with the students and
simultaneously studied there." Perhaps Brezhnev was assigned
to Kamenskoye to help build the school. Such missions were not
uncommon in the early 1930s.

Another possibility is that some senior official either in
Dneprodzerzhinsk or about to go there had been keeping his
eye on Brezhnev and wanted to promote his career.

On the other hand, Brezhnev may have ended up on the
wrong side of the agro-political debate, been dismissed from
the Moscow academy and retreated to Kamenskoye where he
hoped to use friends to start a new career in a potentially more
promising field. The best counter-argument to this thesis is
that Brezhnev survived the 1933 party purge in which nearly a
quarter of the total membership was dropped. Had he been in
serious political difficulties in Moscow, he would have been
affected by that sweep-up.

Finally, the possibility of dismissal for academic reasons
cannot be excluded. That would be the most persuasive
argument for discreetly omitting the Moscow interlude from
his official record. Brezhnev would not be the first politician,
Communist or Western, to have made such a slight cosmetic
change in his biography.

Whatever the facts, by 1931 Brezhnev was studying at the
metallurgical institute and also working at night in the
Kamenskoye *zavod*, by then renamed the F. E. Dzerzhinsky
plant, along with his father and younger brother Yakov. It
was also the year in which he must have married Viktoria, and
the year in which he became a member of the Communist
Party.

Acceptance into the Party – like all members he had under-
gone a 12-month probationary period as a candidate – was a
momentous occasion. What it meant was described by the late
Viktor Kravchenko, a Soviet defector. Kravchenko, a 1930s
acquaintance of Brezhnev, was a student at the metallurgical
institute in Dnepropetrovsk from 1930–34, and like Brezhnev
in those turbulent years, a *Komsomol* activist.

"It seemed to me the greatest event in my life," Kravchenko
wrote in his book, *I Chose Freedom*. "It made me one of the elite

of the new Russia. I was no longer an individual with a free choice of friends, interests, views. I was dedicated forever to an idea and a cause. I was a soldier in a highly disciplined army in which obedience to the center was the first and almost sole virtue. To meet the wrong people, to listen to the wrong words, thereafter would be inadmissible."

One of Brezhnev's assignments in that highly disciplined army, was to run the *Komsomol* organization at the fledgling metallurgical institute.

Kamenskoye and the Dnieper Bend area had changed beyond recognition since his departure in 1923 and were to change even more. North of Zaporozhe, the Dnieper hydro-electric station, one of the first triumphs of "socialist construction", though most of its equipment had been supplied by the General Electric Company, was nearing completion. Kamenskoye itself was a bustling boom town with almost 100,000 population. "You could literally watch it grow," a former resident told me. The old *zavod* had expanded multifold. A chemical combine, a large cement works, a factory making railway carriages and an electrical equipment plant had been built.

Engineer Petrov's polytechnicum had been moved to more auspicious surroundings in a brick building on Ulitsa Pelina. Across the street from it the metallurgical institute was taking shape.

As *Komsomol* chief at the institute, Brezhnev was also responsible for the young Communists at the technicum where he was a frequent but not always welcome visitor. Once or twice weekly he would call on the school's director, a man named Zinchuk, whose former secretary now lives in Western Europe.

"Brezhnev," she recalls, "was aloof, a man who seemed to shun contact with others. He never attended any of the *Komsomol* and student social affairs at the technicum. His manner bordered on arrogance. He was a paragon of party orthodoxy. People were visibly afraid of him. If he is now regarded as gallant toward ladies, then it is a quality he has acquired since I knew him. He never even used to say 'hello' to the women working in the front office and I don't recall his ever asking me whether the director was in or had time to see him. He just went right past me and barged into the office."

For all its growth and boom-town atmosphere, Kamenskoye, like most other cities in the Ukraine in the years from 1931–33, was the quiet eye of a raging storm in the surrounding country-side, a refuge from the horror in the nearby villages that was to engulf Brezhnev as it did all young party activists: forced collectivization and man-made famine.

In the second half of the 1920s, while Brezhnev was in Byelorussia and the Urals, a striking imbalance had developed in the growth of Soviet industry and agriculture. The country-side had become comparatively prosperous with a sharp increase in livestock and industrial crops production. But deliveries of grain, on which government prices had been kept artificially low, lagged behind the demand of the growing cities and industrial centers. By the winter of 1928–29 grain procure-ment from the peasants had decreased so much that bread rationing was introduced in the cities.

The need for collectivization of agriculture had long been accepted by the Party in principle. The critical debate centered on the pace of the changes. A threat of famine in the winter of 1928–29 settled the argument. The Party launched what was to become a ruthless, five-year undeclared war on the peasantry that left a trail of terror, misery and disaster.

The war focused primarily on the Ukraine because it was the USSR's granary and because peasant resistance there was the most violent and most dangerous to the regime. The first step in the struggle, in 1929, called for "liquidation of the *kulaks* (the wealthier, more efficient, more prosperous farmers) as a class". Five million peasants, wives, children and close relatives – approximately half of them from the Ukraine – were uprooted from their lands and homes, beaten, tortured, massacred, imprisoned, deported to concentration camps and banished to Siberia, the Urals and the arctic north. At least a quarter of them perished of hunger, cold and disease on the long journeys. Just as many were killed in their villages and in attempting to defend their property from confiscation and collectivization.

De-kulakization had hardly begun when Stalin launched his drive for full collectivization which was to envelop all peasants, rich and poor alike. The peasants fought back with blind, destructive fury, slaughtering their livestock rather than surrendering it to the *kolkhozes* and transforming their villages into battlegrounds where they fought it out with units of the OGPU, the secret police.

By the spring of 1930 even Stalin realized that the agricultural policy was on the brink of collapse. On 2 March, *Pravda* published his "Dizziness from Success" article which called forcible collectivization to a halt. The gains were consolidated, excesses were halted and the blame for ruthless murder and destruction was shifted to over-zealous local officials.

The lull lasted for only twenty months. Then the drive was resumed with a vengeance with consequences which made the earlier campaign seem mild by comparison. Vyacheslav Molotov himself fired the opening shot. In the fall of 1931 he arrived in Dnepropetrovsk province. Traveling on a special closely guarded train, he went from village to village reinvigorating the collectivization movement. He promised that it would be voluntary. In fact it was carried out under viciously calculated compulsion.

The campaign was two-pronged. To break resistance and destroy the peasant spirit, agricultural procurement quotas were intentionally fixed above what the *kolkhozes* and peasants could produce, thus leaving them nothing to eat and no seed grain for the coming year. A deliberate supply blockade was imposed on those *kolkhozes* and individual landholders who "deviated from the fulfillment of the grain collection plans" or "failed to meet their contractual obligations". When they did comply they were immediately given new and higher quotas. The Soviet euphemism for this policy was "firm assignments". It was a campaign intended to break the peasant will and starve out resistance. Those who survived were not the fittest but the most compliant.

In January 1933, dissatisfied with the way the Ukrainian Communists were handling grain collection and realizing that village soviets and local officials would not stomach further militant action against friends and neighbors, Stalin ordered a number of trusted lieutenants to take over. One of them was M. M. Khatayevich, a secretary of the Ukrainian Central Committee, who was named party chief of Dnepropetrovsk province.

One of Khatayevich's first actions was to organize *buksirniye brigady* – towing brigades. They were composed of 25,000 "workers with adequate political and organizational experience", *Komsomol* enthusiasts and party activists from colleges and factories in Dnepropetrovsk and Kamenskoye. Their purpose was to enforce the policy. Teams of armed, well-fed youths, endowed with full punitive and police powers, their tasks were to see that grain delivery quotas were met by the peasants. Khatayevich called the brigade leaders to a conference at *oblast* headquarters in Dnepropetrovsk city. There were about eighty young men in the hall. Viktor Kravchenko, by his own admission, was among them, as were fellow students, *Komsomol* organizers and young party members from the institutes and factories of the Dnieper Bend. It is a fair assumption that Leonid Brezhnev, the *Komsomol* chief of Kamenskoye's metallurgical institute, was there too.

"Comrades," Khatayevich told the group, "Dnepropetrovsk province has fallen behind. The Party and Comrade Stalin have ordered us to complete the collectivization process by spring. For that the local village authorities need injections of Bolshevik iron. That is why we are sending you.

"The class struggle in the villages has taken the sharpest forms. This is no time for squeamishness or sentimentality. Throw your bourgeois humanitarianism on the garbage heap and act like Bolsheviks. Destroy the *kulak* agents wherever they raise their heads. The *kulaks* as well as the middle-class peasants and the poor refuse to give up their wheat. Your task is to squeeze it out of them, by any and all means. Do not be afraid to employ the most extreme methods."

The brigades were empowered to search for, confiscate and extort every kernel, every potato, every beet, every root they could find. According to a Ukrainian now living in the US, "they went from house to house, day after day, looking for hidden food. They searched attics, cellars, barns, pig-pens, stables, and haylofts. They would measure the thickness of the wall under the oven to find if there was grain concealed in the foundation. They knocked on floors and walls and wherever the sound was dull they would pry the place open. Sometimes whole walls were pulled down, ovens wrecked and the last grain taken away when anything was found. The collection was characterized by wanton destruction and acts of extreme cruelty. Every brigade had its headquarters manned by a special staff. Peasants were hauled to headquarters and there subjected to all-night interrogations, beatings, water-treatment and semi-naked confinement in cold cells. There were many instances of torture."

One can only conjecture whether Brezhnev committed such acts. Regardless of his personal involvement, however, he must have been acutely aware of the horror – starvation, cannibalism, murder and disease – invading the land.

Malcolm Muggeridge, then the *Manchester Guardian*'s correspondent in the USSR, described it as a government war against the peasantry. "On one side there were millions of peasants with bodies swollen from hunger; on the other side soldiers, members of the OGPU, carrying out the orders of the dictatorship of the proletariat. They hurled themselves on the region like a pack of locusts and seized everything edible. They shot and hung thousands of peasants, sometimes whole villages; . . . The Ukraine and the Northern Caucasus were once the most fertile provinces of Russia. Today they look like deserts: the fields are covered with weeds and the people are awaiting inevitable death."

Peasants slaughtered their livestock for food, and when that ran out, dogs, cats, rats and mice. They lived off weeds and grass, barks and leaves and eventually off each other. Cannibalism became almost commonplace that winter. Finding nothing left to eat in the countryside, hundreds of thousands abandoned their homes and villages and dragged their way to the cities and towns where they hoped to beg or exchange their last few possessions for a morsel or two of food.

Through the streets of Dnepropetrovsk, Kamenskoye, Kiev, Kharkov and other cities the miserable hulks of humanity from the villages dragged themselves along on swollen feet or skeletal legs. Each morning wagons rolled along picking up the emaciated remains of the dead. Frozen and stiff they were piled like cord-wood and taken for burial in ravines and mass graves.

The toll, by a careful examination of all estimates and all accounts, was 5.5 million deaths: from hunger and related causes. Nearly all were villagers. In the cities there was plenty to eat. In fact, while millions died the USSR continued to *export* grain. It was a coldly calculated artificial famine designed to break peasant resistance.

"To have let the peasants keep their grain would have encouraged them to go on producing little," a Soviet official admitted to William H. Chamberlin, the *Christian Science Monitor*'s Moscow correspondent in 1933.

Having tyrannized the peasantry Stalin then set out to crush the Party. While no evidence implicates Leonid Brezhnev in that crime he was soon to be one of its beneficiaries.

Brezhnev was still a student when the Communist Party's XVIIth Congress was held in Moscow in January and February 1934. The first difficulties of industrialization had been overcome, collectivization was almost complete and all opposition within and without the Party had been destroyed. Stalin and his supporters were absolute masters. The Moscow conclave was rightfully called "the congress of the victors". But as Khrushchev was to declare more than twenty years later, Stalin's mind was already abnormal: he suspected everyone and everything, saw enemies everywhere and was consumed with a desire to destroy them physically.

His moment to strike came on 1 December 1934 when his friend Sergei Kirov, the party chief of Leningrad, was assassinated.

The circumstances surrounding that murder are mysterious and in his famous "secret speech" in 1956 Khrushchev hinted that Kirov had been killed on orders from Stalin. Whatever the truth about it, Kirov's death triggered the reign of terror that swept the country for the next years. It was an era of fear, lawlessness, inquisition, torture, cruelty and murder that decimated the Party, permanently crippled the Russian psyche, imprisoned millions as slave laborers and sent millions more to their deaths

There are few verifiable facts about Brezhnev's record during the early part of this period. In 1935 he graduated from the institute as a metallurgical engineer. That put him in a special category of party members – those with solid Soviet educations, the "technical intelligentsia". But again Soviet reference sources are contradictory about what he did. According to some, as mentioned earlier, he entered the Red Army. According to others he worked in the Kamenskoye *zavod* as an engineer.

By late 1936, it seems certain, Brezhnev was indeed working in the plant and in the following year he became director of Petrov's old vocational school, the metallurgical polytechnicum. The people in Dneprodzerzhinsk, says the Soviet weekly *Novoye Vremya* (*New Times*) "remember with gratitude how engineer Brezhnev then passed on his knowledge and experience to the future foremen who studied at the metallurgical technical school."

In 1937, too, the terror began to engulf even Stalin's most sincere and loyal followers. One of the first to fall was Pavel Postyshev, the man who for four years had tyrannized the Ukraine. He was recalled to Moscow and eventually disappeared from sight. Khatayevich, the party chief of Dnepropetrovsk *oblast*, replaced him as second secretary of the Ukrainian Communist Party. E. K. Pramnek took the place of Khatayevich as first secretary of Dnepropetrovsk province.

A sweeping purge of party officials at the provincial and local levels followed Postyshev's fall. Two-thirds of the *oblast* and one-third of all the municipal and district leaders were dismissed and replaced that spring. One of the men chosen to fill a suddenly vacated post was Brezhnev. In May 1937 he was named "vice chairman of the executive committee of the Dneprodzerzhinsk city soviet", that is, deputy mayor of his home town.

He was thirty years old, married, the father of two children, locally respected and quite obviously on the way toward a successful new career.

CHAPTER IV

New Pegs for Empty Holes

Pravda on Friday morning, 28 January 1938, displayed a two-column photograph on the top of page one. It showed the broad and smiling face of a balding, fair-haired man in an embroidered Ukrainian shirt: Nikita Sergeyevich Khrushchev.

A tersely-worded, five-line Tass dispatch beneath the picture announced that a plenum of the Central Committee of the Ukrainian Communist Party had elected Khrushchev its acting first secretary.

For Leonid Brezhnev, though he could not have known it then, it was a momentous event. For the next twenty-five years his career was to be interwoven with that of Khrushchev – until he conspired to topple his mentor and take his place. But at that time Khrushchev's name and face were only vaguely familiar to Brezhnev, as to most other young *apparatchiki* in the Ukraine. One of Stalin's favorites, he was formally still party chief of Moscow and best known as the builder of its subway system. But it was no secret that he had been in and out of Kiev during the previous six months doing Stalin's bidding. His appointment as Stalin's new viceroy in the Ukraine could hardly have been unexpected. Yet it must have come as a shock that winter morning. Brezhnev, like other local officials, knew only too well that the Ukrainian Central Committee which purportedly had elected Khrushchev did not exist. It had been physically liquidated four months earlier.

The Ukrainian Communist Party had a special history, steeped in Ukrainian national feeling and in the unique make-up of its membership. Unlike the Russian Party, it was a coalition of Bolsheviks and nationally conscious Left Social Revolutionaries who, until 1920, had an organization of their own called the Borotbist Party.

Time and again attempts to crush this form of Ukrainian

Communist independence had failed. Officials with strong centralizing views, sent by Moscow, modified them over the years, tending to become more sympathetic to Ukrainian policies than the Kremlin's. In the purges that had swept the Soviet Union since Kirov's murder in 1934 the Ukraine, even under leaders loyal to or appointed by Stalin, such as Stanislav Kossior, the party chief, and Pavel Postyshev, the second secretary, provided the last flicker of resistance.

In March 1937, after the second of the big Moscow show trials, it was finally the Ukraine's turn. Stalin began by removing and demoting Postyshev who was shot in 1940.

Soon after Postyshev's fall Stalin delivered a second blow to the Ukraine: the transfer and subsequent execution of General Iona Yakir, the commander of the Ukrainian military district, and a member of the Ukrainian Politburo. Yakir was one of the first Red Army generals and marshals to be liquidated in Stalin's purge of the military.

Undoubtedly Stalin hoped to profit from whatever rivalries the departure of Postyshev would unleash in Kiev. But the Ukrainian leadership held together. At the XIIIth Congress of the Ukrainian CP in late May and early June 1937, nearly all the old guard, including Kossior and Khatayevich, were reelected. Stalin found this team too independent and nationalistic and immediately set about preparing its annihilation.

Scores of NKVD agents were sent into the Ukraine to create an atmosphere of fear and fabricate information about "enemies of the people". In August a special Kremlin commission consisting of Khrushchev, Molotov and Nikolai Yezhov, the NKVD (secret police) chief arrived in Kiev. They charged the Ukrainian leadership with lack of vigilance and failing to "repress" the "enemies" which Yezhov's agents had invented.

Khrushchev, Molotov and Yezhov, distrustful of the local police, were accompanied by train-loads of special NKVD units from Moscow, and military detachments from Siberia. Kiev was turned into a besieged fortress. The district in which the Kremlin team met with the Ukrainian leaders was cordoned off from the rest of the city by NKVD troops directly under Yezhov's command.

At a plenary session with the Ukrainian Central Committee Molotov produced a barrage of accusations, insinuations and fabrications. Then he demanded a vote of no-confidence in Kossior, Khatayevich, N. N. Popov, another secretary of the Central Committee, Grigory Petrovsky, the "president" of the Ukraine, and Panas Lyubchenko, its prime minister, and their expulsion from the Central Committee. He insisted on Khrushchev's election as first secretary.

The Ukrainians refused to comply, arguing that as a legally independent party they were not subject to the Kremlin's dictates. Their negotiations with the emissaries from Moscow – a scene similar to the Soviet confrontation with the Czechoslovak Communist leadership thirty-one years later – dragged out for days.

Of course, Molotov and Khrushchev could have told Yezhov to arrest the entire Ukrainian Central Committee. But before taking so drastic a step they conferred with Stalin who advised them to move the talks to the "mobile" NKVD headquarters which Yezhov had brought with him. Even there the Ukrainians stood firm.

Finally, after consulting the Kremlin again, Molotov offered an alternative. All 102 voting and alternate members of the Ukrainian Central Committee should go to Moscow to discuss the matter with the leaders of the Soviet Party and Stalin personally. That proposal was accepted by the majority, albeit with some dissension. Only one man, Lyubchenko, refused. He shot himself.

On 2 September 1937 the others boarded a special train for Moscow. Of these 101 men all but three eventually were shot or disappeared in NKVD prisons and labor camps. The only prominent member of the Ukrainian leadership to survive the purges, the war and the postwar purges was Petrovsky. Among the full members and candidates of the Ukrainian Politburo subsequently executed were Khatayevich and his successor as party chief of Dnepropetrovsk, E. K. Pramnek.

Soon nearly all the secretaries of *oblast*, city and district committees; provincial and municipal officials; industrial executives; directors of colleges, universities and institutes, and leading figures in the arts and literature were purged from their posts: positions to which many had been appointed just six months before, after Postyshev's fall.

The Ukraine, leaderless, terrorized and demoralized, was

virtually an NKVD fief in which Yezhov's inquisitors and informers denounced, interrogated, tortured, imprisoned and murdered at will.

Until Khrushchev's arrival in January, government in any usual sense of the word had ceased to function. Within the four-month period following Lyubchenko's suicide the Ukraine had had three prime ministers. Following Khatayevich's departure in the spring of 1937 three party chiefs governed Dnepropetrovsk *oblast* before a semblance of stability returned to the province. One of these was Demyan Sergeyevich Korotchenko, a close associate of Khrushchev and patron of Leonid Brezhnev, whose political career was to last into the Brezhnev era. He died in 1969 aged seventy-five. Korotchenko had become Pramnek's successor as Dnepropetrovsk party leader, staying on the job a scant five months until February 1938 when he went to Kiev to become prime minister of the Ukraine.

"Officials came and went so quickly in those months," according to a native of Dnepropetrovsk now living in West Germany, "that the successors of successors were arrested before the names on the office doors had been changed. No one knew who would be next. Today's heroic new leader was likely to be tomorrow's new enemy of the people. The main objective was to avoid arrest and the safest policy was either to keep an almost invisible profile or to endear yourself to the NKVD as a collaborator by denouncing others."

We do not know which course Leonid Brezhnev adopted, but he was one of the few who survived.

The purges had liquidated the first and second strings of party and government leadership. Now it was the third team's turn. Khrushchev was accompanied to the Ukraine by his second-in-command, Mikhail Burmistenko, a leather-jacketed former Cheka man. Together they reconstructed the Ukrainian apparatus. In the spring of 1938 more than 1,600 party members were promoted to fill empty provincial and municipal posts as secretaries and department heads. Brezhnev was one of them.

In May 1938 he was transferred twenty-two miles downstream to Dnepropetrovsk, the *oblast* capital, to become head of the province committee's department of ideology and indoctrination. One year later when the office of *obkom* (*oblast* committee) secretary of propaganda was established, Brezhnev got the title to become the fifth-ranking party *apparatchik* in the second-largest and industrially most important province of the Ukraine: a territory with an area of 12,200 square miles and a population of more than two million.

Brezhnev was not, of course, the only young Communist in the Dnepropetrovsk *oblast* to benefit from Khrushchev's assumption of power in the Ukraine. And a number of them owe their rise in the Soviet hierarchy not only to Khrushchev but to the career of Brezhnev. They are members of the Dnieper Mafia which is one of the vital props of Brezhnev's power today.

In May 1938 when Brezhnev took up his duties in the drab, gray five-story *obkom* building on the corner of Pushkinska Prospekt and Polevaya Ulitsa in Dnepropetrovsk, the first secretary of the *oblast* party committee, Korotchenko's replacement, was Semyon Borisovich Zadionchenko. Like Korotchenko himself, he had once been an *apparatchik* in Moscow's Baumanski district, Nikita Khrushchev's erstwhile power base in the Soviet capital. And like Korotchenko, Zadionchenko was one of Khrushchev's protégés. The *oblast*'s second secretary was Leonid Romanovich Korniets, one of the few "older" Ukrainian party officials who had survived the purges. Korniets was to survive a great deal more in his life. He stayed around just long enough to assign Brezhnev an office and a desk. Then he hurried to Kiev where he became chairman of the republic's Supreme Soviet, that is "president" of the Ukraine. Following Stalin's death, Khrushchev brought Korniets to Moscow as the USSR's minister of procurement, a position which he continued to hold under Brezhnev until his death, at the age of sixty-eight, in 1969.

Shortly after Korniets' departure, Ivan Samoylovich Grushetsky joined the team of *obkom* secretaries in Dnepropetrovsk. A high-ranking Ukrainian *apparatchik* ever since then, Grushetsky was named "president" of the Ukraine and promoted to full membership in the Ukrainian Politburo in July 1972.

Two of Brezhnev's fellow students – Pavel Nikitovich Alferov and Konstantin Stepanovich Grushevoi – also began their climb up the political ladder in those turbulent times.

The same age as Brezhnev, both had graduated from the Kamenskoye metallurgical institute in 1934, a year before Brezhnev, and had then gone to work in the *zavod* as engineers.

Both, moreover, were to play important roles – Grushevoi still does – in promoting Brezhnev's career and strengthening his power base. Alferov was named party chief of the city of Dneprodzerzhinsk in 1937. One year later Grushevoi, who had been working as a shift leader and shop superintendent in the metallurgical plant, took over that position from Alferov. In 1939 Grushevoi went to Dnepropetrovsk as second secretary of the *obkom*, that is Brezhnev's direct superior, a position he held until the German invasion in 1941. Alferov, whose career was less spectacular, died in 1971. But Grushevoi is now a colonel general of the Soviet Army and chief political officer of Moscow Military District. He is one of Brezhnev's vital links to the Soviet military establishment.

In 1939, when Brezhnev was named *obkom* propaganda secretary, Nikolai Anisimovich Shchelokov, a twenty-nine year-old engineer and graduate of Dnepropetrovsk's metallurgical institute, was named mayor of Dnepropetrovsk. He and Brezhnev became close friends and political allies. In the early 1950s Shchelokov followed Brezhnev to Moldavia. Today, as noted previously, he is the Soviet Union's minister of interior and police chief as well as Brezhnev's neighbor on Kutuzovski Prospekt.

In the neighboring *oblast*, Zaporozhe, Andrei Pavlovich Kirilenko was named a secretary, later second secretary of the party committee, the same position he had after the war under Brezhnev. He was Brezhnev's second-in-command during the postwar reconstruction period in that province. Today, a member of the Politburo and a secretary of the Communist Party of the Soviet Union, he is *de facto* Brezhnev's second-in-command in Moscow.

The Dnieper Mafia also includes a number of younger men, *apparatchiki* who joined the Brezhnev bandwagon in Zaporozhe and Dnepropetrovsk after World War Two. But for men like Brezhnev, Kirilenko, Shchelokov, Grushevoi and Grushetsky, the Khrushchev reorganization of the decimated Party in the Dnieper basin was opportunity knocking at their doors: it meant a sudden major step up the political ladder.

For Brezhnev, his wife Viktoria and their two young children, Galina and Yuri, it was also the entrée to an exciting new world. Despite its rapid growth, Dneprodzerzhinsk was hickdom personified. By comparison Dnepropetrovsk, a bustling metropolis of 520,000 population, was a stately, cultured, luxuriously verdant city with its own opera company, university, colleges, institutes and an aristocratic pedigree dating to the golden era of the Romanov dynasty. Its position on a high and lush green bank overlooking the river is breathtaking. The Dnieper is almost a mile wide here.

Founded in 1784 by Catherine the Great, built and designed by her boudoir and throne-room favorite, Prince Grigori Potemkin, as his residence and the government seat of "New Russia", Yekaterinoslav was a totally planned city whose style reflected the ostentatious extravagance that characterized Catherine's reign. Potemkin ordered the construction of a magnificent cathedral in baroque style and a grandiose neo-classical palace. He laid out the three-mile-long Catherine – now the Karl Marx – Prospekt which former residents of Dnepropetrovsk still call, proudly, "the longest, widest, most elegant avenue in all the Russias".

In the late nineteenth and early twentieth centuries Yekaterinoslav developed quickly as one of the major industrial cities of the Ukraine. By 1938, when Brezhnev settled there, it was the metallurgical, chemical and transportation hub of the Dnieper basin. Dnepropetrovsk had also become an important educational center, with its university, founded in 1916, its medical school and college-level institutes of mining, metallurgy, transportation, and chemical and construction engineering. Potemkin's palace was converted into a "student palace of culture", that is, a student union.

As a member of the province's powerful new aristocracy, Brezhnev was entitled to the best Dnepropetrovsk had to offer: an automobile for his private use; shopping privileges in the special well-stocked stores reserved exclusively for *obkom*, city and other high-ranking party officials; a choice of the best theater and opera seats; the most up-to-date medical facilities, and, reportedly, a spacious flat in one of the turn-of-the-century apartment houses on Karl Marx Prospekt.

By comparison others, even members of the local intellectual establishment, lived frugally. Communal apartments with families of three and four people crowded into one room were considered adequate housing even for university lecturers and assistant professors. Although the food supply had improved immeasurably since the mid-1930s, other goods were scarce and clothing was strictly rationed. A former Dnepropetrovsk University faculty member recalls that he once won a ration chit for a new suit as a reward for some innovative research work. Of course, he still had to pay for the suit – the price equalled a month's salary – but at least he was entitled to buy one. An actor who had come from Moscow to join the ensemble of Dnepropetrovsk's Russian-language theater recalls that he could never find underwear in the city's clothing and department stores. He had to order sets from a friend in Moscow whose mother worked in a men's wear shop. Queues, shortages, shoddy workmanship and ugliness of design were the rule, rather than the exception.

One of Brezhnev's tasks as propaganda chief of the *oblast* was to divert public attention from these deficiencies of Soviet life. Another was to implement Khrushchev's Russification policy which had been introduced along with the liquidation of the nationally conscious old guard of the Ukrainian leadership.

In 1938 the Ukrainian school system was ordered to begin teaching Russian and a rudimentary command of the language became compulsory for all citizens. Russian became the official language of local government and party organizations. This represented a complete reversal of the policy adopted shortly after the Revolution when Ukrainian had become compulsory in the schools. Now Russian was depicted not only as the language Lenin had used and the language common to the whole Soviet Union, but as the bearer of an advanced, revolutionary, proletarian culture. The Ukraine's national history and its heroes were de-emphasized and Russia's long colonization and suppression of the Ukraine reinterpreted as a blessing. Among other things, the Dnepropetrovsk Russian-language theater was reinvigorated with an infusion of new talent from Moscow.

Brezhnev was also responsible for indoctrination which was termed "ideological work". It is complementary to coercion and entails securing popular consent to whatever are the leadership's current policies.

Thus it was Brezhnev's responsibility, to stimulate "ideological vigilance" against all manner of saboteurs, spies and enemies of the people who represented a wide spectrum of nemesis: "Ukrainian bourgeois nationalism", "Trotskyist subversion", "rightist deviationism" and German fascism. The last, in particular, was of special concern in the Ukraine, the Soviet Union's westernmost outpost which, so Khrushchev insisted in speech after speech, Nazi Germany was intent upon separating from the USSR.

Brezhnev also had to justify the terror and the purges which, in the language of those days, had "achieved considerable success in the discovery, eradication and annihilation of nests of Trotskyite-Bukharinite and bourgeois-nationalist agents of Polish-German and Japanese Fascism."

Being chief *obkom* propagandist meant supervising the editorial work of the *oblast* party papers, *Dneprovska Pravda* and the Ukrainian-language *Zora*. It entailed organizing agitprop sections in the cities and counties, the factories and *kolkhozes*, the colleges and schools.

Brezhnev was charged with organizing mass meetings, rallies, "spontaneous" demonstrations, parades and celebrations to whip up popular enthusiasm for Stalin and the regime. He had a hand in drafting the countless pledges to increase production, work faster and extract greater yields which were intended to spur "socialist competition" and emulate record breakers like Aleksei Stakhanov, the Ukrainian coal miner who in 1935 had exceeded his production quota fourteen-fold by applying more efficient methods of drilling. Brezhnev was the invisible author of the plethora of slogans and adulations of Stalin on the posters and banners which hung from building walls and across the roads and streets of villages, towns and cities in Dnepropetrovsk province.

"The late 1930s," as an emigrée from Dnepropetrovsk described those years, "were a time for jubilation – artificial jubilation. We read jubilant books, listened to jubilant speeches and saw jubilant movies. All made essentially the same point: Stalin was the wisest, the kindest, the most courageous, the most omniscient and the most prescient. He was our Father whose heart swelled with love for us. And the life he created for us, so we were told and eventually believed, was the best of all possible lives."

It was also a time for Soviet triumphs and heroes whose deeds Brezhnev and his subordinates did their utmost to publicize among the people of Dnepropetrovsk: arctic explorers, non-stop fliers and endurance pilots who, so the people were told, were living proof of the superiority of the Communist system.

Above all there were developments that challenged even the most skilled propagandist's ability to persuade the people of the soundness of the party line. For years Soviet propaganda had portrayed German fascism as the arch enemy. But on 23 August 1939 *Pravda* announced the Hitler-Stalin non-aggression pact. A six-column picture accompanying the report showed a smiling Stalin standing next to Germany's beaming foreign minister, Joachim von Ribbentrop. The propaganda machinery had to be thrown into reverse as the erstwhile enemy became Moscow's ally. Three weeks later the Red Army moved into Poland. Then came the annexation of the Western Ukraine and in November 1939 the start of the bloody, costly war with Finland. It was the Soviet-Finnish war, in fact, which put an end to Brezhnev's role as Dnepropetrovsk's chief propagandist.

The price of victory in that three-months-long conflict was enormous. The USSR had mobilized an army of almost two million men against a nation of only three million people. More than 48,000 Soviet soldiers were killed or listed as missing in action, 158,000 were wounded. Only with difficulty and at a terrible cost had the Red Army defeated a force a fraction of its size.

There were numerous reasons. Stalin's purge of the military had robbed the USSR of its best commanders and demoralized the officer corps. Soviet troops were ill-equipped and badly trained. Red Army tanks were too thinly armored to withstand Finnish artillery.

In April 1940, a month after the peace treaty with Finland, the Supreme Soviet voted an enormous increase in defense spending and Stalin ordered the conversion of countless factories to the production of armaments. The party apparatus was reorganized and secretaries for the defense industry were appointed at all echelons. Leonid Brezhnev was chosen for that job in Dnepropetrovsk *oblast.*

According to official Soviet sources the choice was made at a plenum of the province committee during which Zadionchenko, the first secretary, nominated Brezhnev and praised him effusively. "The secretary for the defense industry should be a man who is energetic, has a technical education and wide experience in production. He must also enjoy the respect of our workers, foremen and engineers." He described Brezhnev as the "only one among us who possesses all those qualities." Brezhnev was chosen "unanimously".

To judge from the laudatory articles and books about his wartime role which have appeared in the USSR since 1970, he was indeed energetic. He worked around the clock, cajoled, exhorted, threatened. He fired off telegrams and letters to Moscow to get more equipment and supplies and made strenuous efforts to cut through the red tape.

Brezhnev was exhausted on Sunday, 22 June 1941 when the Wehrmacht thundered across the Soviet border. He had been busy in his office until long past midnight to complete an urgent report to Moscow on the output of ammunition at local plants. He had risen again at dawn to inspect work at a new airbase under construction near Dnepropetrovsk. There a friend brought him the news: "*Voyna, voyna* – war, war. The Germans have invaded." Brezhnev began a futile two-months-long battle to convert the rest of the *oblast*'s industry to defense work and to evacuate equipment and workers to the Urals and farther east.

Rushing between Dnepropetrovsk and Dneprodzerzhinsk, Brezhnev converted the locomotive plants to the production of truck and tank engines; the Artyom works, a bridge-building enterprise, to making parts for aircraft assembly factories; the Dneprodzerzhinsk *zavod* to casting artillery shells and cannons; the Comintern Combine to manufacturing mortars; clothing factories to turning out uniforms; metal shops to the output of trenching tools and mess kits.

But all to no avail for it was now too late. Stalin had wasted months of the breathing spell which the pact with Hitler had given him. And so by early July, since their advance had met the minimum of resistance, the Germans began bombing and shelling Dnepropetrovsk, Dneprodzerzhinsk, Zaporozhe and the mining centers around Krivoi Rog. Inexorably the front closed in on the Dnieper Bend and the main task became the removal of factory equipment to the east.

There are almost no details on what happened in the Dnepropetrovsk area. But in Zaporozhe the evacuation was carried on without interruption day and night for thirty days.

The dismantling was done during the day and the loading onto railway cars at night, for the Dnieper hydro-electric station had ceased to provide current. The total number of railway cars was 3,500. Not everything removed was usable by the time it reached the Urals for in their haste and determination to evacuate as much equipment as possible, inexperienced and untrained party officials ordered the disassembly and destruction of much that would only work when left intact.

In Dnepropetrovsk *obkom* officials organized the digging of anti-tank trenches, helped to lay mines and even changed the numbers on streetcars and removed street signs to confuse the enemy. Within a month of the invasion the Dnepropetrovsk party committee had recruited five divisions of infantry. They were brave but without tanks or heavy artillery and equipped only with light field guns, rifles, automatic weapons and home-made petrol bombs they were no match for the Germans.

Major General I. T. Zamertsev, then commander of the 225th Division defending Dnepropetrovsk, credits Brezhnev with doing the most to supply his unit with weapons, and ammunition. According to Zamertsev, Brezhnev also made sure "that we had enough of the improvised petrol bombs [or Molotov cocktails as they are called in the West]. Brezhnev ordered all the bottles at the local distillery turned over to us and the vodka poured into the sewers."

Not even that stopped the German advance. By 25 August Zamertsev's division had retreated across the Dnieper, leaving the gutted and scarred city to the enemy. More than half of his division had been killed or captured by the advancing Wehrmacht units of General von Kleist's 2nd Panzer Division.

Where was Brezhnev? A yellowing record in the Dnepropetrovsk *obkom* archives says tersely: "Comrade Brezhnev has left for the army."

CHAPTER V

Heroes are Made, not Born

The Red Army was conceived as a ragged, disorganized band of partisans and volunteers in the crucible of the Civil War. That it triumphed over the Whites and eventually became one of the world's most formidable fighting forces was due as much to the organizational genius of Leon Trotsky as to the introduction of a unique system of ideological control and surveillance of the 20,000 ex-tsarist officers who had been induced and coerced to serve with it by the end of 1918 – political commissars.

Attached to most units of company size and larger, the commissars functioned as the direct representatives of the Party and the Soviet regime. Their primary duty was "to prevent army institutions from becoming nests of conspiracy or employing weapons against workers and peasants". They were charged with directing party work, conducting propaganda among the troops and controlling the activities of the officers. Orders and reports had to be signed jointly by commanders and commissars.

Dedicated and often fanatical men, they stiffened the nerve of unwilling soldiers when the fighting got heavy, kept Moscow informed of troop morale, officer competence and loyalty and provided the Red Army with a coherence and sense of purpose that led to victory.

Trotsky proudly called them "a new Communist order of Samurai which. . . knows how to die and teaches others to die for the cause of the working class."

In the summer of 1941, after the German invasion of the USSR, Leonid Brezhnev entered that order with the rank of lieutenant colonel as deputy chief of the political administration of the Southern Army Group. His immediate superior was the former second secretary of Dnepropetrovsk *obkom*, Leonid

Korniets. In April 1942 Brezhnev was promoted to colonel and transferred to the staff of the 18th Army as its chief political commissar, replacing Zaporozhe *obkom*'s Andrei Kirilenko who had been demobilized and called to Moscow to supervise production of military aircraft. Toward the end of the war Brezhnev was made a major general and became head of the political directorate of the 4th Ukrainian Army Group.

These were by no means as exalted positions as those of Nikita Khrushchev, a member of the military council and the Politburo's chief representative on the Ukrainian and Southern Russian fronts. But they afforded Brezhnev a number of excellent opportunities to prove himself to Khrushchev with whom he forged vital links in the army.

Until a few years ago, virtually nothing was known of Brezhnev's wartime role. A 1959 history of the Great Patriotic War listed Brezhnev together with Stalin, Khrushchev, Kosygin, Mikhail Suslov, Kirilenko and seventeen other party officials as "outstanding organizers and leaders of the armed struggle and the work on the home front".

The 1959 and 1962 editions of the official *History of the Communist Party of the Soviet Union* mention him along with seven other "experienced party leaders" who played important roles during the war.

But just as Khrushchev's personal role in the military operations of World War Two grew with his political power and with each day that the events themselves receded into history, so Leonid Brezhnev's military exploits have loomed ever larger as the challenges to his political supremacy have diminished.

Not surprisingly, it was Defense Minister Marshal Grechko – a wartime comrade-in-arms – who signalled the start of the fulsome campaign to portray Brezhnev as an outstanding military figure. During the war Grechko commanded a number of different armies, among them, for a while, the 18th where he served as Brezhnev's commanding officer.

In his book, *The Battle for the Caucasus*, Grechko expressed frequent and warm praise for Brezhnev's deeds, describing him as an energetic, courageous officer who dashed from front to front to bolster the political morale of the troops. He was also the first to disclose that the present secretary-general of the CPSU was almost killed in 1943 when a small coastal landing craft in which he was riding struck a mine. Brezhnev was "thrown into the sea by the shockwave and lost consciousness", Grechko wrote. "But thanks to the sailors' resourcefulness his life was saved."

Grechko merely opened the sluice gates to what has become a flood of publicity about Brezhnev's wartime activities. The purpose appears to be two-fold: to enhance Brezhnev's image in particular and the reputation of political commissars in general.

Trotsky may have called the commissars Communist Samurai, but their role in Soviet military history has been highly controversial. By the end of the 1920s when most military commanders themselves had become party members and the army's political administration had been turned into Stalin's own instrument, the commissars no longer seemed important. They were revived suddenly in August 1937 in the wake of Stalin's purge of the armed forces.

Commissars were raised to the level of commanders. Both were described as constituting a "single unit in the matter of directing military and political training . . ." Both the commander and the military commissar were to lead the formation into action.

The impracticability of this became painfully evident in the débâcle of the war with Finland. When Marshal S. K. Timoshenko was named commander-in-chief and minister of defense in 1940, political commissars and the dual command structure were abolished. One year later, in July 1941, after many units had panicked and fled before the advancing Wehrmacht, it was reinstituted, only to be modified again in 1942. From then until the end of the war political officers such as Brezhnev ranked as deputy commanders of their units.

Their reputation among combat officers and soldiers was low. Regarded as armchair politicians in uniform, they evoked fear because of their political weight and their obvious links with the NKVD's ruthless "rear security units" and SMERSH, the special section which spied on the military and rooted out "disloyal" officers and men. Among hardened battle veterans the commissars were derided as cowards because they shirked the front lines and remained in the relative luxury and safety of the command posts. Their functions seemed to consist of handing out cards to newly admitted Communist Party members, conducting political seminars, staging indoctrination sessions and holding interminable speeches which exhorted others to go forth to die for the country. But there were some notable exceptions and if we can believe the image makers, Brezhnev was one of them.

Virtually all that is known about his role has been published in newspapers, magazines and the memoirs of certain marshals and generals since 1967, that is, after he became secretary general of the Party. The suspicion of deliberate embellishment as part of the growing Brezhnev personality cult is therefore hard to dispel. Nevertheless, the stories appear to be consistent. The same incidents and witnesses crop up in many of the reports. Moreover, the decorations which Brezhnev received – during the war, not retroactively when he was already a powerful party leader – were usually awarded only for bravery, courage and exceptional leadership in action.

Undeniably, much of Brezhnev's wartime experience *did* consist of typical *politruk* work. One of the earliest photos of him, taken in September 1942, shows a smiling Brezhnev shaking hands with a young Red Army soldier, Alexander Malov, to whom he had just issued a Communist Party membership card. Malov, a tommy gun on his shoulder, is also smiling. Behind them stand other soldiers and officers with rifles and bayonets. Brezhnev attended and organized innumerable conferences at which he appealed to Communist Party and *Komsomol* members to "set examples of bravery and staunchness".

Soviet military historians have access to a fascinating file full of Brezhnev's letters, orders, directives and requests to his subordinates and to his superiors, in particular Khrushchev. These are slowly being made available in articles and memoirs.

A few days before the December 1943 counter-offensive between Kiev and Zhitomir, Brezhnev issued the following directive to corps and divisional commissars:

"You will pay constant attention to the physical fitness and health of your men. They must be supplied regularly with hot meals and hot water. There must be strict control to ensure that supplies issued by the state for the men and officers reaches them. Negligence or inactivity in this respect must be dealt with severely. Particular attention should be paid to the medical corps. The political departments of units will detail special personnel to be responsible for evacuating the wounded and assuring them quick medical aid."

On the same day he sent the following dispatch to 1st Ukrainian Army Group Headquarters, that is, to Khrushchev, its chief political officer:

"The food situation in the units is bad. There is a shortage of meat, fats, fish and canned goods. There are frequent interruptions in the food supply. There is no feed whatsoever for the horses. Ammunition and food deliveries are delayed for lack of motor transport. Until now the motor transport battalion has been *en route* and the first train did not arrive until yesterday. . . We have been issued only 185 tons of gasoline, enough to fill the tanks and armoured vehicles only once. We are badly in need of winter uniforms . . . Please render the necessary assistance on all the points I have enumerated."

A week later he was able to report an encouraging improvement of the supply picture.

According to Ivan Pavelko of Zaporozhe, a former 18th Army major and one of Brezhnev's wartime deputies, the political department was not supposed to be in charge of logistics. "But Colonel Brezhnev believed it was our responsibility not only to inspire the soldiers on the battlefield. . . but to exercise strict party control over supplies. 'First you see to it that the soldier is properly fed and clothed,' he used to say. 'Then you lead him into the attack.'

"He was as demanding of himself as of others: day after day he made the rounds of the units and was always sending us out to report on how things were. When we returned he would question us closely. Did the men have enough bread and sugar? Tobacco? Tinned food? Cereals? Felt boots? Warm jackets? Gloves? Ammo? Hand grenades? And everyone – we in the political departments, the quartermasters, the field commanders – knew that he invariably checked and double-checked supply reports either personally or by telephone."

Brezhnev's frequent visits to forward positions and close escapes from death have become the subject of paeans to his bravery. The most complete and detailed of these began appearing as a six-part article series in *Novoye Vremya* (*New Times*), the Soviet political weekly, in 1971 and 1972. Written by Iona Andronov, one of the magazine's associate editors, the series purports to be a documentary of the 18th Army's battles from the Caucasus to the gates of Prague. In actuality it is a panegyric on *one* of the 18th Army's officers: Brezhnev.

"There was only one way to halt the enemy and raise morale," wrote Andronov, "a way tested in the Revolution and the Civil War. That was for Communists and commissars to be the first to face fire. If a commander got hit, a political instructor immediately took his place. It was no accident that a political instructor was the first man to ascend Mount Elbrus, where German alpine troops had planted the swastika flag. With a handful of soldiers he drove the fascists off the peak and hoisted our red banner with the hammer and sickle."

Brezhnev, according to Andronov, was that kind of commissar. He related a story told by Alexei Kopenkin, a veteran of the bitter fighting around Tuapse, a vital town on the Black Sea coast, in October 1942.
"The Nazis stormed our trenches practically by the hour. Their artillery and aircraft kept us pinned down. For seven days we fought without let-up. The bodies of the dead were everywhere. In spots the river was dammed by corpses and the water turned pink with blood." Practically the entire mortar battalion, of which Kopenkin was a member, was wiped out. Of its second company only ten men remained alive. "When the Germans finally broke through we called our own artillery fire down on ourselves. It seemed the only way out. At that moment I saw a tall, dark-haired commissar come running through our trench under fire and heard him shout: 'Hold on, comrades! Help is coming.'
"That was how I first met Comrade Brezhnev. He came to encourage us. He spent two days with our brigade, cheering up the men, joking with them, assuring them that we would certainly drive Hitler out of our land. We needed those words

as much as we did ammunition. The men believed him because he faced bullets bravely. The strength of his spirit strengthened theirs."

That battle was a turning-point. It stopped the German drive into the Caucasus and to the Black Sea. By the spring of 1943 the Soviets were turning the tide and the 18th Army was in the thick of the fighting on the coast. It was in March that Brezhnev was almost killed when his boat hit a mine.

The details of that episode have been related by Ivan Solovyov (now a lawyer in the town of Anadyr in Magadan) who was then a thirteen-year-old cabin boy on a minelayer operating out of Gelendzhik, on the Black Sea coast.

"We were halfway across Tesemesskaya Bay, after laying mines near Kabardinka, when we spotted a seiner that was directly in our path. Suddenly a pillar of water went up right under its bows. One of the sailors shouted: 'It's hit a mine.'

"It was listing heavily to starboard when we got to it. Several men were swimming in the water. We pulled out some of them. Then other boats approached to help and we all headed toward the shore. A steep cliff there protected us from German shells and a half-sunk barge served as a pier. When all those who had been picked out of the water were on the barge, Dotsenko glanced at one of the officers and exclaimed: 'Well, if it isn't our commissar!'

"Only then did I realize it was Colonel Brezhnev. His demeanor was cheerful but you could see he was pretty well frozen from the icy water. Just then all hell broke loose. Machine guns were crackling and there was the rumble of explosions.

"Everybody dashed away from the water, together with Brezhnev. Ivan Dotsenko (our captain) told me: 'Fetch my emergency rations, boy. The commissar needs to be warmed up. The lads need him now, and no mistake!' He passed his hand over his throat. I ran down to our boat, got a flask of Vodka and took it back ashore to a bunker – the cellar of a vineyard – where the officers, soldiers and sailors stood around Brezhnev. Dotsenko handed him the bottle and said: 'Try some sailors' milk, Comrade Commissar. The weather's foul and it's too cold for swimming.'

"Brezhnev laughed, drank, said thank you, but chided Dotsenko for having sent me, a boy, to get alcohol. There was no time to worry about that, though. German mortars were firing. Brezhnev and some of the other officers ran up the ravine to the forward area. Everybody grabbed submachine guns and grenades and dashed up front. Three German attacks were repulsed that day.

"When we returned to the boats on the shore toward evening to ship out the wounded, I again saw Comrade Brezhnev. Somebody quipped: 'Comrade Commissar, it'd be great to celebrate May Day in Berlin.' Brezhnev smiled: 'We'll be celebrating there eventually.'

"I heard one of the wounded saying: 'That commissar is brave, but he's also rational. He's not the sort of man who risks the lives of others for no purpose. He tries to find out about everything, and he's right there in the trenches. I'm not afraid to fight alongside a man like that.' "

At the end of the summer of 1943 Brezhnev was in on the assault on Novorossiysk and Taman where the 18th Army distinguished itself. In November it was suddenly transferred, by rail and road, nearly 1,000 miles northwest to the Dnieper, Brezhnev's home base, where it became part of General Nikolai Vatutin's and Nikita Khrushchev's 1st Ukrainian Army Group. There Brezhnev was to have his next brush with death.

The decision behind that move was allegedly reached by Stalin on the special train carrying him to the historic November 28th Teheran conference with President Roosevelt and Prime Minister Churchill. With him on the trip from Moscow was his operations chief, Colonel General Sergei Shtemenko, now chief-of-staff of Warsaw Pact Forces, an officer whose oscillatory career has been closely linked to the political fortunes of Brezhnev. Shtemenko has reconstructed the story.

In late October and early November the Red Army had crossed the Dnieper, liberating Dneprodzerzhinsk and Dnepropetrovsk in the south, Kiev further north, and had driven as far west as Zhitomir. There the offensive had run out of steam.

A German counter-offensive by Field Marshal Erich von Manstein's Army Group South began on 15 November 1943, recaptured Zhitomir, threatened Kiev, and menaced the southern bridgeheads at Dnepropetrovsk and Dneprodzer-zhinsk.

To reinforce General Vatutin's and Khrushchev's 1st Ukrainian Army Group there, the 18th Army, was rushed north from the Taman Peninsula on the Black Sea. Its task, according to Shtemenko, "was not only to cut the Zhitomir-Kiev highway, but to launch a counter-offensive".

By the night of 11 December, the situation was fluid, with the Germans providing most of the momentum. The 18th Army headquarters had been established at Kolonchina, a village about twenty-five miles west of Kiev. Shortly before midnight Brezhnev dispatched his officers to various sectors of the front to size up the situation. Then he himself set out in a jeep for the area where fighting was heaviest, accompanied by a driver, a submachine gunner and his aide, Captain Ivan Kravchuk. Kravchuk has retold the story:

"We left the jeep about 1500 meters from the front lines because we were now under heavy German shelling. We jumped into a communications trench and ran forward. The trench, however, was very shallow and we were pinned down by machine-gun fire. Besides, the enemy set off flares every thirty seconds or so. We made the last lap in short dashes.

"At last we reached a trench where some thirty men had just repelled a Nazi attack. . . Suddenly we came under heavy mortar shelling. One shell exploded about ten meters away from me and I saw two men go down. The explosions came one after the other and men were hit right and left. Through the din came the cries and groans of the wounded.

"Someone screamed hysterically: 'We've got to fall back or we'll all be killed.' A young lieutenant loomed up in the darkness and shouted: 'Say that again and I'll shoot you. Don't take one step back.' A steady, calm voice – Brezhnev's – cut him short. 'Put your gun away, lieutenant. Station the Communists all along the trench and the rest of the men between them. There's no time to lose. The Nazis are going to attack again.' Turning to those around him, Brezhnev shouted: 'There can be no retreat, comrades. Kiev is behind us. We've got to hold this line.'

"The Germans opened up again and their infantry attack

began. We had only one heavy machine gun and it fell silent within seconds. Brezhnev rushed towards it and I after him, jumping over men lying motionless at the bottom of the trench. Brezhnev shouted to me over his shoulder: 'You've got a first-aid kit. See what you can do for those men.' Hurriedly I bent over two or three of them, but they were dead. I ran after Brezhnev,

"Just then the machine gun sputtered back to life. When I reached it I saw that Brezhnev had taken the dead gunner's place. I pulled the body aside and pushed the ammo box closer to the gun. We were low on ammunition and the Germans were still advancing. They were only thirty or forty meters away and began lobbing grenades. Brezhnev replied with short bursts to save ammo, taking careful aim in the light of the German flares.

"He seemed to be as calm as ever. Several times I tried to press him down below the parapet when the enemy fire was particularly heavy, but each time he pushed me aside. As he reached the last ammunition belt he ordered me to go along the trench and tell everyone to save the hand grenades until the last and prepare for hand-to-hand fighting.

"I counted about a dozen survivors in the trench, the lieutenant among them. He was no longer nervous. He was firing single shots with his submachine gun, so as to save every round. . . It was obvious to me that we had at the most 10 or 15 minutes to live – until Brezhnev's machine gun fell silent, until the Nazi attackers poured into the trench.

"But as happened so many times in the war, we came through. Our long-range guns and *katyushas* opened up from the rear. A few minutes later a sergeant came up the communications trench with an anti-tank rifle. Soon came a fresh platoon, then a whole company.

"I went back to look for Brezhnev. Behind his machine gun there were now two new gunners and he was sitting on the ground, leaning against the trench wall. Seeing blood on the front of his light sheepskin coat I rushed to him. 'Ivan, have you got a smoke?' he asked, smiling. He was unharmed. The blood, now congealed, was the dead machine gunner's. With shaking hands I rolled a cigarette and put it between his lips, then sat down for a smoke myself.

"We spent the rest of the day in the forward positions. Brezhnev directed the transfer of the wounded to the rear and took part in repelling a panzer attack. Although we were under continuous shell fire, I was somehow no longer afraid. . . After that night, it seemed death would pass us by for a long time to come."

It did, though according to Iona Andronov that was not the last time Brezhnev exposed himself to it. Three weeks later, after Zhitomir had been retaken, the 18th Army drove south toward the town of Berdichev. On the morning of 3 January 1944 Colonel Timofei Volkovich, commander of the 117th Guards Infantry Division, led an assault group towards the German-held barracks in the town. As he approached the stronghold he saw that a group of men, and an officer with a submachine gun, had reached the stronghold before him. It was Brezhnev.

Just as Volkovich reached the scene he saw Brezhnev fire a long burst from the tommy gun, cutting down two Germans who had been sniping from a roof top. Suddenly a German took aim at Brezhnev from a barracks window. Brezhnev would probably have been hit had a Soviet infantryman next to him not pushed him to the ground.

"Colonel," shouted Volkovich, running up to Brezhnev, "you're not supposed to be here. What are you doing?"

"The same thing you are," Brezhnev replied.

"Well, this is no place for you," Volkovich insisted. "Please leave."

"My place," Brezhnev said, "is wherever the situation requires it. Are you aware that our forward units have been encircled in the town? We've got to relieve them. Calm down, Colonel. Let's smoke the Nazis out of these damn barracks together." And they did.

After the liberation of Berdichev the 18th Army fought its way more than 600 miles west, through the Ukraine, a corner of Hungary and into Czechoslovakia, playing a major role in the battle of the Carpathians, one of the bloodiest engagements of the war. More than 21,000 Soviet soldiers were killed there and 89,000 wounded.

It was during the Carpathian operation that Brezhnev first

met Ludwig Svoboda, now the president of Czechoslovakia, then the commander of the Czechoslovak Volunteer Corps which had been attached to the 18th Army in January 1945. Together with Svoboda's corps the 18th Army freed Kosice where the Czechoslovak Government established itself in the waning months of World War Two before the liberation of Prague.

In the summer of 1968, during the Czechoslovak crisis, Brezhnev took time out from the meeting with Alexander Dubcek to visit a military cemetery near Cierna-nad-Tisou where so many of his comrades-in-arms had been buried. He is reported to have wept silently at the site. One wonders whether he also wept a few weeks later when he held one of those comrades, Svoboda, a virtual prisoner in the Kremlin, after having ordained the invasion of a country he once helped liberate.

The 18th Army was not only the first unit to free a large town in Czechoslovakia, it was also the unit for which the war in Europe ended last. It engaged in fighting with Field Marshal Ferdinand Schoerner's army group for several days after the signing of the surrender documents at Rheims. And while the rest of the world was celebrating victory, Brezhnev was still writing front-line dispatches. His last report was drafted late on the evening of 10 May 1945.

"The enemy," he wrote, "refusing to lay down arms, poured a good part of his ammunition on our forward positions on 9 May and then began a hasty retreat. All day on 9 and 10 May our troops pursued the withdrawing enemy and engaged him on one defense line after another."

But then even Schoerner, known as The Devil's Last Field Marshal, gave up. On 12 May the war was over for Major General Leonid Brezhnev. His proudest moment may have come a little more than a month later, on 24 June in Moscow.

To celebrate the victory over Germany, Stalin staged a grandiose parade through Red Square during which hundreds of broken, captured Nazi banners and standards were heaped before the Lenin Mausoleum in a symbolic pile of defeated German ambitions. Representative contingents of the Red Army's most honored units marched in review, including a composite regiment of the 4th Ukrainian Army Group. Among the four generals who led that regiment through the square was Brezhnev.

Although the war was over and Brezhnev no doubt had hopes of returning to Viktoria, their children and to the Dnieper Bend, Stalin and Khrushchev, who had resumed his post as party chief of the Ukraine and become the republic's prime minister as well, had other plans for him. Brezhnev's military service was to continue. He was named political commissar of the Ukraine's Carpathian Military District with headquarters in Lvov. The district chief was General Andrey Yeremenko, the last commander of the 4th Ukrainian Army Group. The first secretary of Lvov *oblast*'s Communist Party committee was none other than Brezhnev's friend from Dnepropetrovsk days, Ivan Grushetsky.

In many respects this assignment may have been one of the most difficult in Brezhnev's entire career. The Carpathian Military District encompassed the territory of Ruthenia, ceded by Czechoslovakia in 1945, and the Northern Bukovina, taken from Romania. The incorporation of those two areas into the Soviet Union involved total economic and social upheaval, the nationalization of property and industry, the forced collectivization of agriculture and the suppression of desperate, armed anti-Communist partisan bands.

If Brezhnev, like other Soviet leaders, has deeds on his conscience to hide, then in all likelihood some of them were committed during this period. Resistance to Sovietization had to be crushed, "bourgeois nationalists" deported and liquidated. It must have been an excellent training ground for the job he was to be called to perform five years later in Moldavia, another chunk of Romanian territory that had become part of the USSR.

Most important, though, his assignment in the Carpatho-Ukraine placed him in an ideal position to receive Khrushchev's continuing notice. By the time he stepped out of uniform in August 1946, Brezhnev was clearly a trusted and chosen member of Khrushchev's entourage.

Part Three

IN THE ANTEROOMS OF POWER

"In the Party there are about 3,000 or 4,000 leading officials whom I would call the Party's generals.

"There are from 30,000 to 40,000 middle rank officials. These are our Party officers.

"Then there are about 100,000 to 150,000 members of the junior Party command staff. These are, so to speak, our non-commissioned officers."

Josef Stalin in 1937

CHAPTER VI

Provincial Power Bases

In 1937 and 1938 political upheavals of which he understood little, and over which he had absolutely no control, had provided the opportunities for Leonid Brezhnev's first hesitant steps up the hierarchical pyramid of Soviet power. In August 1946 another series of portentous events, shaped largely in Moscow, was to wrench him from his peacetime political-military career and launch him into the hazardous, highly competitive generalcy of the party apparatus. Once again, just as they had been for the past eight years, Brezhnev's ascending fortunes were linked closely to the career of Nikita Khrushchev.

Since February 1944 Khrushchev had been both party chief and prime minister of the Ukraine in addition to being a full member of the Politburo in Moscow. He was obviously powerful and undeniably close to Stalin. As Marshall MacDuffie, chief of the 1946 UNRRA mission to the Ukraine, noted: the windows of Kiev art stores featured plaster busts of pug-nosed Nikita Sergeyevich next to those of Stalin and their portraits hung side by side on most buildings. Once, a visiting UNRRA official, conferring with Khrushchev, expressed the almost casual desire to meet Stalin before leaving the country. Khrushchev walked away and returned a few minutes later. "I just spoke to Comrade Stalin on the phone," he said. "He'll see you tomorrow at 2 p.m."

But Stalin's behavior towards his senior colleagues was marked by capriciousness, paranoid distrust and fear. His treatment of them was insidious and devious. Rivalries and jealousies among them were bitter and Stalin deliberately arranged for their areas of responsibility to overlap, so they would maul each other and lessen the threat to him.

Khrushchev's influence on Stalin probably annoyed primarily those other members of the Politburo whose spheres of activity coincided with his. One of these was Georgy Malenkov who from 1943–45 was chairman of a governmental committee on restoring the economy in the liberated areas – of which the Ukraine was by far the most important. In 1946 Malenkov was placed in charge of cadres selection, another job impinging upon Khrushchev's tasks as party chief in the Ukraine. A second senior official was Andrei A. Andreyev, responsible for agricultural policy. The Ukraine was undoubtedly the most important agricultural republic of the Soviet Union and controversies over agricultural policy between Khrushchev and Andreyev were inevitable. Finally, there was Andrei A. Zhdanov. Before the war he had figured as Stalin's most trusted spokesman on cultural and ideological questions. Then he had suffered a partial eclipse. But in 1946 he was making a comeback with a policy of ideological purity – known as the *Zhdanovchina* – which blights Soviet cultural life to this day.

The internecine battles between these four men nearly led to the end of Khrushchev's political career in 1947. They may have played a part in Zhdanov's mysterious death in 1948. They definitely unleashed a factional conflict that not only dominated Kremlin politics throughout the 1950s and 1960s but reverberates upon Kremlin affairs to the present.

Reduced to the simplest terms, in 1946 Malenkov was sparring with Khrushchev; Khrushchev with Andreyev and Malenkov; Zhdanov with Malenkov and Khrushchev. But of the four men – all members of the eleven-man Politburo – Khrushchev was by far the most vulnerable. There were two reasons for this: Stalin's extreme hostility towards the Ukrainians and anything Ukrainian after World War Two, and the chaotic state of Ukrainian agriculture in 1946 and 1947.

As has so often been, and still is, the case in the Soviet Union, agriculture played a vital role in the controversy. Food had been scarce and rationed throughout the war and the immediate postwar period. In fact, relief supplies provided by UNRRA had created almost the only barrier between the Soviet people and starvation. This was a natural consequence of wartime devastation and German occupation of the Ukraine, the USSR's major granary. But the lack of rain and snow in the winter of 1945 and the 1946 summer drought, the worst since 1891, exacerbated the problem.

By late July or early August 1946 a poor harvest was predictable. The chaotic state of postwar Ukrainian farming made it a certainty. "We were short of tractors, horses and oxen," Khrushchev admitted many years later "the land was being worked by cow-drawn, sometimes by man-drawn implements. Frequently *kolkhozniki* harnessed themselves to plows or just turned the soil with spades."

A famine matching those of 1921 and 1933 was imminent. To complicate matters for Khrushchev, a dispute between him and Andreyev arose over the advantages and disadvantages of sowing spring wheat in the Ukraine, traditionally a winter wheat region. Andreyev, backed by Stalin, was for placing all effort on spring sowing, Khrushchev was opposed.

In March 1947 Khrushchev was released from the leadership of the Ukrainian party organization, though retaining his title of prime minister, and replaced by his old mentor, Lazar Kaganovich, then probably the Politburo member highest in Stalin's favor. But Khrushchev's political disgrace did not last long. Ten months later he was back in his position as Ukrainian first secretary and Kaganovich, whom he never really forgave, had returned to Moscow.

The agricultural question was, indeed, important, but it is only recently that Sovietologists have come to realize, as more information became available, that it was merely the visible tip of the controversy surrounding Khrushchev. The real issues ran much deeper – in the rivalry with Malenkov, the conflict with Zhdanov and around the question of Ukrainian nationalism.

The initial dispute between Malenkov and Zhdanov had arisen in the early 1940s over a question as pertinent to Kremlin affairs then as it is today: the ideological versus the pragmatic approach. Zhdanov had been identified with a rigorous, ideological position preaching loyalty to party precepts and the principle of proletarianism. Malenkov had pleaded for a practical, common-sense handling of affairs. "Windbags incapable of handling a live job," he had suggested in a 1941 article, "should be relieved of their posts and placed in less responsible ones, irrespective of whether they are party members or not."

By 1945 Malenkov's view had gained ascendency in the Kremlin and there was considerable relaxation of strict party criteria in a number of fields. Zhdanov, who had spent most of the war years as party chief of Leningrad and away from the centers of power and Stalin's side, made a comeback in 1946 on an opposing platform.

Khrushchev was more or less caught in the middle. His own views were what might then have been described as centrist. His dilemma was aggravated on the one hand by his growing influence on Stalin, and on the other by Stalin's innate distrust of Khrushchev's pro-Ukrainian sentiments.

Although Khrushchev had repressed all manifestations of Ukrainian nationalism, using draconian measures against partisan bands and their sympathizers, his policies apparently were regarded as insufficiently thorough. Wavering Ukrainian loyalties during the war had aroused Stalin's ire. Malenkov and Zhdanov, both eager to improve their own positions in the Kremlin hierarchy, were probably whispering to Stalin that Khrushchev had "gone native", had become a "Ukrainian separatist" and lacked diligence in putting that agriculturally and industrially crucial republic back on its feet. Attacking him from almost diametrically opposed platforms, they both succeeded in making their charges stick.

The "Khrushchev crisis" began fomenting in late July of 1946. The Central Committee in Moscow accused the Ukrainian party organization of having "underestimated the significance of ideological work", of "paying insufficient attention to the selection as well as the political and ideological education of cadres in the field of science, literature and art", and a variety of other transgressions including "serious faults and mistakes" in the field of cadres policy. The charges were tantamount to "political blindness", a crime for which one of Khrushchev's predecessors in the Ukraine, Pavel Postyshev, had paid with his life in the 1930s.

Khrushchev, no novice at interpreting threatening hieroglyphics from the Kremlin, responded speedily to stave off further blows from Moscow. He ordered the arrest of a number of suspected "Ukrainian nationalists" and launched a sweeping purge of the party machine. One of the first to go was the party leader of Zaporozhe *oblast*, Fyodor Semyonovich Matyushin.

Matyushin fell shortly after a plenary meeting of the Ukrainian Central Committee which Khrushchev had convened in the third week of August 1946. Besides Khrushchev there were a dozen other speakers, including Matyushin who cut anything but a brilliant figure. A four-column *Pravda* report of the session singled him out by name as one of the "people who still do not realize their mistakes and have not drawn the right conclusions from the decision of the Central Committee." It accused him of putting forth "muddled arguments".

Within a week Matyushin was out of office and Major General Leonid Brezhnev had been hurriedly recalled from active military service in Lvov to replace him.

Not yet forty, Brezhnev suddenly found himself only eighty-two miles downstream from his native Dneprodzerzhinsk, as party boss of one of the most important industrial and agricultural regions of the Soviet Union. With an area of 10,500 square miles, about the size of Maryland, and a population of almost 1.5 million, Zaporozhe *oblast* is on the fringe of the fertile Ukrainian black earth belt and encompasses the Dneproges dam, first of the large hydro-electric stations to be built in the USSR, and Zaporozhstal, at that time the largest metallurgical complex in the Soviet Union, bigger even than the plant in Dneprodzerzhinsk. In fact, the city of Zaporozhe, formerly Aleksandrovsk, has been appropriately called the "Pittsburgh of the Ukraine".

Brezhnev's primary task as provincial party leader was to rebuild both the hydro-electric station and the steel plant which had been devastated during the war. It was a formidable assignment, whose successful execution, within little more than a year, assured Brezhnev a brilliant future.

The dam across the Dnieper, completed in 1932 with the help of American engineers and equipment, was one of the major symbols of the industrialization of the Soviet Union. To prevent its usefulness to the Germans, Soviet demolition squads had destroyed part of it during their hasty retreat in 1941. In 1943 the Germans shelled and bombed it as they fell back. When Marshall MacDuffie inspected the dam in 1946, the chief engineer showed him two huge rents. Repairs had just begun.

Construction of the Zaporozhstal complex had begun in the early 1930s and by November 1933 the first blast furnace had been blown. Portions of the plant were evacuated before the

Germans thrust into Zaporozhe. The remainder was largely wrecked in the fighting.

To Marshall MacDuffie it had seemed "a mass of twisted girders . . . an empty shell." He said, "I had guessed that the giant steel mill was about 90 percent destroyed, only to hear hopeful Soviet engineers assert that it was no more than two-thirds ruined. In 1946 the phrase 'only two-thirds ruined' was a sign of good luck, something to be glad about."

Zaporozhe city itself was a wasteland in which 300,000 war-weary, desperately hungry and exhausted people sought to make homes in dugouts, squalid huts and the crumbling shells of what had been apartment houses. There were no hotels and no large buildings that had survived the war.

In the midst of these depressing surroundings Brezhnev found at least one familiar face: Andrei Pavlovich Kirilenko, the second secretary of the *oblast* party committee who had returned to Zaporozhe following its liberation in 1943.

Brezhnev was soon to strike up another important political acquaintance in Zaporozhe: with Venyamin Emanuilovich Dymshits, then a 36-year-old construction and metallurgical engineer, who had just been named manager of Zaporozhstroi, the building trust in charge of the steel plant's reconstruction. Another of Khrushchev's protégés, Dymshits has held a number of top-level government posts since 1957, and is now a deputy prime minister of the Soviet Union. Notably, he is also the only Jew in the Soviet cabinet.

It is Dymshits, in fact, who has shed an adulatory light on Brezhnev's role in the Zaporozhstal reconstruction job.

More than 20,000 construction workers were employed on the site and according to an interview Dymshits gave *Ogonyok*, a Soviet illustrated magazine, several years ago, "each one of them felt he knew Brezhnev personally." The reconstruction of the steel works, said Dymshits, "was Brezhnev's entire life. He had his own office there with a controller's communication set-up and even his bed. His knowledge of life and deep understanding of the situation, his great humanity, his sociability and kindness towards people, created an atmosphere of confidence."

Like his wartime role, Brezhnev's performance in Zaporozhe appears to improve with every year that the accomplishments themselves recede into history.

At the time, however, there was no dearth of criticism about progress on the project and the *oblast* committee's desultory management of it. Throughout the fall of 1946 and the winter of 1947, concurrent with Khrushchev's deteriorating position, *Pravda* had published a series of articles sniping at the Zaporozhe party leadership, without however, naming Brezhnev and Kirilenko. That they were the primary targets, however, was obvious even to the most perfunctory reader.

By far the sharpest of these attacks appeared in the 5 February 1947 edition of *Pravda*. Under a headline reading "Rebuild Zaporozhstal More Quickly", the reporter, Yuri Korolkov, today a popular Soviet novelist and short story writer, accused *obkom* officials of placing the blame for deficiencies on subordinates. He criticized the pace of reconstruction, the lack of Stakhanovite competition programs, the slackness of labor discipline and the absence or poor condition of mess halls, laundry rooms, dormitories and tea-rooms.

"Neither the party committee at the construction site nor the Zaporozhe *oblast* committee," he concluded, "seems very interested in the reconstruction of Zaporozhstal whose output the country needs so desperately."

Although his name was not mentioned in the article, Brezhnev responded by cranking up the Stakhanovite movement. Within eleven days of Korolkov's article Zaporozhstroi produced its first Stakhanovite: Ivan Rumyantsev, a brigadier whose construction team had exceeded its pipe-installation quota by 200 percent.

The pressures on Brezhnev were enormous. Besides rebuilding the steel plant, reconstruction of the city, providing adequate housing, dealing with the deteriorating agricultural situation and the constant threat of famine, he was also ultimately responsible for work on the dam at Dneproges where the turbines and generators finally resumed production of power on 4 March 1947, the very same day Khrushchev was replaced by Kaganovich as first secretary of the Ukrainian CP.

But perhaps the greatest pressure came indirectly from Zhdanov in the form of repeated directives and *Pravda* articles which demanded that, irrespective of actual progress on the construction site, the Zaporozhe *oblast* committee should pay more attention to improving "party work" and "ideological and mass political education" at Zaporozhstroi. Brezhnev, as appreciative then as he is now of the benefits of exhortation and "ideological steeling", complied.

On 30 June Zaporozhstal's blast furnace Number 3, the one least damaged by the war, was blown for the first time since 1941. Three months later a rolling mill was back in operation and on 28 September the plant resumed production.

As was customary in the 1940s, Brezhnev, Dymshits and eight other officials connected with the project, reported the news in a three-column, front-page letter to Stalin in the October 3rd issue of *Pravda*. The letter was the first of many such reports and pledges Brezhnev was to sign in the coming years. Mainly a statement of how many million cubic yards of cement, how many millions of bricks, how many hundreds of thousands of feet of electrical cable and miles of new railroad track had gone into the reconstruction project, it closed with the standard salutation: "Long live our dear father and leader, our friend and teacher, Comrade Stalin." On the same page Stalin congratulated Brezhnev and the others on their "great production victory".

Brezhnev wrote one more such front-page letter two weeks later. "It is our pleasure," he said, "to report to you, dear Iosif Vissarionovich, that on 12 October Zaporozhe *oblast* fulfilled the state plan for grain collection of the 1947 crop."

That was to be his last major public act in Zaporozhe. Brezhnev had obviously proven himself. In November he was sent to Dnepropetrovsk as *oblast* party chief and soon coopted into the Central Committee of the Ukrainian CP as a full member.

It was a significant promotion. The *oblast* was larger in area (12,200 square miles) and its population was twice the size (2.5 million) of Zaporozhe. Industrially it was even more important. Conceivably Brezhnev's ability to organize the industrial backing necessary for minimal performance on the agricultural front also helped turn the tide for Khrushchev. A month after Brezhnev arrived in Dnepropetrovsk, Khrushchev returned to power as the Ukrainian Party's leader in Kiev.

The transfer to Dnepropetrovsk was more than just a reward for a job well done, however. Once again Brezhnev had been chosen hurriedly to fill a vacancy left by a purge. But this time the man he replaced was a friend: Pavel Andreyevich Naidenov. Until the war Naidenov had been chairman of the Dnepropetrovsk provincial executive committee, that is, the *oblast*'s government chief. In 1944, after Dnepropetrovsk's liberation from German occupation, he had returned as its party leader.

The story behind Naidenov's fall was not disclosed until many months later, at an *oblast* party conference, about which *Pravda* reported in considerable detail on 6 May 1948. Brezhnev himself read out the main indictment at that meeting.

Naidenov, the article revealed, had been "removed" for "serious failings in the methods of leadership" and for not properly implementing the directives of the July 1946 Central Committee resolution regarding the Ukrainian party organization. To those accustomed to reading between the lines, the long reach of Zhdanov was ominously apparent.

Summarizing Brezhnev's report at that *oblast* conference, *Pravda* said that he pointed out "great blunders and mistakes committed by the *obkom* in directing industry and agriculture. An examination of these errors . . . reveals that they resulted from one-sidedness in the work of the *oblast* committee, in the division of party-political work from the fulfilment of economic tasks. This led to delays in meeting agricultural and industrial goals and to under-fulfilment of plans . . . In this connection the decline in construction and reconstruction and delays in completing important industrial and housing projects are especially serious."

Whatever fumbling Brezhnev himself may have been guilty of when he first arrived in Zaporozhe, he took immediate, self-confident command in Dnepropetrovsk. Why not? He was on safe and familiar ground. He knew the province and its principal cities and industrial centers: Dnepropetrovsk, Dneprodzerzhinsk, Nikopol and Krivoi Rog. He knew the people and the problems. Above all, he had friends and acquaintances in key positions in the *oblast*, in Kiev and in Moscow who could help him do a brilliantly successful job: the nucleus of the Dnieper Mafia which still serves him loyally today.

First and foremost there was Khrushchev himself. Demyan Korotchenko, the former first secretary of Dnepropetrovsk, had just been reappointed prime minister of the Ukraine.

Korotchenko's first deputy premier was none other than Leonid Korniets. The Ukraine's minister of motor transport was Konstantin Grushevoi. Nikolai Shchelokov was crucially positioned as Ukrainian deputy minister of local industry. General Grechko was chief of the Kiev military district and about to become a member of the Ukrainian Politburo.

But there were other friends, acquaintances and useful contacts in important positions. Vladimir Shcherbitsky, now a Politburo member and party chief of the Ukraine, then only twenty-nine, ran the vital "department of scheduled preventive repairs" in Dneprodzerzhinsk. Nikolai Tikhonov, a graduate of the Dnepropetrovsk metallurgical institute, nowadays a deputy prime minister of the USSR, was the managing director of the Southern Pipe and Tube Mill in Nikopol, Ignati Novikov, one year older than Brezhnev and like Brezhnev a graduate of the Kamenskoye metallurgical institute, today also a deputy prime minister of the USSR, was importantly placed in Moscow as head of the main board of spare parts for power plants. Georgy Tsukanov, also a Kamenskoye graduate and since 1960 Brezhnev's personal aide, was working as chief engineer of one of the Dnepropetrovsk steel plants. Georgy Pavlov, another Kamenskoye graduate and now Brezhnev's administrative assistant and chief executive officer of the Central Committee, was party chief of the city of Dneprodzerzhinsk. Andrei Kirilenko had moved on to Nikolaev *oblast*, another Ukrainian province, as party chief. But Zaporozhe was in the safe hands of Brezhnev's and Kirilenko's former deputy, Georgy Yenyutin, who had become that *oblast*'s new first secretary.

Brezhnev's tenure in Dnepropetrovsk was to last more than two years and from the outset, it seemed, he was predestined to perform to Stalin's and Khrushchev's full satisfaction. On the whole, he did.

In his first year the city center of Dnepropetrovsk was rebuilt, in Stalinist baroque style, of course. That achievement won praise from Moscow and Kiev for the speed and efficiency with which it had been completed.

Nikopol, the tube-making center south of Dneprodzerzhinsk, was developed into a thriving new industrial town with wider paved streets, a theater, modern schools and housing projects.

Before the war it had been a horror of muddy and dusty roads where steel workers and their families lived in clay shacks and *zemlyanki* (earth dugouts.)

In Dneprodzerzhinsk a program for heating the city's principal residential sections from a single thermal plant was launched. The Dzerzhinsky combine – the old Kamenskoye *zavod* – was reconstructed and expanded beyond recognition. As a *Pravda* correspondent reported in April 1948: "There is not an enterprise, not a major building in the city that is not being rebuilt or enlarged."

On the agricultural front Brezhnev reported a whole series of successes in several, glowing front-page *Pravda* letters to Stalin. By mid-August 1948 Dnepropetrovsk province had met its wheat harvesting quota by 120 percent and its rye obligations by 104 percent and had delivered a record 30,000 tons of grain to state collection points. In fact, Dnepropetrovsk was the first *oblast* in the Ukraine to complete the 1948 harvest and Brezhnev was given the opportunity to boast of the "Success of Dnepropetrovsk *Kolkhozniks*" in a three-column *Pravda* article that carried his by-line.

During a May 1949 plenum of the Ukrainian Central Committee he went to the rostrum and reported proudly on his achievements in the field of mass political work: more than 25,000 Dnepropetrovsk peasants, collective farm brigadiers and *kolkhoz* chairmen had "established contact with scientific institutions which are helping them to achieve high harvest results."

At another plenary session, two months later, Brezhnev told of "successful measures for strengthening local village party organizations and improving party political work in *kolkhozes*, *sovkhozes* and machine tractor stations". In Dnepropetrovsk province, he reported confidently, 32,000 party agitators "are now working in the field."

But there were problems and troubles, too. In late 1949 a government inspector discovered that there were extensive losses, waste, and excessive inventories in a number of factories. He blamed the chiefs of the *oblast* departments for local and food industries.

The inspection report also mentioned "serious shortcomings" in the work of the province machine and tractor stations where "excessive fuel consumption amounted to 871,400 liters" and 57,700 liters of gasoline and diesel oil had been stolen.

A far more serious matter was a complicated corruption and whitewash scandal in the Dnepropetrovsk city party committee and the mayor's office, on which both *Pravda* and *Izvestia* reported in embarrassing detail. One official was accused of forging a 1,250-ruble check and misappropriating two tons of galvanized iron sheeting that had been requisitioned for repairing the roof of Dnepropetrovsk's city hall. *Oblast* authorities were blamed for having known of the case and not taken action against the man. In an apparently related matter, the first secretary of Dnepropetrovsk *rayon* party committee, A. R. Blinov, was charged with corruption, malfeasance in office and attempting to frame a local *kolkhoz* chairman in a criminal case. *Obkom* authorities allegedly attempted to whitewash Blinov. He was eventually dismissed and reprimanded, presumably on Brezhnev's instructions, but one *Pravda* article about the case accused unnamed "officials" from Dnepropetrovsk *obkom* of "camouflaging the misdeeds and mistakes of associates".

Brezhnev's most serious crisis in Dnepropetrovsk, however, appears to have been domestic – with his impetuous, strong-willed daughter Galina, then just out of high school, who fell hopelessly in love with a circus juggler more than twice her age.

In a sense Brezhnev had no one but himself to blame for that affair. Besides soccer, hunting and driving Brezhnev apparently has always nurtured a passion for the circus and big-top artists – probably ever since those distant pre-Revolutionary days in Kamenskoye when the Truchnaya Circus with its wrestlers used to settle in the town square. One of his contributions to Dnepropetrovsk's postwar cultural life was to revitalize its permanent circus. The director, many of the star performers, including the dashing juggler, were frequent guests at Brezhnev's home. Galina, a gushing teenager, fell for him. That was a domestic crisis of the first magnitude which ended with Galina's brief marriage to the juggler. According to some reports it was not her last romance with a circus performer.

Galina's affair was Brezhnev's last crisis in Dnepropetrovsk. In the spring of 1950, he was ordered to Moscow for reassignment and another important step up the political ladder.

Khrushchev, fully rehabilitated and in Stalin's favor, had left Kiev in December 1949 to return to Moscow as party chief of Moscow and to become, under Stalin, one of the five secretaries of the Central Committee. Brezhnev soon followed him – for a brief tenure in the Central Committee apparatus where, presumably, he was trained and briefed for his next post: party leader of Moldavia, one of the fifteen constituent republics of the USSR.

CHAPTER VII

A New Boyar on the Dniester

With an area of approximately 13,000 square miles, only slightly larger than Belgium, Moldavia is one of the smallest Soviet republics. Comprising the territories of Bessarabia and the Northern Bukovina between the Dniester and the Prut rivers, it is also one of the most artificially delimited. The historical justification for its membership in the Soviet Union is – next to Lithuania, Latvia and Estonia – the most controversial.

The controversy starts with the question: who and what are the Moldavians? According to Soviet historians, "they regard themselves as Slavs." But their language is a Romanian dialect and in Romanian eyes the Moldavians, like the Romanians themselves, are descendants of the Dacians and Roman legionnaires who settled this corner of Europe and intermarried with the local tribes.

"For centuries," so says a propaganda brochure given me on a visit to Kishinev, the capital of Moldavia, "the Moldavians were subjected to pressure from Turkey . . . In their struggle to free themselves from the Turkish yoke, they turned to Moscow for fraternal help. It is no coincidence that nearly three hundred years ago Dosotheus, the Patriarch of Moldavia, wrote: 'Light will come to us from Rus.' . . . In 1812 Russian troops finally liberated the Moldavians from Turkish oppression and Bessarabia became a part of Russia.

"Shoulder to shoulder with the Russians, under the leadership of the Russian proletariat, the working people of Bessarabia fought against tsarism and capitalism. In 1917 Soviet power was established in Bessarabia, as it was in the rest of the country."

But then, the official Soviet version continues, Bessarabian Communism was crushed "on the instructions of US President Wilson who supported the counter-revolutionary activity of the local bourgeois nationalists." Wilson's "infamous Fourteen Points, hypocritically called a 'peace program' but in fact an imperialist program, provided for wresting Bessarabia from Russia and transferring it to Romania ... (which) ... occupied Bessarabia in 1918."

For twenty-two years, so say Soviet historiographers, the Moldavian people resisted that occupation. "It was not until 1940, when Romania returned Bessarabia to the Soviet Union, that the Moldavian struggle for liberation brought the people freedom and independence. They had finally gained nationhood.

In an article he published in *Pravda* in February 1951, Leonid Brezhnev described those twenty-two years of "Romanian *boyar* occupation" in the bleakest terms.

"In those dark times", he wrote, "thousands of unemployed wandered about the cities and villages of Bessarabia and an army of farm laborers migrated from district to district in search of work. Farmsteads lay in ruins and came under the auctioneers' hammers. The native Moldavian land, a land of sunshine, gardens and vineyards, was held prisoner. Mercilessly the working masses were suppressed by the Romanians behind whom stood a rapacious gang of American, British, German and French imperialists who devoured the fruits of the people's exhausting labor and reduced Moldavia to the state of an exploited colony."

Understandably, the Romanian interpretation of Moldavia's history, even the interpretation given by Communist Romania today, differs radically from that offered by Moscow.

As a former official of the inter-war Romanian government put it in a letter to the *New York Times* in 1956:

"The great majority of inhabitants of Bessarabia and Bukovina were Romanians ever since the regions became known historically . . . In 1775 the Bukovina was occupied and annexed by Austria. In 1812 Bessarabia was occupied and annexed by Russia. In spite of the length and terror of the foreign occupation, the population, in its great majority peasant, stoutly maintained its Romanian nationality. Thus it was that in 1918, after World War One, the parliaments elected in both provinces voted to return to the mother country . . .

"In 1940 the Soviet Union, following the secret protocols of the Stalin–Hitler pact, annexed Bessarabia, Northern Bukovina and even a corner of old Romania by means of hold-up tactics."

According to Leonid Brezhnev that was no hold-up at all but "liberation from the imperialist yoke", for which the Moldavian people "offered unlimited gratitude to the Soviet government, to the Bolshevik Party, to our dear Comrade Stalin".

Actually that first Soviet rule, which Brezhnev claimed brought "a free and happy life", lasted less than a year: from August 1940 until the Germans invaded the USSR in July 1941. Romania, allied with Nazi Germany at the time, reoccupied Bessarabia and the Bukovina. But in 1944 the Red Army marched back in and the region – rich in grain, fruit, vegetables and wine, blessed with fertile soil, a benign climate and plenty of rain – came under Soviet rule once more as one of the USSR's nominally independent republics.

Thus began an intense Sovietization campaign, tempered only by the precariousness of Moscow's position in the adjacent Carpatho-Ukraine where armed partisan resistance to Soviet rule had limited *de facto* control to the main urban centers.

Regardless of whether they were Slavs or Romans, the Moldavians were compelled to read and write their Latin tongue, the only Romance language spoken in the USSR, in the Cyrillic alphabet.

Between 1945 and 1950 an estimated 500,000 of the republic's original 3,000,000 population were executed, sentenced to prison camps or deported to "resettlement areas" in Kazakhstan and Siberia. They had collaborated with the Germans or the Romanians, engaged in anti-Soviet "propaganda" or "counter-revolutionary activity", had been "*kulaks*" or had belonged to one of the twelve non-communist political parties. Some 250,000 Russians were settled in Moldavia to replace them and alter the republic's ethnic power balance.

Private enterprise was prohibited; trade and what industry had existed were nationalized. Collectivization of agriculture, begun in 1948, was 80 percent completed by the spring of 1950 though farming remained depressed and the peasants were hostile to Soviet power.

In July 1950 Leonid Brezhnev was sent to Kishinev to

complete the task. It was no job for the pusillanimous. Although popular disaffection marred his entire stewardship – and prevails to the present day in Moldavia – he performed his assignment with toughness and resolution. Within six months after his arrival in Moldavia "the *kulaks* had been liquidated as a class". Sharper penalties for "economic crimes" were introduced. He moved against armed resistance groups that cooperated with partisan bands in the adjacent provinces of the Ukraine. More deportations began, especially from Kishinev and other urban centers, and the cities and towns were completely Russified so that today Moldavians account for only one third of Kishinev's population of 300,000.

Detailed information about Brezhnev's rule has been conveniently camouflaged or obliterated from the record by the usual veneer of Soviet propaganda, secrecy, obfuscation and the passage of time. In fact, the first Western correspondent – Jack Raymond of the *New York Times* – was not permitted to visit Moldavia until 1956, more than three years after Brezhnev had left Kishinev. Even then his movements were carefully circumscribed and his sources of information restricted to official spokesmen.

But the information that is available leads Western observers and the few emigrants from the republic to the consensus that Brezhnev's reign was draconian and represents one of the darkest periods of his career.

As political boss of a large, important province such as Dnepropetrovsk, Brezhnev had, of course, been an influential figure. Nevertheless, he was merely one of scores of provincial prefects whose tasks were to implement a multitude of directives handed down by a confusing, frequently self-contradicting party and government bureaucracy at the national and republican levels above. Moldavia was not much larger or more populous than Dnepropetrovsk *oblast*. Industrially it barely rated. Its Communist Party was ridiculously small, counting no more than 20,000 members until 1953. But as first secretary of its Central Committee Brezhnev became one of a handful of powerful Soviet-style *boyars*, responsible to Stalin personally and thus in the anteroom of Kremlin power.

Just as he had in Zaporozhe and Dnepropetrovsk, Brezhnev came to Moldavia to fill a power vacuum left by a purge.

Only this time, there is reason to suspect, he himself must have participated in conducting that purge from Moscow.

During the latter half of 1949 and early 1950 Brezhnev's predecessor in Moldavia, Nikolai Grigoryevich Koval, and other party leaders had been repeatedly criticized for failing to accelerate the socialization of agriculture and for not eradicating the "remaining vestiges of bourgeois nationalism".

Koval was blamed for "defects in ideological work". It was charged that "bourgeois nationalist distortions and idealization of feudal Moldavia have been permitted in some Moldavian *belles-lettres* and history." According to one report, "insufficient attention is given to training student youth and the educational content of schools is weakly controlled." The republic's party leadership was told to "overcome the remnants of capitalism". There were complaints about preparations for the harvest and the level of grain deliveries. The lack of Communists in the villages and the dearth of rural party organizations were criticized.

What happened subsequently was not revealed until eighteen years later by Sergei Trapeznikov, a party ideologist with whom Brezhnev forged a close association in Kishinev and who today is one of the key *apparatchiki*, certainly the most reactionary and pro-Stalinist in his entourage. According to Trapeznikov's *History of the Moldavian SSR*, published in 1968, the charges against the Moldavian leadership were formalized in a June 1950 CPSU Central Committee decree.

Koval and two other secretaries of the Moldavian CP, F. I. Kashnikov and M. M. Radul, were purged – the first of a series of Moldavian functionaries to be tossed on the political scrap heap. In July Brezhnev moved into party headquarters just off Kishinev's Prospekt Lenina and simply took over.

Legally speaking, Moldavia is a sovereign republic with its own foreign ministry and the constitutional right to secede from the Soviet Union whenever it chooses. Its Communist Party, therefore, is supposed to be as autonomous as, for example, the Communist Parties of Bulgaria, China, France or the United States. For Brezhnev to be named first secretary of its Central Committee would have presupposed that he was a member of that committee, which he was not, and that the committee held a plenum to elect him, which it did not. Indeed, he was still a member of the Ukrainian Central Committee. But then, it was not an era when the niceties of socialist legality were in great demand. Actually, Brezhnev was simply appointed to the job from on high: by Stalin, Malenkov or Khrushchev. Such violations of party statutes, almost routine in the Stalin period, are still committed today and by Brezhnev, too.

Brezhnev arrived in Kishinev accompanied by advisers and people he could trust. One of the first to join him there was his friend Nikolai Shchelokov, the former mayor of Dnepropetrovsk, who as Ukrainian deputy minister of local industry and subsequently as a department chief of the Ukrainian Central Committee, had helped him to run affairs smoothly in Dnepropetrovsk *oblast*. In January 1951 Shchelokov was named first deputy prime minister of Moldavia.

Brezhnev struck new alliances as well. One that has endured to the present was with Konstantin Ustinovich Chernenko, who since 1948 had been head of the department of propaganda and agitation in the Moldavian Central Committee, a job he kept until 1956 when Brezhnev arranged for his transfer and promotion to the Central Committee apparatus in Moscow. He has been with Brezhnev ever since, serving as chief of the Supreme Soviet's Secretariat when Brezhnev was the chairman of its presidium and president of the USSR. Today, as head of the "general" department of the Central Committee, he is one of Brezhnev's closest advisers and aides.

Perhaps the most ominous association for the future of the Soviet Union, was with Professor Trapeznikov. Only thirty-eight years old then, Sergei Pavlovich Trapeznikov was rector of the Moldavian Party Academy, a position he was to retain until 1956 when Brezhnev brought him to Moscow. Since 1965 he has been chief of the Central Committee's powerful and influential department of science and educational institutions: virtual tsar of scientific research and education in the Soviet Union. Whereas Brezhnev has grown intellectually and become ideologically more flexible, Trapeznikov has merely become more rigid. As recently as 1967 he went on record defending and justifying Stalin's 1938 liquidation of Bukharin and Rykov. His influence on Brezhnev in domestic, ideological and foreign affairs cannot be assessed by outsiders. But whatever influence there is, it must be insidious.

Brezhnev's links with Trapeznikov and Chernenko are traceable to his determined efforts in the first months as Moldavian party chief to build up membership, raise the effectiveness and stiffen the ideological posture of existing party organizations and cells, especially in rural areas.

"Although the number of party organizations on collective farms has tripled since 1949," Brezhnev told the Moldavian Party Congress in April 1951, "there are still many farms which have no party organizations at all.

"The district committees pay very little attention to improving the personnel of the rural party organizations . . . There are several thousand tractor and combine operators in the republic, but so far very few Communists among them.

"It is also essential," he said, "to perfect the working methods of party agencies, to improve instruction and check-ups, to develop criticism and self-criticism more boldly, to improve the standards of ideological work."

Between that April 1951 conclave and the IVth Moldavian Party Congress in September 1952, the Central Committee was to meet six times and the same plaintive cry could be heard at almost every plenum. During the September 1951 plenary session the editorial boards of the republic's newspapers were criticized for failing to report on questions of party education. At the meeting in December party organizations were upbraided for devoting too little attention to the political education of tractor drivers. In January 1952 the issue was the desultory and perfunctory approach to the political education of young Communists. During the August session it was revealed that in their rush to get as many new party members as possible, numerous party committees and cells had "failed to consider the practical and political qualifications of the people admitted to membership".

Intellectual resistance to Russification, to Sovietization and to Brezhnev's determined but seemingly futile efforts at tightening ideological discipline and pressing all people into a preconceived Soviet mold punctuate the published record of his stewardship in Moldavia.

"The problems of Moldavian history," Brezhnev told one Central Committee plenum in September 1952, "must be elucidated more broadly from Marxist points of view. Every working person must be made to realize that the reunification of the Moldavian people and the statehood which they have acquired for the first time in their history represent an achievement of the Communist Party's Leninist-Stalinist national policy."

At various plenums Moldavian literary figures and Kishinev's new music and drama theater were repeatedly criticized for "serious ideological faults and errors" and for "depicting the Moldavian past in a distorted way."

Instead of condemning the recent capitalist and Romanian past, Brezhnev charged, Moldavian writers, poets and dramatists were eulogizing it.

"The old patriarchal ways," he said at one session, "the long oppression by the Turkish enslavers and their local minions and the disastrous internecine strife of the *boyars* are frequently depicted as part of an idyllic existence for everyone in a blessed land flowing with rivers of wine."

Historians were singled out for committing "gross errors" because they had treated "a number of historical questions from the bourgeois nationalist points of view" and had repeated "bourgeois lies about some 'golden age' in the Moldavian past". There was frequent criticism of insufficient attention being paid to "the development of the Moldavian language", a Brezhnevian euphemism for the dilatory manner in which the Cyrillic alphabet was being put into use.

At one plenum Trapeznikov took the floor to upbraid Artem Lazarev, the third secretary of the Party, for sanctioning "the appearance of incorrect articles" and committing "major errors" in the "selection and placement of personnel in the field of ideological work".

Oddly, Lazarev, despite strong criticism, was the only Central Committee secretary to survive the full tenure of Brezhnev's stewardship. Of the other four lower-ranking secretaries who had been elected at the Party Congress in April 1951, not one was reappointed at the IVth Congress in September 1952.

Although Moldavia was and is primarily an agricultural region, Brezhnev did bring some light industry to the republic. And, as had been the case in Zaporozhe and Dnepropetrovsk, he proved to be an inveterate builder. "In all the history of

Kishinev," *Pravda* reported in January 1952, "its inhabitants have never yet witnessed such tremendous industrial and other construction as is going on today. The city's central thoroughfare, Prospekt Lenina, is being embellished with large new apartment buildings. Construction of a 120-unit apartment house, the administration building of the ministry of the food industry, the opera house and a motion picture theater is proceeding at full speed . . . The lower part of the city is being radically rebuilt, mainly with apartment houses . . . Extensive work is in progress to plant trees and shrubs and more than two million flowers were planted in 1951 alone."

At times, it seems, the construction work proceeded a bit too speedily. There were complaints of unfinished work, poor quality, badly fitted doors and windows, cracked walls and falling plaster. But the same criticism was heard all over the Soviet Union in those days and has prevailed, unabetted and fully justified, to the present.

Regardless of what he may have done to the Moldavian psyche and language, Brezhnev could proudly claim in 1952 that he was leaving a bigger and better Kishinev than he had found on arrival.

Although there continued to be set-backs – pilfering, harvest failures, poor distribution and some hare-brained cross-breeding schemes – Brezhnev did apparently complete collectivization to everyone's, except the peasants', satisfaction and managed to get a grip on Moldavia's agriculture. Twice in the fall of 1951 he reported on the glorious achievements of Moldavian fruit farmers and winegrowers in front-page *Pravda* letters to Stalin.

But there were troubles for Brezhnev, too, and the nature of some of them remains cloaked in secrecy. On May Day 1951, for example, he was conspicuous by his absence from the reviewing stand on Kishinev's Victory Square. B. A. Gorban, the second secretary, was there to preside over the traditional show and watch the troops march by. Brezhnev was either seriously ill or in great political trouble.

In February 1952 *Pravda* exposed the fact that the chief of the Moldavian Textbook Publishing House was a "sharper" who had plagiarized the works of contributing authors and put his own name on them, passed translation jobs to cronies from

Brezhnev the political commissar during World War II, shown here presenting the party card to a new Communist Party member, Alexander Malov (left). This picture, one of the earliest available, was taken in September 1942 during fighting near Tuapse.

Brezhnev with Khrushchev on the Caucasian front in April 1942.

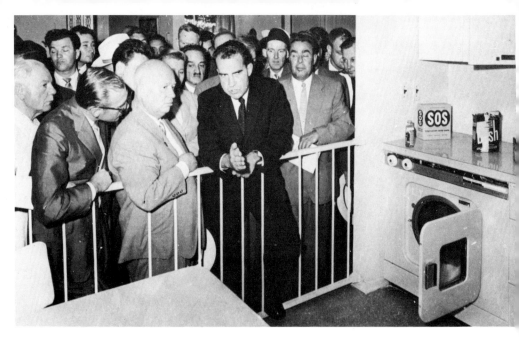

Brezhnev (right) behind Richard Nixon during the famous kitchen debate with Khrushchev in Moscow's Sokolniki Park, July 1959.

Brezhnev (left) during a recess at a session of the XXIInd Party Congress in October 1961, talking with members of the 'Dnieper Mafia': (center) I. T. Novikov, (right) P. D. Rogoza.

Dancing with Tito's wife at a formal dinner given in his honour during a visit to Yugoslavia in 1962.

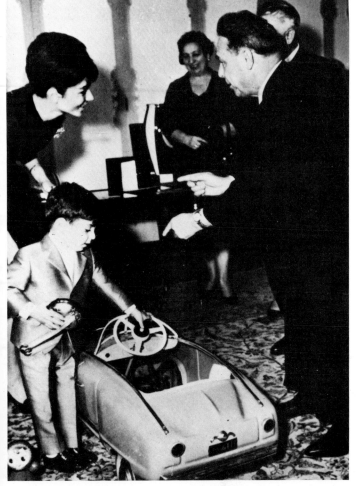

His passion for automobiles extends to his own gifts: here he is seen in 1963 during a state visit to Iran, presenting a toy car to Iranian Crown Prince Reza. Empress Fahra is on the left, Brezhnev's wife Viktoria in the center.

Brezhnev during De Gaulle's visit to the USSR, 1966. Left, Nikolai Podgorny with Maurice Couve de Murville; right, Kosygin approaching De Gaulle. Behind Brezhnev (with glasses) is Ignaty Novikov, a deputy prime minister, and to his right, Boris Ponomarev.

During the Czechoslovak crisis in 1968, Brezhnev, accompanied by other Communist leaders, visited the Soviet war memorial and military cemetery at nearby Slavin where some of his wartime comrades are buried.

Standing proudly behind Kosygin during the treaty-signing ceremony
with Willy Brandt in August 1970.

Brezhnev with
Podgorny on a
hunting trip at
Zavidovo resort.

Brezhnev in relaxed mood, on a yacht off the Black Sea Coast, 1971.

During the XXIVth Party Congress. Brezhnev (far left) looks bored as he listens to Podgorny open the meeting. Kosygin is right of Podgorny and at far right, front row, is Andrey P. Kirilenko, a friend of Brezhnev's since the 1930s.

Revolution Day parade, 1971. Left to right: Defense Minister Marshal Grechko, Podgorny, Brezhnev, Kosygin, reviewing the parade from the top of the Lenin Mausoleum.

In animated conversation with Ruth Brandt, during his visit to Bonn in May 1973.

With his wife Viktoria on a Moscow park bench, summer 1973, with their
first great-granddaughter Galina.

Brezhnev and Nixon signing the joint Soviet-American communiqué in
San Clemente, California, 24 June, 1973.

whom he received kickbacks and had turned "the publishing house into his patrimony and private business". Who was to blame? "The Moldavian Communist Party Central Committee," said *Pravda*, "which has failed to exercise party control over one of the most important fields of ideological work. It has received frequent warnings about this situation but has given no serious attention to any of them and drawn no proper conclusions."

That affair had certain reverberations at the Moldavian Party Congress in September. Lazarev's "errors" in the selection of executives for ideological work again came under fire. But Brezhnev apparently tried to whitewash him. In a rare display of party democracy and political courage, a number of delegates criticized Brezhnev for attempting to circumvent the issue.

In self-defense Brezhnev told the delegates: "We . . . have tried to conduct plenary sessions trenchantly, sparing no one's feelings, no matter what his position."

The remark was met with grumbling and some sneering from the congress floor, leaving *Pravda* to comment afterwards that Brezhnev's assertions "apparently did not reflect the true state of affairs".

A less powerful figure, a Soviet politician with fewer influential friends and protectors in the Kremlin, might have suffered a serious, possibly permanent fall after a verbal altercation like that. But in 1952 Leonid Brezhnev could afford to pass it off with a shrug. He knew where he was heading and what he had to do.

After the Moldavian Congress he went into seclusion for a week to prepare for the most important performance yet in his career: the speech he was to deliver in October at the XIXth Congress of the Communist Party of the Soviet Union – the first such conclave Stalin had called since 1939. That Congress was to vault Leonid Brezhnev into the anteroom of power in the Kremlin itself.

CHAPTER VIII

Steps Forward and Backward

A sense of impending doom punctuated by sinister intrigues, ruthless internecine power struggles and petty bickering pervaded the atmosphere during the last few years of Stalin's life. Among high-ranking party officials, among ordinary workers and simple peasants there was a foreboding that history was about to repeat itself.

The war had occasioned a relaxation of ideology, coercion and threat. It had served as a catharsis for freeing the Soviet people of the most visceral fears acquired during the Great Terror and had welded them, for the first time since the Revolution, into a patriotic, relatively enthusiastic and dedicated whole. But with his growing megalomania and deepening paranoia Stalin did not trust them. He trusted no one.

Publicly he was adored, eulogized, panegyrized and deified as no dictator in the world, no tsar in Russia had ever been before him. His statues stood everywhere, his portraits hung everywhere. He was called "our dear father", "our great leader and patient teacher", "the brilliant architect of communism", "a man of genius", "our guiding light". Cities, streets, factories and *kolkhozes* were named after him. Soldiers pledged their allegiance, school children sang their songs and poets rhymed their verses to him. Writers dedicated their novels, artists their paintings and composers their symphonies to him.

But privately he became, as Khrushchev was to describe in the "secret speech" of 1956, "even more capricious, irritable and brutal . . . His persecution mania reached unbelievable dimensions. . . . He could look at a man and say, 'Why are your eyes so shifty today?' or 'Why do you turn so much today and avoid looking at me directly?' " He suspected almost everyone of his inner circle – including Vyacheslav Molotov, Anastas Mikoyan, Marshal Kliment Voroshilov and Marshal Georgy

Zhukov – of being spies or imperialist agents. "It can happen," Nikolai Bulganin once told Khrushchev, "that you are invited to Stalin's *dacha* for dinner and sit there not knowing whether you will leave the table to go home or to prison."

All those around Stalin were, essentially, temporary people. As long as he trusted them they were permitted to work and live. But, according to Khrushchev's 1970 "memoirs", "the moment he stopped trusting you Stalin would start to scrutinize you until the cup of his distrust overflowed. Then it would be your turn to follow those who were no longer among the living. That's what it was like for all the people who worked with him and struggled beside him in the ranks of the Party for the Party's sake."

As Stalin's suspicion increased, schemes, plots, counterplots and purges among his subordinates multiplied: especially among Khrushchev, Beria and Malenkov and their clients and protégés.

The second dark age of Stalinist terror began in 1946 with Andrei Zhdanov's return to Moscow and the *Zhdanovshchina*. A Communist brimstone and fire era, the *Zhdanovshchina* was a drive for ideological purity and revival launched concurrently with a tightening of the entire administrative structure. Directed primarily at the intellectual community, its objective was to cleanse Soviet minds of liberal wartime influences and "servile adulation of contemporary bourgeois Western culture", to reaffirm basic doctrine and Marxist values in the arts and literature. The poetess Anna Akhmatova was its most famous victim. Zhdanov's purge and policies reverberated throughout the Soviet intellectual, political, administrative and economic structure.

In August 1948, just a month after his arch rival, Malenkov, had returned to a position of power in the Central Committee secretariat after a brief postwar eclipse, Zhdanov died suddenly and mysteriously. Allegedly he drank himself to death, but the circumstances have never been satisfactorily explained and the suspicion of murder has never been dispelled.

The doubts were raised in part by those surrounding the death of his predecessor as Leningrad party chief, Sergei Kirov, in 1934. Kirov was assassinated, but in the "secret speech" Khrushchev implied strongly that Stalin had stood behind the assassin. Kirov's death served as the pretext for the terrible purges of the 1930s. He died while apparently in the highest favor and continued to receive honors posthumously. So did Zhdanov. However within three years of Kirov's death, all his main appointees in Leningrad had been purged and shot. The same happened to Zhdanov's. In 1948 and 1949 his closest associates, protégés and supporters, were arrested and eventually executed, their posts filled by Malenkov appointees. Only one escaped – narrowly – with just a temporary demotion: Aleksei Kosygin, at that time the Soviet finance minister and first deputy premier as well as a full member of the eleven-man Politburo.

Nor was the Leningrad Affair the only one to leave a bloody trail of execution. Other such ones were the uncovering of an alleged conspiracy in the Crimea, and an alleged "nationalist" conspiracy involving the leading party officials of Georgia, home base of both Stalin and his powerful security chief, Lavrenti Beria. Although that case moved along slowly and the record of purges and counter-purges is too complicated to discuss here, the ultimate aim was to gradually lessen Beria's influence and reduce his power.

A pattern was beginning to emerge: disclosure of alleged, though non-existent, conspiracies which were then crushed with mass arrests and executions. Stalin's objective was to lay the groundwork for his last great purge.

Who was an agent for which imperialistic power? The answer varied from one day to the next and depended on Stalin's fertile and patently sick imagination. But for all his mental deterioration, he still understood the basic mechanisms of Kremlin politics: first to divide, then to conquer. Stalin was a master at using the intricate patronage system to build up supports and knock down the other man's props. He knew how to pack the various party and government agencies with enough men dependent upon him to spread the risk and weaken whatever opposition might exist. Those are the basic rules of the Kremlin power game which he devised. He taught them to Khrushchev who in turn taught them to Leonid Brezhnev. They apply today as they did then.

Stalin had ordered Khrushchev to Moscow at the end of 1949 as a counterweight to Malenkov who was becoming too strong. Apart from Stalin himself, the two were the most powerful men in the five-member Central Committee Secretariat. And soon after Khrushchev's arrival in the capital it became apparent that Stalin's ploy was working. Khrushchev was indeed upsetting the power balance in the party leadership – to the detriment of Malenkov.

For the next two years, as Stalin watched with seeming indifference from the sidelines, those two fought it out – largely over agricultural policy. Their feud might have become much bloodier had it not been for Stalin's own plans in the fall of 1952: a new purge that would sweep most of his older associates and allies from power.

Stalin's concept was characteristically circuitous and complex. First he intended to establish legitimacy by convening a Party Congress, the first in more than thirteen years. He would use the Congress to pack the new Central Committee with younger, reliable men and then get them to approve a list for a radically enlarged Secretariat and Politburo in which the position of the old members would be weakened and undermined. Step Two called for the invention of a conspiracy – the Doctors' Plot – that would trigger a new witch-hunt and a mass purge in which the older members of the top leadership could easily be linked to the conspiracy. Finally he would annihilate and liquidate these older associates whose places would simply be taken by the new guard.

Leonid Brezhnev, though he could not have been aware of it, had been chosen as one of the principal beneficiaries of that devious, sinister scheme, the final implementation of which was forestalled only by Stalin's death in March 1953.

And it was in this atmosphere, pregnant with evil, that Brezhnev came to Moscow on 5 October 1952, one of 1,192 voting delegates to the XIXth Congress of the Communist Party of the Soviet Union.

In 1939 Brezhnev had been an insignificant local *apparatchik*, too low on the political totem pole to warrant his nomination to the XVIIIth Party Congress as either a delegate or even a non-voting observer. Now he was a powerful figure who was scheduled not only to deliver a major speech but would sit on one of the ruling bodies of the Congress and emerge from it a member of the Kremlin's ruling elite.

On the opening day he was given the largely honorific task of proposing the Congress Secretariat. He nominated nine men who were elected unanimously. Of the nine, two are still powerful in the party apparatus: Ivan Kapitonov, now a Central Committee secretary, in charge of the party personnel and cadres department, and Antanas Snechkus, then as now party chief of Lithuania. Later the same day Brezhnev was nominated and unanimously elected to the congress credentials commission. Of its fifteen members a number of others were later to reach the pinnacles of party power, but not one is in an influential position today.

The principal speakers were Malenkov and Khrushchev who, respectively, delivered the main Central Committee report and outlined the proposals for changes in the party statutes. Stalin himself kept a stony silence throughout the ten-day conclave, giving only a seven-minute speech at the end.

Brezhnev spoke on the fourth day. His address was a typical paean to Stalin's greatness and a boastful tabulation of Moldavia's postwar achievements, fortified by diplomatically worded suggestions to the government bureaucracy that even more could be accomplished if investments in Moldavia's embryonic industries were to be increased.

" . . . Thanks to the wise domestic policy of the Bolshevist Party and the Soviet Government," said Brezhnev, "and thanks to Comrade Stalin's constant concern for the future of the Moldavian people, the working people of Bessarabia were liberated from the colonial yoke . . . This historic event will never be erased from the Moldavian people's memory; from generation to generation through the centuries the Moldavian people will glorify and pass on the name of their liberator, the great Stalin." At that point, according to the record, he was interrupted by "prolonged applause".

Brezhnev went on to describe the pre-Soviet period as an era of "Bessarabian tragedy" and credited the "constant attention of our Party Central Committee, our Union Government and Comrade Stalin personally" for the "considerable successes" the Moldavian people were able to attain "in advancing the republic's economy and culture".

"Illiteracy among the Moldavian population has been eliminated . . . The people, who for centuries were deprived of the opportunity to enjoy the fruits of culture, are manifesting a tremendous desire under the Soviet system for knowledge and science and are sharing the culture of the great Russian people, the culture of Lenin and Stalin . . ."

Then Brezhnev delivered a laudation typical of the time: "It is the great fortune of our society," he declared, "that the greatest man of our epoch, our wise leader and teacher Josef Vissarionovich Stalin, stands in the forefront of our struggle for the development of the motherland, for the triumph of Communism. Long live our leader and teacher, our great and beloved Comrade Stalin."

It was predictable that on the last day, when the Congress got around to electing a new Central Committee, Brezhnev would be named one of its 125 members.

Unpredictable, on the other hand, was what transpired at that Central Committee's first plenum the following day, 16 October. Stalin himself presided and instead of a Secretariat of five members proposed one of ten; instead of the traditional Politburo of eleven members he nominated a Party Presidium of twenty-five full and eleven candidate members. All, of course, were elected unanimously.

Brezhnev became one of the candidate members of the new Presidium. So, incidentally, did Kosygin, still in partial disgrace following the Leningrad Affair and therefore apparently not worthy, in Stalin's eyes, of full membership. But far more important, Brezhnev was also named one of the ten Central Committee secretaries – along with Stalin, Khrushchev, Malenkov and Suslov.

The older members of the inner circle were stunned by the size of the Presidium. As Khrushchev reportedly said many years later, Stalin himself "couldn't possibly have known most of the people whom he had just appointed." He read off their names from a list he had drawn from his pocket. "He couldn't have put the list together himself."

But apparently he had and as Khrushchev was to remark in his secret speech in 1956: "Stalin evidently had plans to finish off the old members of the Political Bureau. He often stated that they should be replaced by new ones. His proposal at the XIXth Congress . . . was a design for the future annihilation of the old Political Bureau . . ."

For Brezhnev, at any rate, it was an enormous jump. He transferred from Kishinev to Moscow almost immediately moving with Viktoria into a three-room apartment in a grim-looking eight-story building on Mozhaiski Chaussee. For Soviet standards at the time, it was palatial. A compound built in 1939 for senior Central Committee officials, it is the same building in which Brezhnev and his family live today. Only now he has a larger flat and the street has been renamed Kutuzovski Prospekt. The apartment house faces the avenue along which Stalin used to ride in his limousine to the Kremlin from the "Nearby Dacha" in Kuntsevo, a suburban village not far from that where Brezhnev, too, has a country villa today.

Just what his new duties on the Secretariat were has never been disclosed. The fact that he remained a member of the Moldavian Politburo until June 1953 suggests that he may have retained some responsibility and control over that republic from Moscow as well. But he was, undoubtedly, a member of the inner circle. From the time of the large Presidium's inception there were hints of a smaller, more tightly knit, non-statutory group within it. Khrushchev confirmed its existence in 1956. Although its composition has never been made public, Sovietologists believe that it consisted of those party leaders who stood with Stalin atop the Lenin Mausoleum in Red Square for the Revolution Day parade on 7 November 1952. Brezhnev was one of them. Kosygin, previously a familiar face at these annual line-ups and until 1946 a full member of the Politburo, was not.

Brezhnev had barely settled into his new job and apartment when Moscow reverberated with the shock waves of the Doctors' Plot – phase two of what would have become Stalin's last great purge.

The "murderer-doctors . . . monsters in human form," as they were called, were the cream of the Soviet medical profession and nearly all had at one time or another treated the Soviet elite. The essence of the "case" was that they were agents of British intelligence and the Jewish Joint Distribution Committee, described as an "American espionage organization". Of the nine doctors named, five were Jewish. According to the formal charge they had conspired to murder both

Zhdanov and A. S. Shcherbakov, party chief of Moscow, who died in 1945, by prescribing treatment and medication counter-indicated for their ailments. The "criminal doctors", it was alleged, had also "sought to undermine the health of leading Soviet military personnel, to put them out of action and to weaken the defense of the country". Among the five high-ranking officer "victims" were Marshal Ivan Konev, the hero of the battle for Berlin, and General Sergei Shtemenko, then chief-of-staff of the Soviet Army. The doctors were, of course, merely pawns in a larger, more complicated and more sinister ploy.

Eventually, had Stalin lived longer, Molotov, Mikoyan, Beria and possibly Marshal Voroshilov would probably have been linked to the doctors' Anglo-American-Zionist "conspiracy". Perhaps Malenkov, as chief beneficiary of Zhdanov's death, might have been linked with it, too. But certainly not Khrushchev and his clients, most notable among them Brezhnev.

Disclosure of the "plot" on the front page of *Pravda* on 13 January 1953 triggered a witch hunt and vigilance campaign second in intensity and viciousness only to those of the 1930s. For the remaining eight weeks, until Stalin's death, the Soviet propaganda machinery inundated the nation with frenetic, hysterical cries to watch out for spies, saboteurs, swindlers and enemies of the people.

The line, as laid down by articles and editorials in *Pravda* and other party papers, militated against "heedlessness, self-satisfaction and complacency" as a consequence "of the victorious outcome of the war and under the influence of the great postwar achievements".

"The vigilance of some of our officials has become dulled," said the papers. "They have become infected with gullibility ... Comrade Stalin teaches us to watch untiringly for the enemy's intrigues, to be able to recognize an enemy regardless of the disguise he may don [Molotov, Mikoyan, Beria?], to be able to guess his cunning plans in time and to nip his subversive deeds in the bud . . ."

"Gullibility" was labeled "a very dangerous disease" because "it opens the doors to penetration by hostile agents". And "gullible persons" were described as "dangerous because they fall easily for the enemy's tricks and are incapable of exposing hostile intrigues".

Who were these gullible people and deviously disguised enemies to which the whole arsenal of Stalin's propaganda machinery referred? He may have been deranged, but there was an ominous method in his madness.

The most threatening note of all was sounded by frequent references to 1937 when Comrade Stalin "demonstrated how the new type of subversive and wrecker arises – a person who does not dare come forth openly against the Soviet state and the Communist Party but, on the contrary, tries to lull the vigilance of Soviet people by false assurances of his devotion to our cause."

History, it seemed virtually certain, was about to repeat events of the 1930s and only fate intervened to save the Soviet Union from another bloody purge.

Although the arrest of the physicians had not been announced until 13 January 1953, there is persuasive evidence that they had been imprisoned two months earlier, during the first week of November, and there are even suggestions that the entire "case" had been prefabricated some time before the XIXth Party Congress.

Moreover, a number of high-ranking party functionaries, beside Stalin, were at least privy to the fabrication of the whole "case". Khrushchev, it seems certain, was one of them for the minister of state security at the time was S. D. Ignatiev, a political associate, who later came under Khrushchev's protection. Another associate was Frol Kozlov, then second secretary of the Leningrad *oblast* committee. Kozlov had been selected to write the article in the January issue of *Kommunist* magazine which was actually the key policy statement on the purge. Kozlov later became Khrushchev's chosen successor and Brezhnev's chief rival in the party leadership. Whether Brezhnev himself was privy to the facts remains subject to speculation. But somehow it seems more than coincidental that all three men – Ignatiev, Kozlov and Brezhnev – suffered drastic demotions within days after Stalin's death when the charges against the doctors were withdrawn and the preposterousness of the whole plot was exposed.

The dictator died shortly before 10 p.m. on 5 March 1953.

Within twenty-four hours his political heirs had met to reshape the party and government structure they had inherited.

The old guard moved quickly to demote and neutralize the younger men who had been vaulted to great power in October. The enlarged Party Presidium was trimmed down from thirty-six full and candidate members to fourteen. The Central Committee Secretariat was pared from ten to seven members.

Leonid Brezhnev was out of both bodies. One of the numerous terse *Pravda* announcements of the changes on 7 March disclosed that he had been appointed chief of the political administration of the navy ministry. Within a week his career was to take one more dip. The navy ministry was abolished and merged with the war ministry. Brezhnev, in the rank of lieutenant general, became "first deputy" head of the political administration of the new ministry of defense.

It was a severe fall, but Brezhnev could have done worse; as others, in fact, did. Kosygin, for example, became minister of light industry. Moreover, Brezhnev was at least to remain in Moscow in a position that offered some proximity to the reality, if not the trappings, of power.

For nearly a year, until Khrushchev pulled him out of limbo, Brezhnev was in virtual eclipse. He appeared at a variety of receptions and military ceremonies. But usually it was his superior, Colonel General Aleksei Zheltov, the chief of the political administration, whose name made the papers. Brezhnev was mentioned only twice: on 9 August when *Pravda* reported that he had opened the ceremonies for Soviet Air Force Day at the outdoor theater in Moscow's Gorky Park, and on 8 September when, along with thirty-three other high-ranking officers, he signed the obituary for Lieutenant General Boris Vershinin, a prominent armor expert.

But the demotion was to reaffirm a basic principle of Soviet politics as well as revealing a great deal about Brezhnev's particular political qualities and tactics.

Brezhnev demonstrated, first of all, that down for a count does not mean knocked out of the fight. It is an axiom proven by many Soviet leaders before Brezhnev. He was to demonstrate its validity on one more occasion himself and a number o his clients and protégés, notably Shcherbitsky, Shchelokov and Dinmukhamed Kunayev, the present party leader of

Kazakhstan, have reaffirmed the principle under his tutelage and protection. Some day that principle of political resilience could come back to haunt Brezhnev in the guise of those men whose feathers he has plucked since Khrushchev's fall.

Above all, Brezhnev's demotion in March 1953 revealed his remarkable ability to cut losses, to preserve appearances, to make the best of an adverse situation by grasping whatever advantages it offered and to bounce back, ultimately triumphant, on the winning side.

During the hiatus in his career Brezhnev accomplished two important things. First, he made himself uniquely useful to Khrushchev in the post-Stalin power struggle; second, he reforged and extended his ties to a crucial segment of the Soviet establishment: the military. The import of both accomplishments was not to be realized until many years later.

Formally he was only second-in-command of the political administration of the defense ministry. For all practical purposes, though, Brezhnev was the chief *politruk*. General Zheltov, now rector of the Lenin Military Political Academy, though a veteran political officer and a career soldier since 1924, was a nonentity. Brezhnev, on the other hand, was not only a high-ranking *apparatchik* but a member of the Central Committee. Moreover, he was Khrushchev's watchdog and a vital figure in Khrushchev's 1953 power struggle with both Beria and Malenkov.

True, there is no record of Brezhnev's personal involvement in the strike against Beria. In fact, three weeks after Beria's arrest it was Zheltov who presided over the defense ministry party meeting at which "unanimous approval" was expressed of the "timely and resolute measures taken to suppress the criminal activities of that traitor to the fatherland, the bourgeois renegade and sworn enemy of the Party and the people, Beria." But Brezhnev cannot have been far from the decision-making apparatus that pitted army tanks and soldiers against Beria's security troops.

After Stalin's death the ministry of state security (MGB) and the ministry of internal affairs (MVD) had been merged under Beria's command. Together they comprised a formidable force of more than a half million secret police, intelligence and counter-intelligence agents, uniformed civil police, frontier guards, internal security troops, labor camp guards, the coast guard and other military and paramilitary units, including a small police air force. It was estimated at the time that these forces included fourteen well-equipped MVD divisions, some of them mechanized and motorized. Moreover, the entire Kremlin security guard came under Beria's jurisdiction.

The only counterweight was the army and on 27 June it backed Khrushchev, the self-declared architect of the coup against Beria. While Beria was being arrested, Soviet Army anks and troops surrounded and protected the Kremlin and other government buildings and kept the security forces from coming to their chief's aid.

In the ensuing struggle between Khrushchev and Malenkov the army, most of whose marshals and generals detested Malenkov because of the way he had acted as Stalin's spy during the war, remained passive. And that was to Khrushchev's advantage, of course.

Brezhnev, meanwhile, was renewing friendships, reweaving old ties and forging new ones in the defense ministry. The list of marshals, generals and admirals upon whom he can rely today is a veritable who's who of the Soviet military establishment.

First and foremost, of course, there is Grechko, whose unbroken links with Brezhnev date back to the war and who, more or less, owes his position as minister of defense and membership in the Politburo to his erstwhile political commissar in the 18th Army.

Brezhnev's association with Admiral Sergei G. Gorshkov, the commander-in-chief of the Soviet Navy, also dates to the war years, for Gorshkov was deputy commander of the Novorossiysk defense region and commander of the Azov Sea flotilla. Gorshkov's naval units played major roles in the battles for the Caucasus and on the Black Sea in 1942 and 1943 when he and Brezhnev first met. Their association resumed when Brezhnev became chief political commissar of the navy department. Gorshkov, at the time, was chief-of-staff of the Soviet Navy.

The present chief of the general staff of the Soviet armed forces and a first deputy defense minister is General Viktor G. Kulikov, also a wartime comrade. Kulikov is the youngest and perhaps most brilliant officer in the top leadership. A military whizz kid par excellence, he was a brigade commander at the age of twenty-four – in the 18th Army.

Another deputy defense minister and presently the chief of the main inspectorate of the Soviet armed forces, is Marshal Kirill S. Moskalenko whose ties with Brezhnev also date from the war. In 1953, as commander of the Moscow air defense district, later as commander of Moscow garrison, Moskalenko played a crucial role in the coup against Beria. In fact, he was one of the squad of generals who marched into the Politburo chamber and arrested the security and police chief.

The relationship between Brezhnev and Shtemenko, the current chief-of-staff of Warsaw Pact forces, is more difficult to assess. Shtemenko, one of the five officer "victims" named in the Doctors' Plot, has had a turbulent career. A Stalinist general and one of the dictator's closest advisors, he was chief of the Soviet Army general staff until a few days before Stalin's death. Then he was suddenly relieved. His intended role in the forthcoming purge remains obscure, but it seems to have been related to his subsequent eclipse. He was demoted two ranks and did not re-emerge until after Brezhnev had succeeded Khrushchev as party leader. Although there is no evidence of any close wartime association or ties between them in the 1950s, Shtemenko obviously owes his return to authority, not to mention the regaining of his former rank, to Brezhnev.

Until his death in November 1970, Marshal Andrey Yeremenko, Brezhnev's former commander in the 4th Ukrainian Army Group and Carpathian Military District, served as inspector general of the Soviet defense ministry.

General Ivan G. Pavlovsky, presently a deputy minister of defense and commander-in-chief of Soviet land forces, was also a World War Two comrade of Brezhnev. In 1968 Pavlovsky was commander of the units which invaded Czechoslovakia.

Another wartime acquaintance is General Nikolai Lyashchenko, presently commander of the Central Asian military district.

Brezhnev's commander in the 18th Army for part of the war was Anton I. Gastilovich. Now a colonel general, he is deputy head of the Soviet general staff academy.

Konstantin Grushevoi, as noted previously, is now a colonel

general and political commissar of Moscow military district. In 1953 he was a member of the military council of the Moscow area anti-aircraft defense command and involved in the coup against Beria.

Lieutenant General Nikita S. Dyomin, wartime commander of the 18th Army's 17th Rifle Corps, and a close comrade of Brezhnev, now serves as deputy chairman of DOSAAF, the para-military organization of civilian "volunteer assistants of the army, air force and navy".

General Aleksei A. Yepishev is the present head of the main political board of the Soviet Army and Navy, that is, chief political commissar. His ties to Brezhnev pre-date the war when Yepishev was first secretary of the Odessa City Party committee. He was appointed to his present post by Khrushchev in 1962 and is one of Brezhnev's principal links to the high command.

The list is by no means complete. Of the twenty high-ranking military officers elected to full membership of the Central Committee at the XXIVth Party Congress in 1971, at least seven can be considered political allies of Brezhnev.

These associations offer a partial explanation for the latitude Brezhnev seems to enjoy in his *Westpolitik*, his *rapprochement* with Washington and his careful balancing act in the Middle East. They explain, to an extent, the seeming imponderables of Brezhnev's foreign policy in the late 1960s and early 1970s.

Recalling the influential role played on past occasions by the Soviet military establishment, some kremlinologists have repeatedly predicted takeover bids by the Soviet praetorian guard. That was the prognosis in 1969, following the invasion of Czechoslovakia, when the marshals and generals were believed to be in a mutinous mood because the politicians appeared to have turned a brilliantly executed military coup into a political débâcle. The issue was raised once more in the spring of 1972 when President Nixon mined North Vietnam's harbors just before his scheduled summit meeting with Brezhnev: an affront to Soviet military sensibilities which some observers predicted Brezhnev would never survive. The suggestion was made again in April 1973 when Grechko entered the Politburo, the first time in sixteen years that a minister of defense had been named a member of the Party's top executive body.

Indeed, there has been military resistance and foot-dragging, even thinly muffled rumbling of opposition to Brezhnev's foreign policy from Frunze Street, the Soviet Pentagon. But this has never been a serious challenge to Brezhnev's position or to civilian supremacy over the military.

It is true, too, that for decades recurrent tension has marked the relationship between the civilian party leadership and the professional military men in the USSR. One need only recall Stalin's purge of the high command in 1937, his postwar demotion of Marshal Zhukov or Khrushchev's controversies with various marshals, notably Zhukov. Under Brezhnev political-military relations seem to have involved four broad categories of problems: maintaining political control; the issue of economic priorities; the question of international priorities; and how to balance military influence on policy formation against the politicians' increasing need for the professional expertise of the military leadership.

In all this Brezhnev has fared remarkably well. He has consistently reaffirmed the principle of civilian control without liquidating or publicly embarrassing his generals as Stalin and Khrushchev did before him. Most important of all, however, he has forced the military to share responsibility for political decisions by drawing the members of the military establishment into the decision-making process. That is the real significance of Grechko's elevation to the Politburo.

Brezhnev's handling of the brass is a tribute to his political astuteness, to be sure. But would he have been equally successful had he himself not been wearing the old army tie? Many of his political and diplomatic policies could not have been implemented had it not been for his wartime role and those eleven months he spent in limbo after Stalin's death.

CHAPTER IX

Virgin Soil Upturned

While Leonid Brezhnev attended Soviet Army, Air Force and Navy Day ceremonies, Nikita Khrushchev was preoccupied with inheriting the spoils of Stalin's power.

Only a few weeks after Stalin's death *Pravda* had emphasized that "one of the fundamental principles of party leadership is collectivity in deciding all important problems of party work." But behind the headlines and the often oracular editorials a bitter three-cornered struggle for supremacy was taking place between Khrushchev, Beria and Malenkov.

Each man had inherited one of the three supporting pillars of power over which Stalin alone had exercised virtually monopolistic control: Khrushchev, the Party; Beria, the police; Malenkov, the government apparatus.

Theoretically this might have provided the skeletal framework for some type of check-and-balance system. But that would have been expecting too much from a society where total power had been arrogated to one man. It was a foregone conclusion – just as it was after Khrushchev's own fall in 1964 – that eventually, in one form or another, power would again gravitate to one man. The nature of the system dictates that the party chief is that man.

From the outset Beria posed the greatest challenge to the principle of collectivity. Although he had helped to install Malenkov as premier, he had begun to develop his own political support outside the enormous police organization he controlled.

In the first battle Khrushchev and Malenkov forged a tenuous alliance to eliminate Beria. But as soon as he had been destroyed, the two survivors tried to destroy each other.

Although Khrushchev and Malenkov had been rivals for many years, their analysis of the country's basic problems was remarkably similar. Both men agreed, fundamentally, that the Soviet Union as Stalin had left it to them could not continue.

They had already taken far-reaching, but discreet steps to demythologize Stalin and to restore a semblance of legality to Soviet life. The Doctors' Plot had been exposed as a fake and the surviving physicians themselves freed from prison and rehabilitated. Many political prisoners had been amnestied. The vigilance campaign had ended overnight. The ideological stranglehold on literature and the arts had been relaxed. Stalin's name, which before his death had appeared on an average of forty times on a single page of *Pravda*, was rarely mentioned.

Both Khrushchev and Malenkov realized that the economy left them by Stalin was seriously out of balance. In the frantic postwar reconstruction drive and in the effort to create new defense potential, everything had been sacrificed to heavy industry. Soviet workers were badly housed, badly dressed and badly fed. Moreover, the highly centralized methods of industrial planning and control had produced a grossly inefficient and wasteful system, top heavy with bureaucracy. The situation in agriculture was, if anything, even worse. As Khrushchev was soon to point out, in 1953 the USSR possessed 8.9 million head of cattle less than it had in 1928. The potato-growing area had decreased by half since the war, and the total grain output was, after decades of upheaval, only 10 percent greater than in 1913. Worst of all, agriculture was thoroughly inefficient: more than half the nation's population was engaged in it, meaning that a majority was preoccupied with feeding a minority.

It is ironic that, while agreeing on their analysis, the exigencies of the power struggle compelled Khrushchev to take publicly a view opposed to that of Malenkov, a view, moreover, that he was to reverse soon after Malenkov had been defeated and politically crushed.

When Malenkov expounded a new deal for the masses by stipulating that consumer goods production should be developed at the same rate as heavy industry, Khrushchev became the spokesman for the "metal eaters" of the military-industrial complex. Only later, when his position was secure, did he become the prophet of "goulash communism".

Malenkov announced the Government's New Course at the 8 August 1953 Supreme Soviet session. What he said was no less remarkable than what he didn't say, for his speech made only the briefest references to the Party, a clear indication that he intended for the Government to take on virtually alone the task of coping with the economy, and to usurp the Party's traditional role.

Three weeks later, at an epochal plenum of the Central Committee, Khrushchev made his countermove. First of all, he was officially named the Party's first secretary, giving him the power of crucial appointments. But even more important, he rode hard on the state of agriculture which he turned into his offensive weapon.

Khrushchev knew that the countryside and the agricultural economy were more susceptible to guidance and control by the Party than industry. He understood, too, that if he could provide the Soviet people with "an abundance of bread, meat, milk, butter, vegetables and other agricultural products", his predominance would be assured.

The statistics he disclosed on the catastrophic state of Soviet agriculture – the first time even Central Committee members had been exposed to the facts – came as a shock. In a direct assault on Malenkov's area of responsibility, he placed much of the blame on those government ministries concerned with farming.

The solutions he proposed during the plenum and in a series of subsequent speeches, articles and secret meetings called for far-reaching changes: material incentives to farming; drastic increases in the price that the state paid for meat and animal products; and support of private ownership of small plots and livestock holdings. He demanded that more productive crops, especially corn, be grown to increase and improve the meat and dairy products supply. And he ordered 100,000 agricultural experts and 50,000 party officials to the countryside to exercise more political control over the *kolkhozes* and raise economic standards.

But Khrushchev's most sensational and controversial proposal – the first of his spectacular one-man initiatives – was the virgin lands scheme: a daring campaign to plow and sow with grain the unused and potentially arable steppe and prairie country in Kazakhstan and south-western Siberia. The idea itself – expansion of agriculture through virgin lands reclamation – was hardly new. Unprecedented, however, was the scope of Khrushchev's plan: to put 13,000,000 hectars – more than 50,000 square miles, an area larger than the state of Louisiana and equal to that of England – under the plow in 1954 and 1955. Flushed with the success of the first year, Khrushchev was soon to raise his demands, calling for the development of 28 to 30 million hectars by the end of 1956.

The scheme was full of imponderables and fraught with incalculable risks. Hundreds of thousands of experts and volunteers, millions of tons of agricultural equipment, building materials and supplies would have to be sent into a region that had previously been a no-man's land, devoid of transportation or communications facilities. It was questionable whether the USSR had those kinds of resources; moreover, opponents argued that the returns would never equal the investment. Even more serious was the warning by experts that unless correct and carefully adjusted cultivation methods were followed, soil erosion, dust bowls, drought and weed infestation would result.

The focus of attention was on Kazakhstan, second largest of the fifteen Soviet republics, where half of the new lands territory was located.

From the moment Khrushchev had first broached his idea at the September Central Committee plenum, Kazakhstan's party leaders, notably Zhumabai Shayakhmetov, the first secretary, had been opposed. Although they agreed in principle to the extension of arable land, they objected sharply to the scope of Khrushchev's program, arguing that it sought to accomplish too much in too short a period of time. They also realized that implementation of Khrushchev's scheme would bring a massive invasion of Slav settlers, destroy the traditional Kazakh herd and grasslands culture and reduce the Kazakhs themselves to an impotent minority in their own republic.

From mid-September until the end of 1953, while he argued with Shayakhmetov and sought to undermine him by appealing directly to the *oblast* secretaries in what was to become known later as *Tselinny Krai*, the Virgin Lands Territory, Khrushchev shopped around for a man who would do the job for him. What he needed was a personally loyal party *apparatchik* with a proven executive record, experienced in land reclamation and agriculture, familiar with modern machinery, capable of dealing with a non-Slav native population and energetic and young enough to tackle what would obviously be a very difficult assignment.

Among Khrushchev's political allies and protégés whom he had been restoring to positions of power after the September 1953 Central Committee plenum, none met those requirements better than Leonid Brezhnev.

There was one hitch however. When Khrushchev made the choice, at the turn of the year 1953–1954, his own position was not yet strong enough to put Brezhnev formally in charge. The official title went to Panteleimon K. Ponomarenko, an associate of Malenkov. An erstwhile partisan organizer, Ponomarenko had been party chief of Byelorussia before the war and that republic's prime minister from 1944 to 1948. When Zhdanov died, Malenkov arranged for Ponomarenko's transfer to Moscow as one of the five secretaries of the Central Committee. At the XIXth Party Congress he also became a full member of the enlarged Presidium. After Stalin's death he was demoted to candidate membership and was eased out of the Secretariat to become the USSR's minister of culture, a position he held on the eve of his assignment to Kazakhstan.

Malenkov probably had two reasons for insisting on Ponomarenko's appointment. It provided him with a watchdog over Khrushchev and Brezhnev in the virgin lands. Second, if the project succeeded, he could claim credit through Ponomarenko's involvement. In the event of failure it should not be difficult to arrange for Khrushchev and Brezhnev to take the blame.

Ponomarenko, four years older than Brezhnev, was to become the first secretary, Brezhnev merely the second secretary of the Kazakhstan Central Committee. In reality, though, Brezhnev provided the driving force behind Khrushchev's program and within fifteen months he would inherit the formal title to Kazakh leadership – after Malenkov's "resignation" as prime minister and Ponomarenko's abrupt transfer to Warsaw as Soviet ambassador to Poland.

Before either Brezhnev or Ponomarenko could assume their new duties in Alma Ata, however, the matter of a legally constituted, albeit obstructive, Kazakh party leadership had to be disposed of. That called for ruthless political surgery.

On 30 January 1954 Shayakhmetov and the members of the Kazakh Politburo were ordered to Moscow for a meeting with Khrushchev, Brezhnev, Ponomarenko and the Central Committee Secretariat. They were sharply criticized for their behavior and then and there Shayakhmetov and the second secretary, Ivan Afonov, were dismissed. A week later Brezhnev and Ponomarenko arrived in Alma Ata to put the stamp of legality on the Moscow decision at a plenum of the Kazakh Central Committee. When the session ended Ponomarenko and Brezhnev were "elected".

But the purge was by no means over. It continued ten days later at a hurriedly convened VIIth Congress of the Kazakh Communist Party during which Shayakhmetov was charged with "superficiality", "direct violation of party principles" by selecting personnel "from considerations of family and friendship . . ." and "bureaucratic, paper methods of leadership".

Shayakhmetov was "exiled" to Chimkent as first secretary of the South Kazakhstan *oblast*. Even in that political backwater he was to suffer further disgrace. Brezhnev went there in June 1955 to supervise personally Shayakhmetov's removal from the *oblast* leadership and the final destruction of his political career.

With Shayakhmetov out of the way and the rest of the old Kazakh party leadership humiliated, Brezhnev and Ponomarenko were ready to take on the main job itself.

Brezhnev had survived the trials of Revolution, the Civil War, famine, typhus, Stalin's purges and German shells and bullets. He had rebuilt Zaporozhe's war-torn steel industry, revitalized Dnepropetrovsk and brought the hostile Moldavians under Moscow's yoke. His self-confidence should have been almost boundless. But even Brezhnev must have shrunk back at the immensity and the complexity of the task now facing him, especially when he surveyed the meager resources with which to accomplish it.

It was one thing to sit in Moscow and theorize about how many additional million tons of grain could be harvested by plowing up millions of hectars of unused land within twenty months. It was quite another matter when one got to Kazakhstan and saw the land, the poverty, the backwardness, the vastness, the lack of infrastructure and the unpredictable, hostile climate of that republic.

A country one third the size of the United States with only seven million inhabitants, Kazakhstan in the spring of 1954 was a vast expanse of nothingness, rich in minerals and potential but thousands of miles from the sources of supply that could exploit them. Bordering on China's Sinkiang province in the east, on the Caspian Sea in the west, its land was marginal and highly susceptible to the vagaries of nature: the kind of place where one late frost in May or an early rain in August can change the scene from abundance to chaos and frequently does. It was a country with virtually no roads or railways, no air-strips, electricity or communications. In 1954 there were areas of Kazakhstan where the natives had never seen a truck or an automobile and ran in fright when the first jeep, enveloped by a cloud of dust, bounced across the bumpy steppe with a team of virgin-land surveyors.

One such area was in Semipalatinsk *oblast* where a Soviet emigrant, now living in Western Europe, worked as a village grade school teacher when Brezhnev came to Alma Ata.

"There were no houses as such," he explained, "only *semlyanki* (dugouts) with straw roofs and dirt floors. Straw and dried cow and horse dung were used to heat them in winter and to cook . . . We had about fifty of these in the village and the total population was around three hundred. Even the school was a *semlyanka* with a dirt floor. In fact, only two of the huts were laid out with wooden planks: the *kolkhoz* chairman's and the party secretary's.

"In the school we had no books, no paper, no educational materials to speak of. During the winter of 1954–55 animal fodder was so scarce that we stripped the straw off the school roof to feed the livestock and held no more classes until late spring.

"The population consisted primarily of Volga Germans who had been deported there during the war, Chechens, some Poles and the descendants of nineteenth-century Ukrainian settlers and of political deportees whose ancestors had been exiled there by the tsarist police.

"We had no running water, only a well, and the village was

not electrified until 1956. The school itself did not receive electric light until 1959.

"It was fifty miles to the railroad line, more than twenty to the town where we had the nearest service facilities such as a barber shop and post office. In summer you could travel there over a dirt road by truck, jeep or wagon. But in winter the only means of transport was by *kolkhoz* sleigh. I recall that once, in the winter of 1955–56 I had to attend a teachers' conference in the county capital and bribed the *kolkhoz* chairman with two bottles of vodka to let me use the sleigh and a couple of oxen with which to get to town.

"At that conference, in the assembly hall, I saw a huge portrait of Brezhnev and a slogan beneath it: 'Forward to the Victory of Communism.' "

Brezhnev's and Ponomarenko's assignment was to transform backward regions like this into a rich new granary.

To cultivate 6.3 million hectars of virgin Kazakh soil during the first twenty months of the program, that is from the time it was formally promulgated in March 1954 until the end of 1955, nearly three hundred new state farms – *sovkhozes* – each encompassing a minimum of 50,000 acres of land, were to be created.

The scope of the logistical support needed to accomplish this is staggering. But no one can claim that the Soviet state stinted its efforts.

During the first year Kazakhstan was to receive an additional $50 million (at the official 1954 exchange rate) for building those farms and providing the infrastructure. The initial party and government edicts called for shipping in 5,000 combines and harvesters, 10,000 trucks, 6,000 cultivators, 3,000 harrowers, more than 50,000 tractors and thousands of tons of additional agricultural hardware. More than 1,200 miles of new railway lines, most of them narrow gauge, and hundreds of miles of roads had to be laid.

The Party's vast propaganda machinery was cranked up to lure *Komsomol* youths, demobilized soldiers, tractor drivers and combine operators, *kolkhozniki* and *sovkhozniki* to Kazakhstan. A variety of inducements was employed to draw young people. There were appeals to their patriotism and the promise of high pay and generous credits if they agreed to settle permanently. But there were also the more subtle means of coercion available to party officials who wished to oversubscribe their quotas of "volunteers" for the virgin lands.

And come they did, some starry-eyed, some mercenary, but most of them true volunteers. They came in tens and hundreds of thousands. By June 1954, as Brezhnev reported, 55,000 tractor drivers, brigade leaders and other agricultural machinists had arrived in Kazakhstan. By the end of 1956 more than a half million new *sovkhozniki* had moved to the republic.

To house, feed and clothe them required the same organizational skill and vast supply apparatus that it takes to field an army. Merely to accommodate the first wave, the Central Committee had decreed that 500 field kitchens, 225,000 square meters of pre-fab housing and nearly 4,000 multi-man tents should be shipped to Kazakhstan.

The plans were grandiose, but as had happened so often and still occurs so frequently in the Soviet Union, there was a yawning gap of confusion, disorganization, apathy and corruption between promise and reality.

Komsomoly arrived, raring to operate tractors, but there were no instruction manuals with which to train them. Experienced operators arrived from the Ukraine only to discover that the machinery in Kazakhstan was of a new design and no one knew how to service it.

A *Pravda* "investigative" correspondent reported from Kustanai that the daily arrival of dozens of freight cars with new equipment and the absence of off-loading machinery had caused such a jam at the local railway station that new implements were just being strewn on the ground and left to rust.

"Everywhere you look," he wrote, "you see different types of machinery and supplies dumped down in disorder right in the dirt . . . and . . . the wreckage of tractor plows, bent metal panels from haying combines, new-but-already-disabled diesel engines . . . The freight yards have but one small crane, which is frequently out of order because of clumsy handling. As a result new tractors are used to haul new machinery from the flat cars and everything gets broken."

Equipment not pilfered outright or stripped for spare parts on the long journey to Kazakhstan, was inevitably damaged during unloading at provincial stations, or broken on the bumpy trips to the distant farms and then conveniently dumped by the wayside. Within a year the *Tselinny Krai* was indeed producing grain, but it had also become a vast junkyard of rusting, unserviceable machinery.

These were by no means the only complaints. Impure seed was being sent to many *sovkhozes* and when it was pure there were frequently no trucks to carry it. Or the trucks lacked fuel, for deliveries of diesel oil and gasoline repeatedly fell 40 to 50 percent below allocations. During the first harvest thousands of tons of grain were lost, because there were no sacks for it nor tarpaulins with which to cover it in open dump trucks. In some areas road conditions caused up to 100 pounds of grain to be lost from each truck-load as the vehicles hit moonscapes of potholes or got stuck in the mud.

The saddest stories, however, were being told by the volunteers and new settlers. The plan had foreseen the construction of enormous amounts of new housing. Practically none was being built. By the end of the first harvest, it has been estimated, 75 percent of the "virgin-land toilers" were still living in tents. Lumber that had been allocated was never distributed. Window glass that had been earmarked for distribution simply disappeared before it reached its destination.

Those fortunate enough to complete houses or move into dormitories before the winter set in, had no furniture or housewares because the retail trade was on the brink of chaos.

"Our people sit on boxes and eat off them, too," complained one *sovkhoz* engineer in Kustanai *oblast.* "We all make good money but we can't buy chairs, tables or bedsteads. In the evening there is no light. We installed electricity but the co-op store has neither lamp sockets nor light bulbs."

From all over Kazakhstan similar complaints could be heard: no furniture, kitchen utensils, dishes, cutlery, pots, pans, washtubs; not enough felt boots, padded jackets, caps or mittens; no soap, matches, sugar, tea. And as one *traktorist* moaned with a specially mournful sigh: no chess sets nor dominoes, either. Service facilities were virtually non-existent, and trips of up to forty miles for a shoe repair, a haircut and medical care were commonplace.

A year after the campaign got started 700 physicians, hospital directors, sanitation inspectors, pharmacists and nurses from the virgin lands districts gathered in Alma Ata for a conference. Brezhnev sat on the platform and listened glumly as Kazakhstan's minister of health, S. R. Karynbayev, delivered his report. Seventy-eight district hospitals had no doctors, he said, forty were without midwives or gynaecologists, thirty-three without pediatricians. More than three hundred doctors had left the republic in 1954, the majority from the rural districts, because of living conditions.

Brezhnev and Ponomarenko had spared no efforts to bring scores of top-rate Moscow and Leningrad artists and entertainers to the virgin lands. They sponsored conferences of Kazakh writers who were encouraged to describe a bright, optimistic future in their novels and stories. Delegations from India, China and Afghanistan arrived to observe the work. The central press reported on the grand transformation of the Kazakh steppe and published countless testimonial letters from happy young *Komsomoly* urging their "friends back home" to join them on the new frontier.

But for hundreds of thousands of volunteers the reality of Kazakhstan was the rotting grain because someone had failed to provide trucks or storage facilities; the broken drive shafts on their harvesters for which there were no replacement parts; the cold nights in the tent or dugout; the lack of soap and water; the shortage of mittens and warm boots or the letters from home that never reached them because no one bothered to deliver the mail.

And yet, it was a triumph. By August 1954 Khrushchev was so emboldened as to raise the targets for the plowing of new lands. And when the harvest results were reported in November, Kazakhstan alone could boast that it had delivered almost twice as much grain as the year before.

Those were precisely the figures Khrushchev needed for his victory over Malenkov, a victory in which Leonid Brezhnev was not only to play an eminent role but to share significantly.

The battle had been shaping up for weeks in the form of esoterically worded debates in the press and the discreet but unmistakable erosion of Malenkov's power base through the removal of his allies and supporters. It reached a climax during a week-long plenary meeting of the CPSU Central Committee in January 1955. Brezhnev as a member of the Central

Committee, was in Moscow for the kill. One week later, on 8 February, Malenkov submitted his "resignation" as prime minister to the Supreme Soviet, stating that he was "incompetent" to handle the job. Khrushchev nominated Nikolai Bulganin for the premiership.

After that Khrushchev went about methodically purging what remained of Malenkov's machine. It was only a matter of a few months before Ponomarenko, too, fell. In May he was shunted to Warsaw, the start of a long, ignominious descent. In 1957 he was transferred from Warsaw and became ambassador to India. In 1959, after a brief interlude in Nepal, Khrushchev assigned him as Soviet envoy to the Netherlands. There he made the headlines one last time. In October 1961 he was involved in a fist-fight with police at Amsterdam's Schiphol airport over a Soviet woman defector. Ambassador Ponomarenko, who walked from the mêlée with a bloody nose, was declared *persona non grata*.

For three more months after Ponomarenko's departure from Alma Ata, Brezhnev was the republic's acting first secretary. He inherited the title formally at a meeting of the Kazakh Central Committee in August 1955. Meanwhile he had also been making friends and striking new political alliances of which the most important and durable was with Dinmukhamed Kunayev, who was named prime minister of Kazakhstan in March 1955.

In Kunayev, six years his junior, Brezhnev found a soul brother. Half-Kazakh, half-Russian, born in Alma Ata, Kunayev is a brilliant metallurgist and engineer who holds the Soviet equivalent of a doctorate. From 1952 until his election as premier, he was president of the Kazakhstan academy of sciences.

Significantly soon after Kunayev's election as prime minister, Brezhnev's attention began to waver from the virgin lands program and agriculture to Kazakhstan's other exciting frontier: the exploitation of its mineral riches and the development of its mining and engineering industry. At the August 1955 plenum, which formally elected him to the Kazakh party leadership, Brezhnev devoted the major portion of his report to industrial themes.

Volunteers, millions of rubles, thousands of tractors,

harvesters, trucks and tons of equipment continued to pour into Kazakhstan and 9 million hectars of new land – 1.5 times as many as in 1954 – were being plowed up. But by August it was evident that the 1955 harvest would be a failure: the first of many that were to beset Kazakhstan. Brezhnev could hardly be blamed. A severe drought had visited the region. Fortunately for Brezhnev, and Khrushchev, it was offset by a near bumper crop in the USSR's traditional grain-growing areas. In 1956, on the other hand, Kazakh grain deliveries reached a near all-time record of 16.1 million tons, offsetting a drought in the Ukraine and giving the USSR an excellent harvest. Brezhnev can hardly take credit for that, since he left Alma Ata in February to return to Moscow and the inner circle of the Kremlin leadership.

Nevertheless, he acquired a reputation as something of an agricultural wizard and is still regarded as the only Soviet politician – next to Kunayev, perhaps – who has made the virgin lands scheme work.

That accolade is no more justified than the popular allegation that the virgin lands were Khrushchev's great folly. But it is indisputable that Brezhnev is virtually the only man to have come out of a Kazakhstan assignment with his plumage intact.

In the Soviet Union political fortunes tend to rise and fall with the annual harvests. Since Kazakhstan's harvests are especially vulnerable to the caprices of nature in addition to human error, the republic's first secretaryship – at least until Khrushchev's fall – had gained an odious reputation as a graveyard of political dreams and ambitions. Of the seven men who served in the post during the past two decades only one other man besides Brezhnev avoided the political junkyard: Kunayev. And Kunayev, it is important to note, had the job twice. In January 1960 he moved from the premiership to the party leadership, lasting until December 1962 when a mediocre harvest, compounded by a power struggle between Brezhnev and Frol Kozlov, resulted in his dismissal and transfer back to the prime minister's office. In December 1964, seven weeks after Khrushchev's fall, Brezhnev arranged for Kunayev's return as the Kazakh Party's first secretary, which he has been ever since.

Kazakhstan and the virgin lands plagued Khrushchev for

many years of his rule, just as they continue to preoccupy Brezhnev today. Some observers have suggested that the catastrophic harvest in 1963 was a primary cause for Khrushchev's fall and they were quick to imply that Brezhnev might suffer the same fate because of the 1972 crop failure.

Although striking parallels can be drawn, for example, between the enormous grain purchases Khrushchev was forced to make in 1963 and Brezhnev in 1972, the issue is far more complicated than that.

The basic question is whether the virgin lands scheme really was a folly. In principle it was not. Khrushchev's mistake was to get carried away by his own exhilaration and to ignore the agricultural experts who warned him to leave a much greater percentage of these lands fallow. The result was disastrous. Following the excellent 1958 harvest a steady decline set in, not only in overall production but in per acreage yields. The whole project was jeopardized by erosion, dust storms and loss of soil fertility. Moreover living conditions for the much fêted "virgin lands toilers" continued to range between abysmal and marginal, and hundreds of thousands, brought in at great expense, left again.

Brezhnev set out to correct these mistakes within a few weeks of assuming power in 1964. In fact, he may have taken over just in time to save Khrushchev's great scheme from Khrushchev's foibles.

Through careful management and by listening to scientists instead of charlatans, Brezhnev has succeeded in repairing the damage. He has increased Kazakhstan's average annual tonnage output and per acreage yields by 50 percent over that of the last five Khrushchev years, turning Kazakhstan into a major bread basket.

To whatever degree the agricultural débâcle contributed to Khrushchev's fall, it must be seen in the rare concatenation of two harvest catastrophes within the same year: a major crop failure in both Kazakhstan *and* the traditional grain areas of European Russia and the Ukraine. In a country the size of the Soviet Union such combinations are highly unusual.

In 1972 the crop failed in the Ukraine – thanks to one of the worst winters in a century and one of the hottest, driest summers since the Revolution. But Kazakhstan came through with the biggest harvest in its history: 27 million tons or 16 percent of the Soviet total crop. And Brezhnev was right on scene, touring the virgin lands for nearly two weeks at harvest time in a desperate bid to offset the losses he knew were imminent in the western part of the country.

This does not mean, of course, that Brezhnev's agricultural difficulties have been solved. On the contrary, as a later chapter will show, they are increasing. Moreover, even as he hopped from one Kazakh *oblast* to the other in August and September of 1972, the papers were reporting the same disorganization and mismanagement, the same sad tales of spillage and spoilage that seem to be endemic to Soviet agriculture in general and virgin lands farming in particular.

But in his own curious way, Brezhnev was demonstrating that Kazakhstan is still his special preserve. That fact had been underscored two years earlier, in August 1970, when he had visited Alma Ata for the Kazakh republic's fiftieth anniversary celebration. Kunayev, introducing him as the key speaker, delivered a laudation that would have made even Khrushchev or Stalin blush.

"We are very pleased," he said, "that you Leonid Ilyich have found time to share in our festivities despite your tremendous work load. We note with particular pride that you headed the Communist Party of Kazakhstan during one of the critical periods of our republic's development, when millions of hectars of virgin lands were being opened up. With your dynamic and tireless activity in those years you made a huge personal contribution to the opening up of the virgin lands and to the development of the whole economy of Kazakhstan."

A bit too thick? Perhaps. But it had, after all, been the scene of one of his greatest triumphs, not to mention that it was the crucial stepping-stone for his return to power in the Kremlin after a three-year hiatus.

Part Four

BREZHNEV, THE KHRUSHCHEVITE

"The peoples of the Soviet Union. . . see in these successes the fruitful activity and Leninist perspicacity of . . . that talented organizer and outstanding leader of the Communist Party, the Soviet State and the entire international Communist and workers' movement: Nikita Sergeyevich Khrushchev."

Leonid Brezhnev, 22 April 1959

CHAPTER X

To Moscow! To Moscow!

Sentries saluted smartly as the black ZIS limousine rolled through the Borovitsky Gate towards the Great Kremlin Palace. In the back seat of the cumbersome-looking, old-fashioned automobile, surveying the familiar but never dull view inside the ancient Russian fortress, sat Brezhnev.

He had passed this way many times: for meetings of the Supreme Soviet to which he had been a deputy since 1950; as a delegate to the Party Congress in 1952; to attend numerous receptions. But not in the same style as on this Tuesday morning, 14 February 1956, from a new position of strength, as one of Nikita Khrushchev's most loyal and successful supporters.

Ever since Malenkov's "resignation" a year earlier, Khrushchev had been making a more or less unconcealed bid for supremacy. He was counting on the XXth Congress of the Communist Party, whose opening session Brezhnev was attending that morning, to provide him with a commanding majority in the Central Committee, the Secretariat and the Presidium.

Khrushchev was to fall short of his aim, not consolidating his position until some sixteen months later. But it was a memorable conclave nevertheless for on its last day Khrushchev would deliver his "secret report" about the crimes of Stalin, thereby writing the opening page of a new chapter in Soviet history. And for Leonid Brezhnev the Congress was to become the providential turning-point of his political career.

The initial success of the virgin lands program was certainly a quintessential element of Khrushchev's attempt to win complete control. And considering that Brezhnev had played an instrumental part in making that success possible, his report to the Congress as Kazakhstan's party leader was remarkably brief and devoid of the boastful claims one might have expected. The disappointing 1955 harvest may have been partially responsible for that tone of moderation.

The most probable reason however is that he was following Khrushchev's explicit instructions, for in his scant forty-five-minute speech Brezhnev merely brush-stroked the subject of agriculture. Instead, he devoted himself to the complex question of the development of Kazakhstan's heavy industry and the exploitation of its mineral treasures: more specifically, to their inadequate exploitation and development. Brezhnev was merely echoing the Khrushchev line which called for the promotion of heavy industry and reaffirmed the Party's supremacy over the governmental-managerial bureaucracy.

"Kazakhstan," he said, "is one of the richest regions in the Soviet Union . . . Two thirds of all the lead, about one half of all our copper and cadmium and huge reserves of iron ore, coal and oil are located there. Every opportunity exists to make Kazakhstan one of the Soviet Union's mighty industrial and power centers . . . However, we are not yet taking full advantage of those opportunities."

Brezhnev then began to enumerate the shortcomings, the errors and failings. Who was to blame for these? Why, naturally, the central planning agencies and the various industrial ministries which had been, until February 1955, under Malenkov's, and since then under Bulganin's, direction.

The Congress continued for another week after Brezhnev's speech and on 25 February, after hearing Khrushchev's epochal secret attack on Stalin, elected a new Central Committee. Brezhnev, of course, remained a member.

On the following day when the Committee met to choose the Party's new leaders Brezhnev at last received the assurance that he would be returning to Alma Ata only briefly: to wind up his affairs, help select a successor and move his family back to Moscow – to the apartment on Kutuzovski Prospekt. He had been named a secretary of the Central Committee and a candidate member of the new Presidium (Politburo).

Three years after Stalin's death Brezhnev was back in the ruling circle – precisely where he had stood before his March 1953 demotion. He was almost fifty – hardly what one could describe as a rising young star on the political horizon. For the next four years – until he suffered another set-back to his career in May 1960 – his political fortunes remained on the ascent.

Those were to be turbulent years of lasting historical significance, pregnant with events that Brezhnev was to shape and that were to shape him: the Hungarian revolution and the Poznan riots in Poland; the 1956 Suez crisis; the showdown with the anti-party group and the political destruction of Malenkov, Molotov and Kaganovich; the first *sputnik* and the beginning of the space age; the banning of Boris Pasternak's novel *Doctor Zhivago*; then the beginning of the second cultural thaw in the USSR; the 1958 Berlin crisis; Richard Nixon's visit to the USSR and Khrushchev's trip to the United States in 1959; the beginning of the Sino-Soviet schism, and, finally, the U-2 spy-plane incident which was to have far-reaching repercussions for Khrushchev and Brezhnev.

Including Khrushchev and Brezhnev, the Central Committee had elected eight secretaries. With the exception of Khrushchev, the first secretary, their specific functions and duties were never publicly disclosed, but all the evidence indicates that in his first year or so on the new job, Brezhnev was in charge of relations with foreign Communist parties.

In this capacity he soon formed associations with two men who to this day play crucial roles in the Kremlin power structure: Yuri Vladimirovich Andropov, Brezhnev's neighbor and KGB chief, and Boris Nikolayevich Ponomarev, the present Central Committee secretary in charge of relations with "non-ruling" Communist parties. Andropov is a full member, Ponomarev a candidate member of the Politburo.

Andropov, forty-two years old when Brezhnev returned to Moscow from Kazakhstan, had been Soviet ambassador to Hungary since 1954 and remained in Budapest right through the Hungarian revolt until March 1957. Then he was recalled to Moscow to become head of the Central Committee department for relations with "ruling" Communist parties, that is with those parties which are in power. The department was under Brezhnev's jurisdiction.

Ponomarev, one year older than Brezhnev, a historian and veteran Comintern and Cominform executive, headed the Central Committee's department for relations with non-ruling parties.

Almost immediately after taking on his new duties Brezhnev was catapulted onto the diplomatic stage. He attended receptions, banquets, luncheons and conferences. He met famous foreign leaders and their elegant wives. He traveled abroad. A fascinating, glittering new world opened up: a world he could not have dreamed of back in Kamenskoye, a world he hardly knew existed.

Within a few weeks after his appointment Brezhnev received his first assignment abroad: as head of a CPSU delegation to the IIIrd Congress of the North Korean Labor Party in Pyongyang. He delivered a speech and brought the "cordial fraternal greetings" of the CPSU. He did not say anything unexpected or original. It was an address any Moscow official could or would have given. But it was the beginning of a new Brezhnev image.

By the autumn of 1956 he had met such prominent international figures as Indonesia's Sukarno, India's Radhakrishnan, Cambodia's Prince Sihanouk, the Shah of Iran and France's Guy Mollet.

In late September even Viktoria appeared briefly on the international stage, accompanying Brezhnev to Yalta for a "vacation" meeting with Khrushchev, Yugoslav President Josip Broz Tito and his wife Jovanka, and Hungary's party chief Erno Gerö. Other participants included Premier Bulganin, Marshall Grechko, KGB-chief General I. A. Serov, the Ukrainian Party leader, Aleksei Kirichenko and Ukrainian Premier Demyan Korotchenko – most of them accompanied by their wives. As *Pravda* reported the event on 1 October, it was a social affair complete with pleasant strolls in the balmy breezes on the sea front. In fact it was a crucial meeting intended to prevent another Yugoslav-Soviet break. The objective was to enlist Tito's support for Gerö as Hungarian party chief. Tito hesitated for two more weeks. By then it was too late and the Hungarian crisis was already irreversible.

That is the only record of Brezhnev's involvement in the events surrounding the Hungarian revolution. But as the party secretary responsible for relations with other Communist parties, he must have been in on the decision-making process which led to the Soviet intervention. One wonders how much of that experience he remembered twelve years later during the Czechoslovak crisis.

On 19 December 1956 – while the Central Committee was in an important plenary session – Brezhnev had his fiftieth Birthday. He was awarded the Order of Lenin; this was the first of the four such medals he now holds.

On the surface everything seemed calm enough. Actually a political holocaust was brewing, for that December plenum signaled the last-ditch effort by Khrushchev's opposition to topple him: a campaign that reached its climax with the coup by the so-called anti-party group in June 1957.

The December Central Committee meeting had strengthened Malenkov's position in the leadership again and had made one of his allies, Mikhail Pervukhin, virtual dictator of the Soviet economy, thus reducing Khrushchev's and the party apparatus' wide-ranging area of authority.

In February, at another plenum, Khrushchev struck back. He announced a major decentralization of economic management through the creation of regional economic councils – *sovnarkhozes*. The effect would be to undermine the power bases of his chief opponents and raise the role of the top party organs at the expense of the central government bureaucracies.

For Brezhnev – though it is inconceivable that he recognized it at the time – that February plenum had also brought forth a powerful new figure who was to come within reach of the leadership of the Soviet Union: Frol Romanovich Kozlov. Khrushchev, as part of the compromise he had had to strike, assented to the promotion of Kozlov, party leader of Leningrad, to candidate membership in the Presidium.

Kozlov was the man who had been closely linked to the fabrication of the Doctors' Plot and Stalin's planned 1953 purge. Like Brezhnev, he had suffered a major reversal after Stalin's death and was slowly climbing back up the rungs of power. In February 1957 he was indeed an ally of Khrushchev. But unlike Brezhnev or some others, his career had not depended exclusively on Khrushchev's protection. Thus his promotion to candidate status in the Presidium was a compromise of sorts between Khrushchev, who considered Kozlov reliable enough, and his opponents who hoped that Kozlov would not support Khrushchev in any extreme moves towards one-man rule. In effect he did. But within a few years Kozlov himself was to emerge as the primary challenger to Khrushchev's supremacy, as well as Brezhnev's chief rival. In fact, had fate not intervened in 1963 with a cerebral stroke, Kozlov would probably be sitting where Brezhnev is today.

For the next few months after that February plenum Khrushchev moved ahead on a broad front with a variety of economic and organizational measures to solidify his position. By June opposition to Khrushchev in the eleven-member Presidium had crystallized. He no longer enjoyed a majority. At least six members, led by Malenkov, Kaganovich and Molotov, were arrayed against him. On 19 June they forced a showdown.

On the pretext of discussing the celebration of the forthcoming 250th anniversary of Leningrad, the leaders of the coup had requested a special meeting of the Presidium. When it convened in the Presidium chamber of the Central Committee building on Staraya Ploshad (Old Square), a block from the Kremlin, they unleashed their attack. They charged Khrushchev with pursuing opportunist and Trotskyist policies and insisted on a complete reshuffle of the government and party leadership. A list of new leaders, which they had prepared beforehand, excluded Khrushchev. They called for an immediate vote and publication of the decision in the press.

Khrushchev resisted, arguing that since the Central Committee had elected him, only the Central Committee could remove him. Certain that he could muster a majority there, he played for time, demanding that a plenum be convened.

The battle over procedure raged for three days behind the leather-padded doors of the chamber. By all accounts, Brezhnev, as a candidate member of the Presidium with no vote, was not privy to it. Like other Presidium candidates, including Marshal Georgy Zhukov, the minister of defense, he spent most of the time in the hallway where an ever-increasing number of Central Committee members was congregating to find out what was happening.

As the debate between Khrushchev and his peers dragged out, Zhukov arranged for Soviet air force planes to bring virtually all provincial, non-resident Central Committee members to Moscow. By the time Khrushchev's opponents

agreed to throw the whole matter into the hands of the Central
Committee, 309 of its full and alternate members had arrived
in the capital.

The crucial plenum opened on Sunday, 22 June and lasted
for eight full days. In an unprecedented – and never to be
repeated – display of democracy, sixty members actually took
the floor to speak. When the marathon session ended on the
following Sunday, Khrushchev not only emerged victorious but
the principal opponents who had sought to oust him – Molotov,
Malenkov, Kaganovich and others – were themselves voted
out of the leadership and the Central Committee itself.

Brezhnev's role in crushing the "anti-party group's" coup
remains obscure. It is noteworthy, however, that in the many
public discussions and debates on the subject that were to
continue for quite a few years, Brezhnev's condemnation of
the group was remarkably moderate in tone. While others
referred to the group as "criminal", "loathsome", "perfidious",
"base", "despicable", "treacherous" and "dirty", the worst
words Brezhnev could find to describe it were "anti-Leninist"
and "politically bankrupt". But he was undoubtedly one of the
principal beneficiaries, entering the newly elected Party
Presidium as one of its fifteen full members.

Brezhnev was not the only man to benefit from Khrushchev's
victory. Kozlov, too, had moved up a rung. Demyan Korotchenko was named a candidate member of the Presidium as
were three men who still share power in the Politburo with
Brezhnev today: his friend Andrei Kirilenko, Kirill T. Mazurov,
then party leader of Byelorussia, and Aleksei Kosygin. For
Kosygin, in fact, it was the first step back into the inner circle
since Stalin's death.

Khrushchev moved quickly to consolidate his strengthened
position. In March 1958 he assumed Bulganin's role as premier,
becoming, like Stalin before him, chief of both the Party and
the Government.

As Khrushchev's stature and power rose, so did Brezhnev's.
In 1958 he became deputy chairman of the party bureau for
the Russian Federation. Russia, as distinct from the other
fourteen republics of the USSR, does not have its own nominally
independent Communist Party. Instead Russian Republic
party affairs are managed by a special bureau within the

Secretariat of the CPSU. Brezhnev's new position was one with enormous influence and great leeway in cadre assignments and patronage.

Brezhnev's friends, confederates and protégés were also beneficiaries. Georgy Yenyutin, his successor as party chief of Zaporozhe *oblast*, had been named chairman of the powerful new Commission for Soviet Control in the Council of Ministers. Konstantin Chernenko was ensconced in the Central Committee apparatus. Georgy Tsukanov had joined the staff as Brezhnev's aide. Pavel Alferov had an influential job as a member of the Party Control Commission.

Increasingly, too, Brezhnev came to be identified with heavy industry. Because the Hero of Socialist Labor award he received in 1961 makes specific references to his contribution to the Soviet space and rocket program, it is likely that his responsibilities included this highly secret enterprise as well.

In January 1959 Khrushchev convened a special Party Congress, the XXIst, to scrap his lagging five-year plan and substitute a seven-year plan. Brezhnev, naturally, was one of the principal speakers. His address was devoted almost entirely to the problems of expanding and modernizing the Soviet metallurgical industry. It was a no nonsense, no frills, no party-gobbledegook speech: the kind that made an engineer's heart beat faster. And as Brezhnev well knew, there were plenty of engineers among the congress delegates.

Noting that some plants had been under construction for as long as ten years, he said: "This practice can no longer be tolerated . . . The plan provides for concentrating funds on key projects and accelerating the schedules." He stressed the need for "economical expenditure of metal" and the introduction of "new, highly efficient technological processes and production methods." Labor productivity in the Soviet metallurgical industry, he said, was lower than in the United States "because a larger number of workers are occupied with various ancillary operations and repair and auxiliary jobs in our plants. . . We have much to do in introducing mechanization and automation."

In April he received the supreme honor of being the key speaker at the annual Lenin birthday celebration in the Bolshoi Theater. His address was a two-hour panegyric of

Khrushchev – who was notably absent – and a *tour d'horizon* of Communist achievements, especially during the period of Khrushchev's ascendancy which he called "a turning-point in the life of the Soviet Union". For all its repetition of standard Soviet concepts and hopes, the speech also expressed Brezhnev's personal political style: compromise, an attempt to satisfy as many disparate interest groups as possible.

While praising Khrushchev he also gave Stalin credit for a large part of the USSR's "industrialization . . . collectivization (and) cultural revolution" which had achieved "the socialist reorganization of society". He spoke about the reinstitution of Leninist norms but then mentioned the "many class enemies within the country and their agents inside the Party – Trotsky-ites, Zinovievites, Bukharinites, bourgeois nationalists – [who sought to frustrate] socialist construction and did their utmost to divert the Party from its Leninist course." While reminding his listeners that the USSR must remain on guard and be strong militarily, he stressed the hope for peaceful coexistence. "We do not need wars, conquests and the armaments race," he said. "What we need is peace to build communism." American capitalists, he warned, were the greatest obstacle to that goal because "the arms race is useful to their economy".

Three months later Brezhnev met one of the "capitalist-imperialist Americans": Richard Nixon, then Vice President of the United States. For the first time Brezhnev penetrated the Western consciousness. During the historic "kitchen debate" between Nixon and Khrushchev at an American exhibition of consumer goods in Moscow's Sokolniki Park, Brezhnev stood slightly to the left and behind the then Vice President. His square-jawed face set in a mask of grim silence, he listened stonily as Khrushchev and Nixon exchanged threats, boasts and bluster. Only once did Brezhnev break his rocklike stance: to nod energetic encouragement as Khrushchev, wagging his finger in Nixon's face, bragged loudly, "We too are giants. If you want to threaten, we will answer threat with threat."

Whatever his other duties, Brezhnev was clearly one of Khrushchev's principal trouble shooters. By the end of 1959 Kazakhstan was very much in trouble and Brezhnev rushed to Alma Ata to straighten it out. As his own successor he had chosen Ivan D. Yakovlev to head the Kazakh Party. During the first year Yakovlev had done very well, reporting a record harvest. But in 1957 catastrophe struck the virgin lands: grain deliveries had decreased by 75 percent. Khrushchev had purged Yakovlev in December 1957 and ordered his chief agricultural advisor, Nikolai I. Belyayev, a full member of the Presidium, to Alma Ata as Kazakhstan's first secretary. Belyayev's first harvest, 1958, was excellent. But in 1959 deliveries again had fallen off. In January 1960 Brezhnev arrived on scene to fire Belyayev, putting his friend Dinmukhamed Kunayev, the Kazakh prime minister, into the post of party leader.

Brezhnev's personal intervention in Kazakhstan confirmed what Kremlin watchers had been suspecting for some weeks: that he was moving into the number two position in the party hierarchy as Khrushchev's heir presumptive and successor to Aleksei Kirichenko.

Kirichenko, a friend and protégé of Khrushchev, had been party leader of the Ukraine until 1957. Several months after the defeat of the anti-party group Khrushchev had called him to Moscow where, in addition to his seat on the Presidium, Kirichenko became a Central Committee secretary. It was soon apparent that he was *de facto* the Party's second secretary. He was in charge of cadres, next to Khrushchev's the most powerful and influential job. Kirichenko was the acknowledged heir. Suddenly, in January 1960, he was sacked and sent to Rostov-on-Don as *oblast* first secretary.

The reasons for this demotion have never been given. One version that circulated in Moscow at the time was that his "style of work" had been "defective". Another was that he had irritated other influential Presidium members, notably Anastas Mikoyan, with his curt manners. There may also have been clashes over policy. What is highly unlikely is that Khrushchev himself instigated Kirichenko's demotion, for in Kirichenko he lost perhaps his most loyal and devoted lieutenant. Most likely a combination of Kirichenko's errors had brought forth a heterogeneous coalition against him.

Whatever the cause or causes, Kirichenko's fall in January 1960 opened up new opportunities for Brezhnev. But as Michel Tatu pointed out in his excellent study, *Power in the Kremlin,*

Kirichenko's fall also "opened a new phase in Khrushchev's reign".

On the surface everything had seemed calm enough in those first weeks of 1960. Actually a new storm was brewing. By May it was to engulf Leonid Brezhnev.

CHAPTER XI

Mr President

When Leonid Ilyich Brezhnev graduated from Kamenskoye's *Trudova Shkola* in the summer of 1921, conditions were hardly conducive to producing a class yearbook with promising prognoses about the boys' future careers. Nor were the speeches and farewells that had been expressed over the cups of hot sugar water during the candle-lit "graduation ceremony" ever recorded for posterity. But assuming they had been, it seems unlikely that anyone – the teachers, his classmates or Iosif Shtokalo, the principal – would have predicted that Brezhnev might some day become president of the country.

Nevertheless, in May 1960 he was named the Soviet Union's fifth head of state – successor to Yakov Sverdlov, Mikhail Kalinin, Nikolai Shvernik and the great cavalry hero of the Civil War, Kliment Voroshilov.

In most countries, when a man becomes president he has reached the apex of power and the zenith of personal honor and prestige. But in the Soviet Union where the Party is the fount of all power and plays "the leading role" in society, the "presidency" is little more than an honorable pasture of political impotence.

Brezhnev had no cause whatsoever to rejoice. His election to the chairmanship of the Presidium of the Supreme Soviet on 7 May 1960 represented a major setback, as grave in its potential consequences as his demotion had been in 1953.

Moreover, just as in 1953, Brezhnev was a victim of political circumstances beyond his control. Through no particular fault of his own, other than being Nikita Khrushchev's fastest rising and most influential protégé, he had become a scapegoat of a massive reshuffle that shook the Soviet leadership a few days after the CIA's U-2 spy plane, piloted by Gary Powers, had been shot down over Sverdlovsk. The political upheaval which followed that seemingly unrelated Cold War incident was directed not so much against Brezhnev as against Khrushchev whose policies a coalition of opponents sought to undermine and whose power they were determined to circumscribe.

Until 1 May, when Powers was brought down, Brezhnev stood the best chance of stepping into the number two party position left vacant by the mysterious demotion of Aleksei Kirichenko. Although he was no longer totally subservient to Khrushchev, Brezhnev had displayed infinitely greater loyalty than any other man in the top leadership. But the U-2 incident and Washington's inept diplomacy deprived him of that chance. At least for the next three years.

Actually, the events that led to Khrushchev's difficulties and Brezhnev's reversal in May 1960 had been germinating for a number of months.

The issues were crucial: Khrushchev's policy of *rapprochement* with the West which was scheduled to culminate in a Paris summit meeting on 16 May and a subsequent visit to the USSR by President Eisenhower; his plans to demobilize 1.2 million men, including 250,000 career officers, generals and admirals; the incipient rift with China; his economic decentralizing program.

Khrushchev's foreign and military policies in particular had been under fairly consistent and only thinly-veiled attack since his return from the US and the Camp David talks with Eisenhower in September 1959. The opponents were a conglomerate coalition of guardians of Communist orthodoxy, members of the military establishment and cold warriors. Their persistent criticism had produced a stiffening of Soviet foreign policy well in advance of the U-2 incident. The two leaders who had pressed most vehemently for a hardening of policy were Mikhail Suslov and Frol Koslov. The downing of the U-2 and Powers' capture merely brought the internal debate to a climax. Ineluctably the incident also shook the foundations of Khrushchev's power structure.

For months Khrushchev had been maintaining that the US could be trusted. He had based this assertion in part on his "friendship" with Eisenhower and the accord he claimed to have reached with the President during the Camp David meeting. But the capture of the spy plane made American policy appear deceitful and Khrushchev was ridiculed for having been gullible enough to believe the President. When Eisenhower admitted that he had personally authorized the espionage flights over Soviet territory he blindly compounded Khrushchev's dilemma and embarrassment. As Khrushchev told a group of foreign journalists in Moscow: "The American militarists have placed me, the man responsible for arranging the visit of the President to the Soviet Union, in a very difficult position."

The difficulty of his position became apparent on 4 May at a Central Committee meeting which ratified a sweeping change in the leadership, aimed at reducing Khrushchev's power. The Party Secretariat was drastically reduced in size and placed under the *de facto* control of Frol Kozlov, until then a deputy premier. Three men who owed little or nothing to Khrushchev were promoted to full membership in the Party Presidium: Aleksei Kosygin, who was also named a first deputy prime minister; Nikolai Podgorny; and Dmitry Polyansky.

Khrushchev's closest ally in foreign affairs, Anastas Mikoyan, suffered a serious defeat and Brezhnev was elbowed away from the levers of power by being "kicked upstairs" to the presidency of the USSR.

For the first time since the anti-party affair in 1957 Khrushchev's position had been seriously threatened. Moreover a new opposition, centering around Suslov, Kozlov and Kosygin, had been born. It was still inchoate and fate was to alter its complexion drastically within a few years. Nevertheless it offered a new pole of attraction to all those who objected to Khrushchev's policies and to those who, having no alternative policies of their own, merely chafed under his high-handed style of leadership, his callous public embarrassment of subordinates, his bumptious and *ne kulturny* manners, and the new personality cult to which he made them subscribe.

It seems doubtful that the question of overthrowing Khrushchev had seriously been broached in May 1960, but those opposed to his policies and monopoly of power had demonstrated that he could be stopped and even forced to retreat. True, there had been a compromise of sorts. The leadership changes reflected an attempt to take the army in hand and to reaffirm the primacy of political authority over the military command. On the other hand, the military had achieved one of its basic aims: the stiffening of foreign policy. Khrushchev's detractors – the Chinese; the marshals and generals who wanted greater appropriations; the economic planners who demanded greater centralization; the conservatives in the state and party apparatus – were emboldened. They had shown that Khrushchev could be forced to share power. For Khrushchev it was a tocsin that heralded the beginning of the end. Only the weakness of Frol Kozlov's cardio-vascular system prevented that end being Brezhnev's too.

Brezhnev fought tenaciously and his demotion came in stages. The decision to shift him to the "presidency" was obviously reached at the 4 May plenum. Another two days passed before it was confirmed in the Supreme Soviet itself. But he was not yet out of the Party Secretariat.

From 11 to 14 May a mammoth conference on political work in the Soviet Army was held in the Great Kremlin Palace. The meeting dealt with the structure of party organization at the battalion, regimental and divisional level and, in general, with the question of civilian political control. The principal military speakers were Defense Minister Marshal Rodion Malinovsky and General F. I. Golikov, the chief political commissar. Three "civilians" were on the platform, too: Suslov, Nikolai Ignatov, another Khrushchev protégé who had just been demoted, and Brezhnev. Of the three Brezhnev was the only one who spoke, a hint of the importance the marshals and generals attached to his role in the Secretariat. But two months later Brezhnev was relieved of his functions in the Party Secretariat.

For an ambitious man it was a reversal of mammoth proportions. But just as he had done in other personal crises of power, Brezhnev demonstrated a remarkable ability to exploit adversity. He became the only Soviet politician thus far to return to real power from the graveyard of the presidency.

Almost immediately he transferred the most trusted advisers on his personal staff from the Central Committee building on Staraya Ploshad to the Supreme Soviet offices in the Kremlin: Georgy Tsukanov, the Kamenskoye engineering graduate, who had been his personal aide since 1958, and Konstantin Chernenko. Fortunately he was also assigned a brilliant foreign affairs adviser: Andrei M. Aleksandrov-Agentov, a career diplomat and expert on German affairs who, since 1970, has emerged in public as "Brezhnev's Kissinger".

Moreover, Brezhnev soon discovered that the chairmanship of the Supreme Soviet Presidium was not, or at any rate was no longer, quite the sinecure it was generally believed to be. It offered the enormous advantage of exposure. Next to Khrushchev, Brezhnev became the man seen most frequently on TV. He was mentioned almost daily in the press. He greeted foreign visitors, received ambassadors and exchanged messages with foreign heads of state. He signed all laws, decrees and international treaties ratified by the Supreme Soviet. He dispensed medals and awards by the thousands.

Above all, he traveled abroad. He traveled as no Soviet president had: fifteen trips in three years. He went to Morocco, Ghana, Guinea and the Sudan, to Iran, India and Afghanistan, to Finland and Yugoslavia, and to Hungary, Poland, Romania, Bulgaria, Czechoslovakia and East Germany.

The beginning of his peripatetic career was hardly auspicious, though. On 9 February 1961, 130 kilometers north of Algiers, while flying to Rabat, Brezhnev's Ilyushin-18 was buzzed and fired at twice by a French Air Force jet fighter. The incident touched off an angry exchange of diplomatic notes between Moscow and Paris in which the Soviet Union accused the French of "international banditry" and the French replied weakly that the plane had been off-course and the interceptor was "seeking to establish its identity".

What Brezhnev felt as the French jet's cannons began firing has not been recorded. But the brief brush with death failed to daunt his lust for travel. Nor did it seem to worry his wife, Viktoria, who accompanied him on a state visit to India later the same year and to Iran in 1963.

Viktoria left no indelible mark as Brezhnev's traveling companion – in contrast to their daughter Galina who accompanied him to Yugoslavia in 1962 and titillated gossip columnists and foreign correspondents with her stylish dresses and urbane manners.

On the whole Brezhnev left impressions that contrasted sharply with those made abroad by his choleric chief, Khrushchev, and his irascible rival, Kozlov, Brezhnev's hosts may have wondered just where he stood in the Kremlin power sweepstakes, and some may have regarded him as little more than a figurehead. But Brezhnev was clearly neither a peasant nor a boorish *apparatchik*. He was, if anything, a paragon of polite diplomatic behavior.

He also seemed to be aware of problems. "Two years of independence is a very short time," he told a beaming Sekou Toure in an exchange of toasts in Conakry. "So it is all the more gratifying to see how in that time you have moved forward, have strengthened your state and have started large-scale economic and cultural construction."

Ghana's Kwame Nkrumah was equally pleased when Brezhnev told him: "I have heard that in Africa there is a saying that 'even a lion can be stopped if forces are joined'. Thus if the socialist states and the independent countries of Africa, Asia, Europe and Latin America will stand guard over peace together, this will be an immovable barrier in the path of those who are fond of military adventures."

During those years away from tangible political power Brezhnev certainly grew in stature. His horizons broadened, his tastes became more sophisticated and expensive. He saw something of the world and its peoples and he began to view them with different criteria from those with which an *apparatchik*'s life along the Dnieper, in Kishinev, in Alma Ata or the austere offices of the Central Committee had equipped him. He was also granted the emoluments and perquisites of high station: another Order of Lenin, a Hero of Socialist Labor award for his "outstanding service in the development of rocket technology and the successful flight of a Soviet man in space", and, most important of all, perhaps, a larger apartment in the building on Kutuzovski Prospekt.

But what good would it do him? He was in his mid-fifties, full of energy, with a zest for life, consumed by ambition, but fettered by the ineptitude of his own patron whose bungling seemed merely to strengthen the hand of Brezhnev's arch rival: Kozlov.

The May 1960 selection of Frol Kozlov – allied to the metal-eating lobby of the Soviet military industrial complex, an exponent of a tougher line in foreign and domestic affairs – had obviously been a compromise between an outspoken Khrushchev supporter such as Brezhnev and an opponent backed by the hard-line opposition, for example, Suslov. But compromise or not, Kozlov had wasted no time filling the power vacuum with his own clients and protégés to the detriment of those friends and allies of Brezhnev who remained in office. A number of important leadership changes at the XXIInd Party Congress in October 1961 served to weaken further Brezhnev's position and strengthen Kozlov's.

True, the group of Brezhnev's friends, confederates and protégés in the Central Committee increased. Thus Marshal Grechko, then commander of Warsaw Pact forces, and Admiral Gorshkov as well as a number of other marshals and generals were elected to the committee. Ivan Grushetsky became a full member. So did Venyamin Dymshits, whom he had first met in Zaporozhe, Ignati Novikov, Nikolai Tikhonov and Lev N. Smirnov, who had headed a research institute for the defense industry in Dnepropetrovsk and was then chief of a state committee for the armaments industry. There were others as well: Nikita Tolubeyev, then first secretary of Dnepropetrovsk *obkom;* Ivan Yunak, then as now party chief of Tula *oblast* who until 1961 had been government leader of Dnepropetrovsk, and Vladimir Shcherbitsky. Incumbent members of the Central Committee who were Brezhnev allies included Kunayev, Korotchenko, Kirilenko and Yenyutin.

But on the other hand, two of Brezhnev's strongest supporters – Korotchenko and Kirilenko – were removed from the Party Presidium. Kirilenko was in fact replaced by Kozlov's successor as Leningrad *obkom* leader, Ivan Spiridonov, who became a party secretary. Spiridonov's place in Leningrad was taken by another Kozlov client: Vasily Tolstikov who held that position until 1970 when Brezhnev finally managed to "exile" him as ambassador to Peking.

Soon after the congress Kozlov also used his new power to encroach on Brezhnev's provincial power bases. He struck first in Moldavia. In May 1962 Nikolai Shchelokov was dismissed as the republic's first deputy prime minister and appointed one of several deputy premiers. Some months later Shchelokov's career suffered a further setback and entered a period of "phased demotion" which was halted only by Kozlov's physical collapse.

Next, using another poor harvest as a convenient pretext, he moved in on Brezhnev's old Kazakhstan fief where, in December 1962, he personally supervised a two-day session of the Central Committee in Alma Ata that culminated in Kunayev's demotion from the party leadership and reassignment to his pre-1960 job as prime minister. Kozlov's protégé, Ismail Yusupov, became the new first secretary.

The Kazakh purge was especially acrimonious in tone. Kozlov had accused Kunayev of "poor management". Yusupov, without naming them, charged top officials with drunkenness, gambling and embezzlement. A massive removal of Brezhnev's old machine soon began. Kozlov clients and supporters were appointed to the vacant positions.

After Khrushchev's fall in 1964 Brezhnev acted quickly to restore Kunayev as party leader of Kazakhstan, but the consequences of Kozlov's sweep of the Kazakh apparatus were to plague Brezhnev for many more years, largely because Kozlov's machine had in the meantime become Nikolai Podgorny's.

In April 1963, when Kozlov suffered his ultimately fatal stroke, many Kozlov protégés and supporters in Kazakhstan crept under Podgorny's protective wing. Podgorny proceeded to develop a Kazakh power base of his own, thanks to the assistance of his client Vitaly N. Titov. Kozlov, at the height of his power, had installed Titov as chief of the cadres division of the CPSU Central Committee. Titov was thus in one of the most powerful positions in the apparatus and used his power to place Kozlov and Podgorny clients in key positions around the country, including, of course, Kazakhstan. It took Brezhnev until 1965 to move Titov out of Moscow – but he was able to shunt him only as far as Alma Ata where he became, of all things, second secretary of the Kazakhstan Communist Party, that is, number two man to Kunayev. Titov's influence in Moscow had been eroded, but he had plenty of power left in Kazakhstan. Kozlov-Podgorny men were, for the most part, beneficiaries of his protection. Brezhnev and Kunayev tried a number of ploys to ease them out of power, including extensive gerrymandering of *oblasts* and districts in Kazakhstan. Not until March 1971, when Titov was finally removed as second secretary of Kazakhstan, did Brezhnev succeed in restoring his control over the republic. A decade had passed since Kozlov had moved in on the Kazakh fief.

For Kozlov, of course, these sorties against Brezhnev's bastions were merely secondary to the essential struggle: the one with Khrushchev himself. Khrushchev was a masterful actor and the personality cult he had fostered provided perfect scenery for a performance that deluded most of the world into believing he was at the height of his power and virtually unchallenged – until that fatal day in October 1964 when he disappeared from the stage. But it *was* merely an act. In reality he had reached the pinnacle of success in 1959 and from May 1960 he was in decline. What confused most observers, perhaps, was the fact that he resisted skillfully. A tenacious and complex holding action, fought in a series of skirmishes over many issues with shifting personal alliances, clouded the real situation on the battlefield.

Broadly speaking, and leaving aside for the moment his quest for personal power, Khrushchev's dilemma since 1953 had been rooted in his pursuit of two basic objectives: de-Stalinization and providing the Soviet people with a better life. Both were fraught with enormous complications and like any leader anywhere who faces multiple pressures and impulses, Khrushchev sought to avoid the hard choices and eventually responded to events and pursued policies with contradictory implications.

To de-Stalinize meant, first of all, to come to grips with the society which the dictator had molded: a society founded on fear, suspicion, poltroonery and obsequiousness, cruelty, intrigue and bureaucratic hyper-centralization. It also entailed grappling with the multitude of vested interests whose power and perquisites more or less depended on the continuation of the system which Stalin had created. Finally, de-Stalinization implied unleashing forces at home and abroad over which Khrushchev soon lost control. The uprisings in Hungary and Poland in 1956 were but one consequence. In effect, Khrushchev triggered the breakdown of discipline and touched off the disintegration of the empire, of the world Communist movement, which Stalin had created. He had let a genie out of the bottle. It is still out. He floundered in his efforts to force it back into the flask, conjuring new troubles in the process. His successor, Brezhnev, has proven himself no more capable of doing that job than Khrushchev was.

Khrushchev's second objective, adopted after Malenkov's political defeat, was to satisfy the widespread yearning for a rapid improvement in the standard of living. It compelled him to divert resources from armaments and heavy industry to agriculture and consumer goods and to seek an arrangement with the West which would enable him to relieve the Cold War pressures upon the economy. Khrushchev was frustrated in this effort by the opposition of powerful interests at home: the military and the magnates of heavy industry who constituted somewhat of a state within the state. He was also opposed by the ideologists who feared *rapprochement* and who had been taught by Stalin to equate industrialization with the building of Communism itself. Finally, his policies presupposed an agricultural basis for which he had neither the skills, the complex modern machinery nor the required system of incentives

As resistance to his policies mounted and his schemes began to fail, Khrushchev began to lose the backing of those members of the Communist party apparatus who had supported him to an extent. Moreover, in the pursuit of his foreign policy aims and in his repeated failure to achieve them, he laid the foundation for the rift with China.

The specific issues which led to the erosion of his authority and power in the 1960s were the following:

1 *Foreign policy and military strategy:* Khrushchev had professed an unquestionably real desire to reach agreement with the US so that he could concentrate greater resources on internal development. He was thwarted by continuing opposition at home and by constant vacillation on the part of the United States who questioned his motives.

Like John Foster Dulles, Khrushchev practiced brinkmanship, but he was just not as good at it. His most notable failures were the Congo adventure; the ultimatum over Berlin and the military showdown in the divided city after the Wall had been built; the Cuban missile fiasco which, while leading to the nuclear stand-off that governs US-Soviet relations to this day, made a fool of Khrushchev and the USSR.

2 *Relations with the Communist World:* That the Peking-Moscow schism was irreparable after 1960 was obvious to most Soviet leaders. The issue on which they differed, however, was the question of tactics and the degree to which the rift should be permitted to develop. Khrushchev opted for a tough line; Suslov, and possibly Kozlov, advocated either mollifying the Chinese or at least finding a *modus vivendi* that would defuse the crisis and perhaps paper over the crack.

3 *Agriculture:* Although Khrushchev's virgin lands program was sound in principle, its application and his refusal to listen to expert advice had resulted in decreasing yields. Moreover, he experimented incessantly with agricultural projects, the best-known example of which was a crash drive to plant maize. The essence of Khrushchev's policy was to raise the meat and animal products supply. Failing to get the results he wanted from the new lands, he turned to maize which he had seen being used successfully in the United States. Maize was indeed a crop with high potential for human nutrition as well as animal fodder. But Russians were not used to it. Moreover, Khrushchev got carried away by his own enthusiasm and ordered a corn campaign in areas unsuited to the crop. In 1963 he brought the country to the brink of agricultural ruin. In a belated effort to face up to some of his problems he launched a large-scale program for expansion of the chemical industry, the building and importation of many fertilizer plants, the increased output of agricultural machinery and the construction of irrigation facilities. All these measures required substantial new capital and infringed upon the privileged preserves of the metallurgical and armaments industry.

4 *Centralization versus regionalization of the economy:* To assert the Party's control over the economy and to reinvigorate the heavily bureaucratized and centralized economic machinery, Khrushchev had taken a bold step in 1957. He abolished some twenty technical ministries and created 105 regional councils – called *sovnarkhozes* – whose tasks were to run industry on a regional basis instead of from the center. For thousands of unhappy managers and bureaucrats it meant moving to pro-

vincial backwaters where amenities were few. For central planners and the technocrats in the former ministries it spelled the erosion of their traditional power bases. During the first few years this reform yielded good results. But resistance mounted and an increasingly complex, bureaucratic structure resulted with the establishment of state committees and supra-regional councils which were, in effect, surrogates for the disbanded ministries. Upon Kozlov's and Kosygin's advent to power in May 1960 a drive for recentralization began.

5 *Division of the Party:* In November 1962 Khrushchev launched the most daring and perhaps most ill-conceived of his numerous reforms. He abolished the *rayon* (district) party committees which left tens of thousands of functionaries unemployed and divided *oblast* and republican party committees and governments into two independent and equally powerful parts, one for agriculture, one for industry. His aim was to reinforce the Party's total control over the economy. In effect, however, he created chaos and thousands of enemies plus an even more complex bureaucratic structure. Every *obkom* secretary who hitherto had managed an entire province suddenly found himself controlling only half of it, either the agricultural or the industrial part, with no one really responsible for the wide intermediate range of activities such as ideology, police control, education and science. One of the better jokes circulating in the USSR at that time concerned a party member who complained to his "agricultural" *obkom* secretary that another comrade had hit him on the head with a hammer. "I'd do something about it, Ivan," replied the agricultural secretary, "but it's not my area of responsibility. Now if he had cut you with a sickle then . . . "

6 *De-Stalinization:* History will remember Khrushchev best for his stubborn effort to destroy the "cult" of Stalin and to restore a semblance of legality and justice in the USSR. But Khrushchev's motivations were not entirely humane. De-Stalinization was also an effective weapon in Khrushchev's hands to purge his putative rivals and consolidate his power. In 1956 he had used it sparingly. In 1961, at the XXIInd Party Congress, he unsheathed it again with devastating results.

The dictator's embalmed body was removed from the Lenin Mausoleum and re-interred in a simple grave next to the Kremlin wall. His name was virtually obliterated from the history books and the maps. The liberals, especially in the cultural field, were delighted, for the new policy also heralded the Soviet Union's second cultural thaw which culminated in Khrushchev's decision to publish Alexander Solzhenitsyn's novel *One Day in the Life of Ivan Denisovich*. But the Chinese and the USSR's own Stalinists and neo-Stalinists were incensed. The reaction among orthodox ideologues and Communist conservatives was vehement and by the spring of 1963 Khrushchev was forced to retreat, unleashing a new crisis that nearly toppled him.

7 *His style of leadership:* An entire catalogue of grievances ranging from Khrushchev's shoe-banging behavior in public to the nepotistic advancement of Aleksei Adzhubei, his son-in-law, had come under this heading. The man who had shouted the loudest for collective leadership after Stalin's death had himself become a new autocrat, the focus of an adulatory personality cult which threatened to surpass even the dead dictator's. Khrushchev's portraits hung everywhere. No speech could be given, no article written without uttering paeans to his greatness. He was a simple ebullient man, full of enthusiasm, whose effervescent personality contrasted sharply with that of the dull, plodding, unimaginative and fearful *apparatchiki* who surrounded him. And they loathed and resented him. But he was also crude and rude, given to tirades of colorful profanity and to interrupting his associates' speeches with sarcastic remarks that appealed to the gallery. He was contemptuous of the vast bureaucracy Stalin had created, but clearly oblivious to the fact that his power depended on it. He was disdainful of science, relying instead on charlatans, yet professed to be the leader of a party that claimed to be based on scientific principles. He was a braggart and a know-all, a self-proclaimed expert on everything from planting corn to nuclear physics. He experimented wildly, dashing from one reform of society to the next. His heart, I am sure, was in the right place and he did much to change the USSR for the better. In his zeal to move mountains, however, he cut a wide

swath through a field of enemies. By the early 1960s they had encircled him.

Between the spring of 1960 and mid-1963 Khrushchev had come within inches of being toppled several times. Those clearly identified with Khrushchev, such as Brezhnev, were also in danger of being sucked into the vortex. By the winter of 1962–63 Brezhnev had reached the brink of political oblivion. His position as head of state still entitled him to a front seat at official functions, but in matters of real importance and party protocol, he was treated according to his true political weight which was then close to nil.

The attention kremlinologists pay to who stands where on the Lenin Mausoleum or whose portrait hangs in which order on a building's facade may strike non-specialists as an exercise in futility. But experience has shown that these niceties of protocol are extremely important indicators of who is up and who is down in the Kremlin sweepstakes. It is, for example, *de rigueur* when an important party official leaves or returns from a trip abroad for other officials to see him off and to meet him again at the airport or railway station. The more weighty the official, the bigger and more important the delegation of greeters will be. In December 1962, when Brezhnev went to Prague for a Czechoslovak Communist Party Congress, not a single member of the Presidium was on hand to see him off at Vnukovo Airport or to greet him on his return. That was an ominous sign.

Khrushchev, too, was receiving ominous signs and in mid-February 1963 had a precariously close brush with political death. According to rumors circulating in Moscow at the time, he had been out-voted and placed in a minority during a Presidium meeting, purportedly held on 15 or 16 February. Allegedly even his resignation had been considered, but then shelved.

We may never know whether this is true or not, but there is conclusive evidence that Khrushchev's policy line on three or four issues altered sharply after that purported meeting. Only a few days after the session is supposed to have taken place, the Soviet attitude towards China softened perceptibly. The recentralizers of the economy and the metal-eaters scored an important victory. Finally, Khrushchev's policy on de-Stalinization and the cultural thaw, underwent a complete reversal, leading to a sudden campaign of strict party control over art and literature.

Reportedly, the attack against Khrushchev at that Presidium meeting had been led by Kozlov, supported by Suslov. Some weeks later, in mid-March, Khrushchev dropped out of sight on vacation at his retreat in Gagra. Less than a month passed before Kozlov, too, dropped out of sight: forever.

Kozlov was last seen in public, together with Brezhnev, Kirilenko (who had made a comeback in 1962), Mikoyan, Polyansky and Suslov, at a congress of artists some time during the day on 10 April. That evening, according to the rumors circulating in Moscow and now generally accepted as the most plausible version, Khrushchev telephoned Kozlov from Gagra. There was a violent verbal clash over a number of issues. Kozlov, who had a record of heart disease, became so agitated that he suffered a stroke.

For Leonid Brezhnev it was a stroke of luck. For Nikita Khrushchev it was a stay of execution. Kozlov's illness could not be kept secret long. His absence from the Lenin Mausoleum reviewing stand at the May Day parade had to be explained. On 4 May – precisely three years after he had been elevated to the Secretariat – *Pravda* confirmed he was ill.

As occurs frequently in cerebral hemorrhage cases, Kozlov's condition apparently improved somewhat, but by mid-June it was evident that he was permanently disabled. He remained a member of the Presidium and the Secretariat until the re-shuffle after Khrushchev's fall, but was never politically active again. He died in February 1965.

On 21 June 1963 Brezhnev celebrated a comeback. Although retaining his post as president, he was re-elected to the Central Committee Secretariat. By implication he became Khrushchev's third successor-designate – after the disgrace of Kirichenko and the incapacitation of Kozlov.

It was, however, a qualified triumph, for along with him Nikolai Podgorny, the party leader of the Ukraine, was also appointed to the Secretariat. Podgorny, though not exactly a client, was definitely an ally and supporter of Khrushchev. Moreover, his rise from provincial leadership to the center of power was certainly more spectacular than Brezhnev's return to a position from which he had been demoted three years earlier.

Did this mean two heirs presumptive instead of one? Events soon demonstrated that it did and that Khrushchev had obviously learned an important political lesson. By dividing power among two "second" secretaries he was reducing their challenge to him.

During the first few months it became increasingly difficult to predict which of the two would triumph. While Brezhnev, as president, was preoccupied with functions of state and the Supreme Soviet which diverted his attention from repairing his battered machine in the Party, Podgorny was busily constructing an apparatus of his own, based on his Kharkov and Ukrainian associations and those of Kozlov's supporters who had rushed to him for protection. Khrushchev had every reason to be pleased.

But it was also obvious that Brezhnev stood higher in Khrushchev's esteem. After President Kennedy's assassination Khrushchev told US Ambassador Foy Kohler: "It's too bad I couldn't send Brezhnev to the funeral. I want him to get to know America." Brezhnev happened to be on a state visit to Iran.

That remark was also a hint of the dilemma facing Brezhnev who was in fact holding down two full-time posts. Despite his apparent resilience and readiness to invest countless sixteen-hour days, it was clear that, physically, he could not go on with both jobs forever.

Khrushchev had, indeed, learned a lesson. Whether or not he merely forgot it again or whether circumstances compelled a change in tactics we do not know. But on 15 July 1964, at the Supreme Soviet session, Khrushchev opted for Brezhnev who was relieved from his duties as president so that he could "concentrate on his activity" in the Secretariat. Anastas Mikoyan was chosen the new chief of state. Leonid Brezhnev was at last confirmed as crown prince.

Could Brezhnev have known that his vicarship was to last merely three months? That seems doubtful. Had Khrushchev just committed the cardinal error of his political life? Perhaps, but he could not have known it. Podgorny may have been the more compliant man, but in July 1964 Khrushchev had little reason to suspect Brezhnev. Brezhnev was no longer the docile client he had been in the 1940s and 1950s. But he appeared loyal nonetheless. And perhaps he really was.

But Khrushchev must have sensed that his days were numbered. He had even told Averell Harriman that he intended to retire on his seventieth birthday (17 April 1964) and had made similar allusions once to the Polish party leader, Wladyslaw Gomulka. The birthday came with a public display of adulation second only to that accorded Stalin on his seventieth birthday in 1949. Yet Khrushchev stayed on, apparently blissfully oblivious of the extent to which his authority had eroded.

Despite the disintegration of Khrushchev's power, however, there was no sign in the late summer or early autumn of 1964 to suggest that his fall was imminent. But as Michel Tatu, the former *Le Monde* correspondent in Moscow, stressed in his analysis of Khrushchev's decline, there must have been a "last straw" that provoked the subsequent events. What that straw really was remains open to speculation.

Some observers at the time suggested that it was the deterioration of relations with China and Khrushchev's intention to bring the Sino-Soviet schism to a climax with a December conference of the world's major Communist Parties. Others contended that the decisive issue had been Khrushchev's incipient *rapprochement* with West Germany and his plan to visit Bonn, capital of the militarist *revanchists*, Moscow's most tangible enemies. Yet a third theory points to a September 1964 clash with the recentralizers of the heavy industry lobby.

Finally, there was the sheer madness of Khrushchev's space race with the United States, in particular the three-man Voskhod space shot of 12 October. To keep ahead of the Americans, Khrushchev had ordered Soviet space experts to launch a three-man capsule before the US sent up its first Gemini with a two-man crew. The scientists had neither the time to develop such a capsule by the 7 November deadline which Khrushchev had set nor the rockets capable of hoisting it. But they obeyed his edict nevertheless – at grave risk to the cosmonauts. The standard one-man Vostok capsule, in which Yuri Gagarin had made his epic flight, was stripped down. Its life-support and communications gear were reduced to the minimum and three pint-sized cosmonauts, wearing nothing but their underwear, were squeezed into it like sardines in a can. Luck was probably the only thing that saved their lives.

While all four of these issues were undoubtedly contributing factors, it is unlikely that any or all of them were of sufficient weight to persuade the plotters to take the ultimate risk of a confrontation with Khrushchev. As they knew only too well, the minimum consequence of failure would be political death. There had to be yet another issue which induced them to act.

In all probability, the decisive straw was Khrushchev's plan to reshuffle the party leadership at a Central Committee plenum scheduled for some time in November. Ostensibly that plenum was to deal with agricultural questions, but leaks to foreign correspondents in Moscow and thinly-veiled hints in the party press suggested that, under the pretext of discussing agriculture, Khrushchev actually intended to upset the delicate equilibrium of power in the Presidium and Secretariat and divest other members of the oligarchy of their remaining responsibilities.

"You will see," a reliable Moscow source told Tatu, "the November plenary session is going to be very interesting. There will be many changes at the top. Almost all the leaders *except Khrushchev* will be affected."

In other words, a purge was pending. To forestall it, the ruling "collective" had to purge Khrushchev. Either he or they had to disappear, and the imminence of the November Central Committee plenum dictated fast action. Khrushchev's fall was inevitable. What no one could have predicted was the timetable.

Equally inevitable was Brezhnev's ascendancy to the party leadership after Khrushchev's disappearance. He towered over his peers as the logical candidate. Neither Podgorny nor Kosygin could match him for breadth of experience or popularity within the Party's apparatus. Nor were they as adept at political in-fighting. Nearly three decades of internecine political warfare had taught Brezhnev plenty.

This is not to say that Brezhnev played the decisive part in the coup which felled Khrushchev. On the contrary his role remains obscure. As on so many occasions in the past, however, he was unquestionably the principal beneficiary.

As we know now, the man Khrushchev should really have been watching was Mikhail Suslov: the Kremlin's *eminence grise*, the myopic professor, the ultra-conservative ideologist who had been a secretary of the Party without interruption since 1947, senior even to Khrushchev in that elitist circle of Soviet power; Suslov, the recurrent king-maker who had been either privy to or instrumental in every important reshuffle in the hierarchy since Stalin's death. In the ninety days between Brezhnev's anointment as Khrushchev's crown prince and the coup itself, it was Suslov who engineered the plot that ended Khrushchev's political agony and opened the pages of history to the Brezhnev era.

Part Five

POWER IN THE KREMLIN

"You do not know – you cannot know – the difficulty of a politician's life. It means every minute of the day or night, every ounce of your energy. There is no rest, no relaxation. Enjoyment? A politician does not know the meaning of the word. Moreover, you never know what is going to happen next."

Nikita Khrushchev, Glen Cove, Long Island
October, 1960

CHAPTER XII

Caretaker or Leader?

The *dvortsovy perevot* – the palace revolution – that unseated Nikita Khrushchev and vaulted Leonid Brezhnev into the leadership of the Communist Party of the Soviet Union was carried out with stealth and intrigue in a manner reminiscent of a Florentine court: proof that those who master-minded it had learned a lesson from the abortive coup of the anti-party group in 1957.

The crucial prerequisite was to remove Khrushchev from Moscow, away from the multifarious switches of power he could throw in his favor. On 30 September 1964 the plotters dispatched their unsuspecting prey on a vacation to his Black Sea residence at Sochi. No one would have challenged the suggestion that he needed it. During the past month or so he had become increasingly irascible and capricious.

No sooner had Khrushchev left than the cabal went into action. They were to engage in considerable improvisation before the coup could actually be carried out. In fact, the evidence indicates that the precise timetable for the strike was not decided upon until 10 October.

For this reason alone, if no other, it seems certain that Brezhnev had not been initiated into the *details* of the plot when he flew to East Berlin on 5 October as head of a delegation (which included his friend and ally Ivan Grushetsky) to participate in the fifteenth anniversary celebration of the founding of the German Democratic Republic.

Brezhnev was, however, aware of the *general* plan. The ambiguous tenor of the speech he delivered during the festivities in East Berlin on 6 October leaves no doubt that he knew of Suslov's intentions. But Brezhnev is a prudent man and he kept a verbal path of retreat open should the ploy fail.

Careful not to slam the door on the tentative overture

towards West Germany which Khrushchev had broached, he took pains nevertheless to placate the worried East Germans. "As you know," he admitted, "we ourselves are in favor of mending relations with the Federal Republic." But then he reassured his listeners that "you and we have the same views on how the German question should be settled . . . The Soviet Union fully supports the program the GDR has proposed for normalizing relations between the two German states."

Brezhnev's treatment of Khrushchev was even more equivocal. He dared not pass over him in silence as Suslov had done at a Soviet-East German friendship rally in Moscow the day before. That would have been courting disaster if the plot misfired. But neither did he extol and eulogize him as some other leaders, notably Podgorny, were doing in public appearances right up to deadline. In his hour-long East Berlin speech Brezhnev circumspectly mentioned and quoted Khrushchev once, but only once.

When Brezhnev's Ilyushin-18 touched down at Moscow's Vnukovo Airport on Sunday, 11 October, the welcoming group that met him – contrary to traditional Soviet protocol – was not the same as the one which had seen him off. Standing there in the little knot of senior officials was the master schemer himself: Suslov. Was this Brezhnev's first inkling of the coup? That seems implausible. Surely, what Suslov told Brezhnev on the ride from the airport to their dachas was not a revelation. It must have been a briefing to tell Brezhnev what had developed during his week-long absence from Moscow. There were, as Suslov must have explained, just two days left before the strike.

On Monday, 12 October, Voskhod with its three-man crew was launched and Khrushchev had his last opportunity to shine in public. Outwardly everything appeared routine but there were nuances of change in the public procedure which adumbrated the historic events to follow.

Shortly before the 10.30 a.m. launching, Khrushchev telephoned the crew at the Baikonur space center from his villa in Sochi to wish them good luck. In an unprecedented and barely noticed move Brezhnev did the same from his Moscow office. The would-be-successor was demonstrating that he was around too.

Later in the day, during Khrushchev's traditional radio call to the orbiting space capsule, an even more unusual thing happened. Mikoyan, who seems to have been at the Sochi retreat on-and-off in the preceding ten days, was at Khrushchev's side. Speaking to the crew commander, Vladimir Komarov, Khrushchev suddenly said: "I am turning the microphone over to Anastas Ivanovich Mikoyan. He is literally tearing it from my hands. I can no longer refuse him."

Sovietologists have spent countless hours analyzing that remark and searching for its hidden meaning. Possibly there is none. But it was certainly symbolic in view of the momentous transfer of power soon to come.

During the conversation with the cosmonauts Khrushchev had warned them of a "no less difficult" task still facing them: the tumultuous welcome being prepared for them in Moscow upon their return. Confidently Komarov signed off: "Goodbye, dear Nikita Sergeyevich . . . We understand you – you will wait for us on earth and we shall meet with you."

They never did, for by the time they arrived in Moscow a week later, Khrushchev was already an "unperson". In the capital meanwhile, as Voskhod was circling Earth for seventeen orbits, the Party Presidium had convened and presumably ordered Khrushchev to come back for the showdown meeting.

The end came quickly. On Tuesday morning, 13 October, Khrushchev had his brief session with Gaston Palewski, the French space and science minister, breaking off the conversation after only thirty minutes with the announcement that he had to leave Sochi. Right after Palewski's departure from the villa, Khrushchev, reportedly under heavy escort, left for Moscow, arriving around 2.30 p.m. Allegedly Vladimir Semichastny, the KGB chief, and Semichastny's predecessor and mentor, Alexander Shelepin, were at the airport to meet him. Khrushchev was rushed to the Central Committee building where the Presidium was waiting for him. Suslov opened the attack.

Was it 1957 all over again? Not quite. This time Khrushchev had no opportunity to override the Presidium by mobilizing a majority in the Central Committee. Most of the Committee's members were already in town and the plotters had reassured themselves of their support. When the plenum met early on the morning of 14 October it merely listened to Suslov reel off his catalogue of charges while Khrushchev, according to one report, sat there flushed and clenching his fists. Then it ratified the decision.

The Committee accepted Khrushchev's "resignation" as first secretary and a member of the Presidium "in view of his advanced age and deterioration in the state of his health". The only thing wrong with his health at that moment was that his blood was boiling with rage.

Then, as the official communiqué phrased it, "the plenary session . . . elected Comrade L. I. Brezhnev, first secretary of the Central Committee of the CPSU."

Brezhnev's initial acts were to telephone the news to some of his new "peers", the leaders of the East European Communist Parties, personally. Their reaction was mixed.

Czechoslovakia's Antonin Novotny, a staunch Khrushchev supporter, retorted angrily that he had met with Khrushchev just six weeks before and he had appeared in perfect health then. Moreover, Novotny pointed out that Nina Khrushchev just happened to be taking the waters at Karoly Vary right then and when she had last spoken to her husband a few days earlier he had not complained about his health.

Poland's Wladyslaw Gomulka was hosting Hungary's Janos Kadar at a mass rally in the Nowa Huta steel and iron combine near Cracow. Both party chiefs were on the platform in the plant auditorium and Gomulka was about to speak when an aide rushed in and escorted him to a nearby phone. Brezhnev was on the line and promised to be in Poland within a few days to explain.

Gomulka dashed back to the assembly hall, whispered into Kadar's ear, grabbed a microphone and announced that the rally which had not really begun, was over. The two party leaders hurried back to Warsaw.

Of course, other formalities had to be settled before the world in general could be told. For example: Khrushchev's "resignation" as prime minister and Kosygin's "election" as his successor. The Presidium of the Supreme Soviet took care of that matter some time on Thursday, 15 October.

Even then there was no immediate announcement. Outwardly Moscow was quiet: no tanks, no troops, no overt hints that history had been made. Cuba's President Oswaldo Dorticos had arrived for a state visit the preceding afternoon, shortly after Khrushchev had been ousted, and had accompanied Mikoyan to a concert in the Kremlin's Palace of Congresses as if nothing had happened.

But the city *was* thick with unconfirmable rumors and perspicacious observers recorded some unusual signs. Smaller Western embassies, for example, which had been without police guards for several months, reported that the policemen, inexplicably, were back in front of the gates on Thursday. (One might add that they have remained there ever since, for the Brezhnev regime is infinitely more secretive and security-conscious than was Khrushchev's.) The official wire agency, Tass, announced that there had been a luncheon at the Kremlin for Dorticos. It listed virtually all members of the hierarchy present, except Khrushchev. Another lunch for Italy's visiting foreign trade minister, scheduled for 1.30 p.m., was delayed for two hours without explanation.

Later that afternoon passers-by noticed several burly workmen remove the forty-foot portrait of Khrushchev which had hung on the façade of the Moskva Hotel near the Kremlin in preparation for the cosmonauts' home-coming. To cap it all, *Izvestia*, the government paper, edited by Khrushchev's high-living son-in-law, Aleksei Adzhubey, had failed to appear as usual at 6 p.m. Callers at its editorial offices were told gruffly that it would come out simultaneously with *Pravda* early the following morning.

Pravda's coverage of the story on Friday, 16 October, was limited to a banner headline, fifty-six terse lines of text and two pictures, one of Kosygin, the other of Brezhnev, taken when he was at least a decade younger. That is all that 230 million Soviet citizens were ever told officially of the change in their country's leadership.

Within hours Khrushchev's portrait disappeared magically from hotel lobbies, restaurants, stores and government offices. His books were hastily removed from store windows and shelves.

One more day was to pass before the people of the USSR and the rest of the world learned by inference what they had suspected all along: that Khrushchev had not resigned but had

been deposed. His name was never mentioned but one para-
graph in a lengthy editorial, cryptically entitled "Unshakeable
Leninist General Line of the CPSU" on the front page of
Pravda Saturday, 17 October, told the story.

"The Leninist Party," it read, "is an enemy of subjectivism
and drift in Communist construction. Wild schemes; half-
baked conclusions and hasty decisions and actions divorced
from reality; bragging and bluster; attraction to rule by fiat;
unwillingness to take into account what science and practical
experience have already worked out – these are alien to the
Party. The construction of Communism is a living, creative
undertaking. It does not tolerate armchair methods, one-man
decisions or disregard for the practical experience of the masses."

In Russia it is a political tradition to paint an opponent in
the blackest terms, to denounce anyone who is not a full ally
as a total enemy. Given that tradition and given that extremist
trait of the Russian character, it might conceivably be a sign
of Leonid Brezhnev's integrity that revilement of Khrushchev
ended with that single paragraph on the front page of *Pravda*.
In the nine years since Khrushchev's fall hardly another
opprobrious word has been uttered in public, and not one has
been linked to Khrushchev by name. The text of Suslov's
critical Presidium and Central Committee speech was never
published.

Besides the loss of power itself, the only fate Khrushchev
suffered was the penalty of total silence, complete oblivion.
Would Khrushchev have been as charitable to Brezhnev had
events taken a different course? It was a new kind of liquidation: erasure from memory, from the pages of history. But was it
more humane? After all, not even Leon Trotsky, Communism's
devil incarnate, had suffered that fate. On the contrary, he
remains a spectre for ideologists to conjure at will. We do not
know how Brezhnev felt when he transformed Khrushchev,
to whom he owed so much, into an invisible man. But surely
Brezhnev must ask himself whether his successor – whoever it
may be – will subject him to the same ignominy.

Predictably, many Russians took the change of leadership
in their stride with no more indication of how they felt than a
shrug of the shoulder or a quizzically raised eyebrow.

"How unexpected this is," one Muscovite laconically told

an American reporter. "And I thought *Khrushchev* was going to meet the cosmonauts in Red Square when they come to Moscow."

And the cosmonauts came: shortly after noon on a cold, foggy Monday, 19 October. Seven MIG jets accompanied their silvery Ilyushin as it landed at Vnukovo for the big welcome Khrushchev had promised them. Khrushchev's was the only face missing from the crowd, but if the cosmonauts noticed it, they did not let on. Three abreast – Colonel Komarov in uniform, Konstantin Feoktistov and Dr Boris Yegorov, both in sharply-tailored Western clothes – they marched bareheaded along a red carpet from their airliner to the reviewing stand in front of the VIP reception building. "Mission accomplished," Komarov reported.

It had always been Khrushchev who received returning cosmonauts with a grandfatherly hug. This time it was Leonid Brezhnev who embraced Komarov and placed a kiss squarely on the colonel's mouth.

The hugging, hand-shaking, congratulations and the playing of the national anthem over, the trio and their wives jumped into a flower-laden ZIL convertible. With a flying wedge of five police motorcycles they began the twenty-mile procession down Leninsky Prospekt, past flag-waving, cheering crowds, to Red Square.

Khrushchev had always ridden with the returning heroes in their open car, basking in the accolades and returning the cheers with his toothy smile and waving his pudgy hands as if he had been the one who had flown in space. The new leaders – Brezhnev and Kosygin – followed behind the cosmonauts in a long, black bullet-proof limousine. That was but one of several subtle changes in the style of leadership noticeable that day. Not the least of these were the tight security precautions. One Western correspondent reported that he had shown his credentials and invitation card to eight inspection lines before he could enter cordoned-off Red Square.

There, atop the Lenin Mausoleum, the main attraction was no longer the Voskhod crew but Leonid Brezhnev who delivered the welcoming address. His first performance in public as party leader was a pronounced departure from his predecessor's style – a deliberate demonstration of modulation and moderation. No lambasting of the West or the Chinese, no off-the-cuff quips or vulgarities, just measured words about avoiding war, striving for co-existence, tightening Communist unity and raising living standards at home. Brezhnev sounded thoroughly business-like and very much in command of himself and the country.

Only once did he allow a hint of criticism of the man who was so noticeably absent: he referred to his risky ventures, in particular to the one that had surrounded the space flight just completed.

"We are pleased, of course, that our country is ahead in the exploration of space," said Brezhnev, knowing perhaps only too well that despite the seeming triumph this was not really the case. "But we Soviet people do not regard our space exploration as a goal in itself, as some kind of 'race'. The spirit of reckless gambling in the great and serious matter of exploring and mastering space is deeply alien to us." At the time most observers read those remarks as a propaganda blast at the United States. Evidence available today leaves little doubt that they were directed at members of his Soviet audience.

After a two-hour parade, the heroes, the elite of Soviet science, industry and the military establishment, the senior leadership, Kosygin and Brezhnev adjourned to St George's Hall in the Grand Kremlin Palace for a reception in honor of the cosmonauts and their families. More than a thousand guests attacked the tables which were heavily laden with caviar, meats, pastries, vodka, wine, champagne and fruits. And while Kosygin moved discreetly around the crowd, seeking out Western ambassadors whom he assured that there would be no sharp turn in Soviet foreign policy, Brezhnev set out to mend political fences, slapping backs, shaking hands, reassuring provincial party barons, telling anecdotes and laughing heartily at new ones he heard.

The Soviet Union's new ruler had clearly passed the first test. There were many more to come.

Within hours after the news of Khrushchev's fall, Soviet officials hastened to assure Western diplomats and correspondents that little, if anything, would change. Brezhnev's and Kosygin's intentions, they suggested, were to practice Khrushchevism without Khrushchev.

Initially it seemed as if the new leaders knew only what they did not want. Brezhnev's 6 November speech on the eve of the forty-seventh anniversary of the Revolution, though a sign of his growing personal power within the new oligarchy, sounded like an SOS from a man with no concept of where to go or what to do, the desperate plea of a politician faced with problems and dilemmas he had not bargained for.

In fact, the word "problems" recurred so often in this "state of the union" message that it was difficult to keep count. He spoke of "unsolved problems", "new problems", "a number of problems", "problems that need to be resolved", as well as innumerable "shortcomings", "requirements", "necessities", "lags to be overcome", and "tasks to fulfill". His proffered panaceas were "objective appraisals", "correct utilization", "necessary measures", "scientific approaches", and "harmonious development". Small wonder that foreign observers regarded Brezhnev as a caretaker instead of a new leader.

Then as now, he preferred to postpone solutions rather than face difficult decisions, but gradually Brezhnev and Kosygin took hold.

The first and most dramatic switch was the attempt to explore once again the possibilities of *rapprochement* with China. Khrushchev had been driving relentlessly towards a final, formal break amid a high-pitched anti-Chinese press campaign and a club-wielding effort to dragoon other world Communist Parties into some kind of showdown meeting where Peking could at last be labeled, officially, as an outcast. Upon Khrushchev's fall the Soviet propaganda machine went silent. The pressure for an international meeting was relaxed and Chou En-lai came to Moscow, for Brezhnev's Revolution Day speech, to see if some compromises could not be hammered out.

That none were and that the Sino-Soviet rift widened, leading eventually to armed confrontation on the Ussuri in 1969 and the current state of acrimonious exchanges, was – at that moment – due in large measure to Peking's intransigence. Responsibility was to shift decisively to Moscow in later years. But in November 1964 Brezhnev and Kosygin were willing to seek compromise. They were not, however, ready to cut off their collective head and present it on a platter to Mao Tse-tung. Chou flew back to Peking with empty hands.

With *rapprochement* clearly out of the question, the Kremlin launched what was definitely a non-Khrushchevian policy, and is pursuing it to this day: trying to regain in China's Asian backyard the influence that Nikita Khrushchev had been ready to renounce as too dangerous, too unprofitable and too likely to bring the Soviet Union into direct conflict with the United States. In February 1965 Brezhnev dispatched Kosygin to Hanoi and Pyongyang, with a stop in Peking on the way back for an icy and apparently position-hardening meeting with Mao Tse-tung. The die for the next few years – more Soviet aid for and involvement in Vietnam – was cast. With it the chances for *detente* with America were shelved: chances, one must add, that had hardly improved with President Johnson's decision to start continuous bombardment of North Vietnam at the precise moment when Kosygin was visiting Hanoi trying to restore a Russian "presence" there.

Until his fall in October 1964, the dominant theme of Khrushchev's foreign policies had been a tempestuous, often strife-ridden, but recognizably consistent attempt to come to some sort of *modus vivendi* with the USA. Against strong opposition from some of his colleagues, powerful pressure groups such as the army and East Germany's Walter Ulbricht, Khrushchev was also clearly moving towards some form of accommodation with what was then the USSR's most feared rival: West Germany. Indeed, with the Sino-Soviet feud at white heat, Khrushchev seemed to have decided to do the maximum to relieve the pressure on his Western and European flank.

It is ironic that in 1970, five years later – albeit under more fortuitous, as well as more pressing, circumstances both at home and abroad – Brezhnev was to pursue precisely the same policy as Khrushchev and bring it, so it seems at the time of writing, to a successful conclusion.

But in 1965 events quickly showed that Brezhnev could not have everything simultaneously – not renewed influence in Asia and Vietnam, renewed authority in the Communist and developing world, improved relations with the United States and *rapprochement* with Bonn.

For a while the new leadership took the anguished line that Soviet-American *detente* was still desirable but obviously impossible while Washington was bombing a fraternal Communist state. When Washington made its choice and continued to bomb, Moscow made its own. The idea of a *detente* was put into deep freeze. With it went Khrushchev's attempts at better relations with Bonn. Brezhnev simply did not have the power, or the desire, to carry through so thorny an issue so early. Thus there were, within a few months after taking power, pronounced departures from Khrushchev's foreign policy.

Domestic de-Khrushchevization was no less conspicuous. To no one's surprise, the artificial division of the Party into industrial and agricultural sectors was the first of Khrushchev's programs to be scrapped. The Party was "reunited" and *rayon* party committees were reestablished in November 1964 at the first Central Committee plenum following Khrushchev's fall. Dismantling Khrushchev's *sovnarkhozes*, that is, his system of regionalization of the economy, proved to be a more complicated task, in part because the lines of support and opposition were by no means clearly drawn. It took until September 1965 to scrap that program which had been such an explosive issue upon its introduction in 1957.

Just as Khrushchev had done after Stalin's death, Brezhnev sought to establish himself as an agrarian reformer shortly after Khrushchev's fall. During his November 1964 address Brezhnev hinted at a new deal for the Soviet peasantry. He unveiled his program in detail during a three-hour speech at the March 1965 Central Committee plenum.

The most important of Brezhnev's promises was that there would be no more agricultural "campaigns" like Khrushchev's corn-growing or virgin lands drives. The emphasis in the future, he pledged, would be on farm autonomy, on adopting those methods of agriculture that were most suited to local conditions, subject only to the requirement that the *kolkhozes* would have to deliver certain amounts of certain products to the state.

Since their inception in the 1920s, *kolkhozes* have been required to deliver specific annual quantities of grain and certain other products to the state at an abnormally low price. One might describe this as a tax. Under Stalin, especially in the early years of collectivization, these mandatory delivery quotas had often exceeded production or the requirements for seeds. Even under Khrushchev grain delivery quotas had been set at unrealistically high levels. The results were either human tragedy and impoverization of the *kolkhozniki* or deleterious long-term agronomic effects.

Brezhnev did not go so far as to abolish the quota system as such. But he did set a fixed annual grain quota of 55.7 million tons which, he promised, would not be raised for the next six years, that is, not before the end of 1970. Moreover, the quota amount was very low. The figure of 55.7 million tons was well below the known needs of the economy and substantially less than the 68.3 million tons which had actually been procured in 1964.

The effect of this was that in the future the state would have to *buy* more grain from the *kolkhozes*. Simultaneously, Brezhnev also raised the prices for grain and other farm products, thus compelling the state to *pay* more for above-quota deliveries. Concurrently the prices which *kolkhozes* had to pay for industrial goods and services such as tractors, agricultural machinery and electric power, were reduced. In essence, it was an incentive system designed to raise the income of collective farms and induce them to produce more at a profit.

Furthermore, he called for a series of welfare measures that would raise the standard of living of *kolkhozniki*: old age pensions and a guaranteed minimum monthly income. The improvements were tangible, despite the fact that *kolkhozniki* still earn less than salaried agricultural workers on *sovkhozes* (state farms) or industrial blue-collar workers.

Moreover, in order to raise the incomes of *kolkhozniki* as well as to provide the urban population with a greater food supply, Brezhnev eased restrictions and reduced taxes on private plots and private livestock holdings, thus encouraging a flow of fruits, vegetables and meat into the free peasant markets of the big cities. In this connection it must be stressed that at the present time private peasant plots account for only 3 percent of all the cultivated land in the USSR and privately owned animals represent only 25 percent of the USSR's total livestock population. Yet, Soviet consumers today obtain more than 60 percent of their potatoes and eggs, 40 percent of their fruits, vegetables, meat and dairy products and even 30 percent of the wool they use from this private agricultural sector.

Brezhnev's proposal also called for heavy investments in

agriculture, extensive irrigation and land reclamation projects and increased production of fertilizers, tractors, trucks, harvesters, combines and other agricultural machinery.

The plan was a good one. Unfortunately it failed to take into account the inherent weaknesses and the built-in disincentives of the entire Soviet economic system. Brezhnev's tragedy, so to speak, has been his failure to keep the promises he made in 1965. To note just a few examples: by the end of 1970 fertilizer production was 15 percent below the planned level, tractor production 19 percent and farm truck output 35 percent below the targeted level. The way the Soviet economy has been performing since 1970, there is not much reason to believe that the goals for 1975 will be met.

One consequence of this has been that, on balance, Brezhnev's agricultural record does not look much better than Khrushchev's. During the first five years of Khrushchev's rule, from 1953 to 1957, gross agricultural product had gone up by 50 percent. During the last five years of the Khrushchev era, the increase was only 13 percent. The initial effect of Brezhnev's reform was also beneficial and growth rates were substantial, but over the total eight years that his program has been operative gross agricultural product increased by a scant 24 percent: that is, an average of 3 percent annually, just a little more than the population growth.

The seemingly perpetual malaise of Soviet agriculture is personified in the case of Vladimir Matskevich, the USSR's stop-go agricultural tsar. Once regarded as the brightest star on the agricultural horizon, Khrushchev made him minister of agriculture in 1955, only to fire him in desperation in 1960. In February 1965 Brezhnev brought Matskevich out of limbo and reinstated him, only to sack him himself in February 1973. There is, it seems, a perniciously repetitive pattern on the farm front.

If Brezhnev's agricultural reform program was sound in principle, Aleksei Kosygin's September 1965 economic reform was even sounder. But also only in principle.

The concept of reform was hardly new, nor was it Kosygin's. The basic idea of reform of a Communist economy – that is, introducing profitability, the market forces of supply and demand, material incentives for both labor and management as well as genuine cost accounting – had originally been advanced by Oskar Lange, a Polish economist, in 1956.

In the Soviet Union, Lange's ideas had been enthusiastically adopted and propagated by Yevsei Liberman, a Kharkov University professor. Although by no means the only Soviet reform economist, it was Liberman whose 1962 *Pravda* article, personally approved and endorsed by Khrushchev, set out the principles of what became known as economic reform, or Libermanism, in the entire Communist bloc.

Libermanism, of course, sharply contradicted the essence of the existing Stalinist economic system which recognized only one law: that of *val* or production expressed in physical units regardless of quality or cost, and one method of running the economy: that of direct command and unquestioning obedience by lower echelons. Under the Stalinist economic system, factory managers had been relegated to the role of bureaucratic errand boys whose only job was to meet the production plan imposed from above. That plan invariably emphasized quantity and tonnage rather than the quality or usefulness of the products. The output of farm tractors, under this system, might be measured in tons of tractors, thus serving as an inducement to build heavier, more cumbersome tractors with which to meet the plan targets more easily.

Moreover, manufacturing enterprises, all subordinated to central ministries, were not only told how many pieces or how many tons of a given product they were to make, but also how many component parts, how many workers, how much in wages, how much in capital investment they were to put into producing it. Enterprise managers and plant directors literally received instructions on the number of nuts and bolts they could use to assemble a steam shovel, how many buttons should be sewn on a shirt, how many nails to hammer in a packing crate.

This system deprived the economy of competitive motivations and to compensate for them, a complex arrangement of moral incentives, appeals to patriotism and pseudo-competitive techniques had been introduced and raised to the level of a quasi-religion.

Some of Khrushchev's "hare-brained schemes", such as the abolition of the central ministries and the establishment of the regional *sovnarkhozes*, were designed to alter this top-heavy, unproductive Stalinist economic system.

Liberman's reform proposals, which Khrushchev had endorsed, recommended that enterprises be freed almost entirely from the external planning and control to which they were subject. Under the Liberman system only two mandatory plan figures would be dictated to plant managers: total production in terms of numbers and fulfillment of delivery dates. The only criterion for efficiency would be profitability which in turn would determine premiums and wage increases for both labor and management. Reinvestment capital, instead of being allocated and budgeted by the state, would derive from profits. Market forces – that is the law of supply and demand – were to prevail. Suppliers and manufacturers, manufacturers and wholesalers, wholesalers and retailers were to deal directly with one another instead of channeling deliveries and requisition orders through the bureaucratic ministerial structure which theretofore had determined the exchange of goods on the basis of pre-planned indexes, not on actual demand and supply.

In August 1964, shortly before his fall, Khrushchev had approved the experimental implementation of the Liberman system in two textile plants – Bolshevika and Mayak. Two days after Khrushchev's fall, Kosygin ordered an extension of the Bolshevika and Mayak experiment to other plants and began working out a reform program for the entire economy.

There was considerable opposition to the reform idea because it threatened to shake not only the complex ideological foundation of the USSR which Stalin had created, but posed a dangerous challenge to the vested interests of a variety of powerful groups in Soviet society: the Party, the governmental bureaucracy, the managerial caste and the military-industrial complex. Moreover, if carried to its logical conclusion, the reform would certainly upset the delicate power balance between the Party and the Government, that is between Brezhnev and Kosygin.

This struggle between the Party and the Government, so similar to the one between Khrushchev and Malenkov after Stalin's death, seems pointlessly illogical in a state where only one party is permitted and all members of the government belong to it. But virtually since the USSR's inception both bureaucracies, the Government and the Party, had developed a momentum and life of their own, becoming in many respects competing elements of the whole. Both have evolved as separate vehicles of power, competition between which subsides only when the leadership of both is unified in one man.

The threat posed by Libermanism to the Party is fairly easy to recognize. If managers are given the authority to run their enterprises almost autonomously according to the dictates of profit and the laws of supply and demand, then they tend to become an independent force in the society and jeopardize the Party's proclaimed "leading role" and traditional control of the economy. That explains why Brezhnev opposed the reform.

To the Party's orthodox ideologists, with whom Brezhnev identified, the reform proposals were anathema because they conjured visions of "goulash communism" in which "economism" prevailed over the "great ideals of Marxism-Leninism". Those "ideals" equated Marxism-Leninism with a science, and of course, it would not be very scientific to let free market-type forces such as supply and demand or cost accounting influence the economy.

Western observers expected most of the managers of Communist factories to favor the reform idea. Rigidly controlled since the late 1920s by either the Government or the Party or both, they should have been delighted at the prospect of displaying initiative. They were not, for taking the initiative was alien to them and they feared that under the reform they would suddenly face responsibilities for which they were not trained or equipped. They certainly did not want a continuation of the dozens of scattered and contradictory supervisors which Khrushchev had imposed on them. But what they wanted least of all was a system with no supervisors at all. Their preference, actually, was for a system with a single, reliable supervisor: either a government ministry or the local party committee.

Ultimately Kosygin himself provided the greatest contradiction. He wanted the reform, yes. But he also wanted to restore the central ministerial bureaucracy which Khrushchev had dismantled. It should have been obvious to him that the reform idea was wholly incompatible with recentralization of the economy.

Yet, the reform plan which Kosygin introduced and which was adopted at the 29 September 1965 Central Committee plenum encompassed this very contradiction. The reform, on paper at least, was approved. But all the central industrial and technical ministries which had been abolished in 1957 were reestablished. In fact, a quarter of the "new" ministers were men who had held the same posts eight years previously. Nearly all of them were disciples of the Stalinist school.

Moreover, the reform was a compromise which reflected the protracted internecine struggle between Kosygin and Brezhnev, between the governmental and party bureaucracies, between pragmatists and ideologists, between liberals and conservatives. It was such a watered-down version of Libermanism that it was destined to fail. And it has failed.

Nevertheless, it can be seen that despite the promise of Khrushchevism without Khrushchev the new leaders had already gone to great lengths within a year after Khrushchev's fall to dismantle most of his policies.

The most striking departure from the Khrushchev course, however, was the halt which Brezhnev called to Khrushchev's de-Stalinization program. Not only was de-Stalinization interrupted abruptly within a few weeks after Khrushchev's fall, but the policy that replaced it can be described as creeping re-Stalinization.

De-Stalinization had been not only Khrushchev's greatest achievement but also his most daring undertaking, for it had threatened the vested interests of so many. Hundreds of thousands of Stalin's beneficiaries were just waiting for an opportunity to have Khrushchev's indictment of Stalin reversed. Brezhnev provided that opportunity.

We do not know how Brezhnev really feels about Stalin, no more than we knew how Khrushchev really felt despite the many statements that he made on the subject. Was Brezhnev's aim to rehabilitate Stalin *per se* or simply to de-Khrushchevize? Did he merely intend to halt the attacks on the Stalin cult? Did he realize that this approach, ineluctably, would lead to castigation of those who had condemned Stalin? Or was his aim just to restore confidence in the wisdom of the Party and its top leaders, all of whom of course, Brezhnev included, had risen to power under Stalin?

One can only conjecture. But it is a fact that the Brezhnev era has been characterized by persistent re-Stalinization for which Brezhnev himself must take major responsibility.

The first ominous sign was the climate of secrecy that enveloped the new leadership within hours after it came to power. It has become increasingly secretive in the years since Khrushchev's fall. Just as had been the case under Stalin, officials were dismissed and replacements appointed without disclosure in the press.

Then began a systematic rehabilitation of Stalin's image. In April and May 1965 the memoirs of three military leaders were published. Not one of them contained the usual criticism of Stalin. Subsequently General Sergei Shtemenko, the Stalinist general *par excellence*, was appointed deputy chief of the general staff and restored to all his military glory. On 8 May 1965, at a rally devoted to the twentieth anniversary of VE Day, Brezhnev delivered a four-hour address in which he endeavored to depict Stalin's wartime leadership as beyond reproach. His mention of the dictator's name was applauded enthusiastically – for the first time in eight years.

In September 1965 Brezhnev's pro-Stalin friend Professor Sergei Trapeznikov was named chief of the Central Committee's department of science and education. Trapeznikov hastened to explain where matters stood. In an 8 October article in *Pravda* he described the Stalin era as "one of the most brilliant in the history of the Party and the Soviet state. It is full of the richest experience in the theoretical and practical activity of the Party, in the persistent struggle for the ideological purity of its ranks."

What doubts remained were dispelled by the new freeze in the arts and the retrenchment on the cultural and literary scene which Brezhnev imposed. A week after Trapeznikov's arrival in Moscow, the writers Yuli Daniel and Andrei Sinyavsky were arrested and the summer cottage of Alexander Solzhenitsyn who had already been relegated to silence, was searched. The dissident movement – a reaction to Brezhnev's systematic rehabilitation of Stalin and reintroduction of Stalinist practices in Soviet life – was born.

Throughout 1965, of course, Brezhnev was still fighting to consolidate his position. He was in that uncomfortable interstice of power between caretaker and leader. The interregnum was to end with the XXIIIrd Party Congress in March and April 1966. More than a mere confirmation of his new authority, that Congress set the neo-Stalinist tone of the years to come. The Party's Presidium was renamed the Politburo – as it had been known through most of the Stalin era. And the Party's new leader assumed the title Stalin had held: Secretary-General.

CHAPTER XIII

The Making of a Secretary-General

"Collectivity of Leadership!" That was Moscow's halcyon cry in the autumn of 1964. Thrice *Pravda* had shouted the reassuring slogan in its 17 October condemnation of Khrushchev, stressing that collectivity "is one of the most important of the principles worked out by V. I. Lenin . . . one of the greatest political inheritances of our Party."

The Voskhod cosmonauts were billed as the new "cosmic collective" and the TV crew that filmed the trio's welcoming ceremony described itself as a "television collective". Even sports-writers joined the chorus, referring to the USSR's athletes at the 1964 Tokyo Olympiad as "our Olympic collective".

But behind the façade of collectivity which the new leadership upheld so assiduously and still attempts to maintain, a struggle for power began taking shape before Khrushchev had time to clear the nicknacks and souvenirs from his desk. In many ways it recalled the contest after Stalin's death, but in other, more important respects it differed from the battle of the 1950s because the rules of the game and the times were changing.

First of all the Presidium, or Politburo as it was to be called again, became the focus of the power struggle as Brezhnev attempted to pack it with clients and allies to obtain a working majority in support of his policies.

Second, except for identifiable members of Khrushchev's entourage, there were virtually no purges. Although relative weight within it has changed primarily to Brezhnev's benefit, the inner circle of the party leadership remained remarkably stable over a period of more than eight years. It has been enlarged, but there have been few demotions. Among the first to go were the ailing Frol Kozlov; Khrushchev's cultural tsar

Leonid Ilichev; and Khrushchev's last agricultural wizard, Vasily Polyakov. Two members of Khrushchev's last Politburo, the venerable Nikolai Shvernik and Anastas Mikoyan retired honorably from active political life in March 1966 at the XXIIIrd Party Congress. Podgorny's ally Vasily N. Titov had been purged in 1965. Another Central Committee secretary, Aleksandr Rudakov, died in July 1966. In fact, it was not until the autumn of 1972 that demotions of any far-reaching consequence began shaking the Politburo. The first to go was a candidate member, Vasily P. Mzhavanadze, who had been dismissed as party chief of Georgia in the wake of a corruption scandal. In April 1973 two full members, Gennady Voronov and Pyotr Shelest, were ousted from the Party's top executive and policy-making body. Theirs were the first "genuine" demotions since Khrushchev's fall.

Third, Brezhnev avoided what may have been one of Khrushchev's cardinal errors: he selected neither a second secretary powerful enough to undermine his authority nor did he choose an heir presumptive. During the first year Nikolai Podgorny undoubtedly aspired to be both and more, but Brezhnev outmaneuvered him. Periodically Western kremlinologists have ascribed that role to Andrei Kirilenko, only to reverse their judgment as they watched Kirilenko, who is the same age as Brezhnev, grow older without any significant or dramatic enhancement of his political power. In fact, from the minute he became party leader, Brezhnev took pains to keep the pack at a safe distance. If they wanted to massacre each other, that was their business, he reasoned. But he remained aloof.

Finally, Brezhnev acted speedily to restore victims of Khrushchev's caprices or Kozlov's purges to their previous niches in the hierarchy. Coincidentally, most of them were also his clients, friends or confederates. Thus by December 1964 Dinmukhamed Kunayev was reelected party leader of Kazakhstan. In February 1965 Brezhnev resuscitated the political corpse of Vladimir Matskevich who was reinstated as minister of agriculture. In May he brought Fyodor Kulakov, a 1960 victim of one of Khrushchev's rampages, out of limbo, naming him chief of the Central Committee's agricultural department. In October Brezhnev rescued Vladimir Shcherbitsky from political oblivion, helping to restore him as prime minister of the Ukraine, a post from which he had been dismissed in 1963, and arranged for his reentry into the Politburo as a candidate member.

In October 1964 Brezhnev had little more than a title, a legal mandate from the Central Committee, some clients and allies in important positions and the experience of years of political infighting. It took him more than a year to win a solid bridgehead and the path was often rough. So rough, in fact, that on several occasions Brezhnev was fighting with his back to the wall and there were strong doubts that he would last that year as first secretary.

The first reshuffle took place a month after Khrushchev's fall at a 14–16 November plenum of the Central Committee. Adzhubey, who had already lost his editorship of *Izvestia*, was voted out of the Committee. Kozlov was relieved from his posts as Secretariat and Presidium member on health grounds. Polyakov, the agricultural expert, was dismissed from the Secretariat.

The dismissals hardly mattered, though, being predictable and unimportant. However, three significant additions were made to the Presidium.

Pyotr Shelest, Podgorny's successor as party leader of the Ukraine and his occasional ally, was promoted from candidate to full membership. Shelest was to play a crucial role during the 1968 invasion of Czechoslovakia and in 1972 attempted to block the summit meeting with President Nixon. Alexander Shelepin, the former *Komsomol* and KGB chief, was elected to full membership without having been a candidate. That was obviously Shelepin's reward for having lined up the security forces behind the plotters. But it also placed Shelepin in a position of unprecedented advantage with a base on three pillars of power: the Presidium; the Government in which he was a first deputy prime minister; the Secretariat of which he was a member and in which he headed the increasingly puissant watchdog Committee for Party and State Control. Moreover, Shelepin's protégé, KGB Chief Vladimir Semichastny, was elected to full membership in the Central Committee. The only straw of solace Brezhnev could draw from that November 1964 meeting was the election of Pyotr

Demichev, the secretary for the chemical and light industry branch, to candidate membership in the Presidium. Demichev was not a Brezhnev ally. But neither was he an opponent.

At the next Central Committee meeting in March 1965, Brezhnev fared a little better. The only demotion was of Leonid Ilyichev, who was relieved from the Secretariat. Once again the promotions were what mattered, and they were highly unusual ones.

Kirill T. Mazurov, until then party chief of Byelorussia, was promoted to full membership in the Presidium and appointed first deputy prime minister, on a protocol par with Shelepin. Dmitry Ustinov, Stalin's armaments minister and the spokesman for the defense industry, was relieved of his post as a deputy prime minister and elected a secretary of the Central Committee and a candidate member of the Presidium. Mazurov, a veteran party *apparatchik* with little previous government exposure, became Kosygin's second-in-command. Ustinov, a man with no previous experience in the party apparatus, became a member of the Secretariat.

A compromise had been reached in the simmering party-government strife. With Ustinov, Kosygin had a toe in the Secretariat, with Mazurov, Brezhnev a party foot in the Council of Ministers. Not that Mazurov was a Brezhnev man: on the contrary, as a disciple of Panteleimon Ponomarenko, Brezhnev's old chief in Kazakhstan, Mazurov's loyalties were questionable. But his entry into the Government was nevertheless a qualified victory for Brezhnev. Moreover, Brezhnev had other men in the Government on whom he could depend: for example, Ignati Novikov and Lev Smirnov, both members of the Dnieper Mafia and both deputy prime ministers.

Only a few more changes were to be made before Brezhnev consolidated his power at the XXIIIrd Party Congress in March–April 1966. But behind a curtain of seeming unity, the battle had hardly begun.

The initial conflict was with Aleksei Nikolayovich Kosygin. In many ways it was analogous with Khrushchev's contest with Malenkov in 1953. It differed in the very important respect that Kosygin, for all his many years in government and for the positions at the apex of power which he had reached during and shortly after the war, had never, like Malenkov, been a party *apparatchik* nor an influential secretary with a coterie of clients and allies. Malenkov *had*, after all, been the chosen heir and upon Stalin's death he attempted to inherit the whole mantle of leadership over both the Government and the Party. Kosygin had neither the political strength nor, probably, the ambition to compete with Brezhnev for leadership of the Party. He was interested primarily in gaining a free hand for his managers to run the economy. Moreover, there was no record of personal rivalry and animosity between him and Brezhnev as there had been between Malenkov and Khrushchev.

In Kosygin, nevertheless, Brezhnev had a formidable opponent. No man could have become a deputy premier of the USSR at the age of thirty-six, prime minister of the Russian Federation at thirty-nine, and a full member of the Politburo – on a par with Stalin – at forty-two without being fairly skilled at the sort of combat required for survival in the Kremlin. Moreover, this premier with the permanent hang-dog look is, by consensus, the most intelligent, most able and most urbane of the Soviet leaders. Inclined to choose his friends from among intellectuals, artists and writers; devoted to cool jazz and Baroque music; somewhat puritanical; reserved and publicity shy; every inch a family man – Kosygin is tough, resilient, indefatigable and a brilliant administrator who spends up to sixteen hours at his desk each day. He knew what he wanted and wasted no time after Khrushchev's fall setting about obtaining it.

Within a few days of becoming prime minister, Kosygin, on his own authority and, apparently without consulting his colleagues in the Presidium, especially Brezhnev, ordered an extension of the Bolshevika-Mayak economic reform experiment to a sizeable number of other enterprises in the textile field. That was the first sign of discord in the collective leadership.

Brezhnev rejoined almost instantly. At the welcoming ceremony for the Voskhod cosmonauts on 19 October he told his Red Square audience: "We shall go forward *increasing the responsibility of the Party and its leading and organizing role* in the life of society." Anyone reading between the lines immediately understood that he had in mind his *own* responsibility as first secretary. He pressed his point at the next opportunity, the Revolution Day speech when he called upon party members to "continue to control the activity of the governmental, economic and social organizations". He had gone too far, however. The published version of the speech, when it was distributed by Tass, was slightly modified. Instead of "continue to control" it quoted Brezhnev as having spoken of "effective control". The party leader had obviously been censored by the prime minister's friends in the editorial offices.

The press, in fact, became the main battlefield of the Brezhnev-Kosygin contest. Adzhubey's successor as editor of *Izvestia* was Vladimir Stepakov, a Kosygin ally, and that paper took the government line. The Party's arguments were expressed most forcefully by the journal *Kommunist* whose editor was Vasily Stepanov. As Stepakov and Stepanov stabbed at each other with eloquently poisoned pens, Aleksei M. Rumyantsev, the first post-Khrushchev editor of *Pravda*, attempted to mediate. The director-general of Tass, Dmitry Goryunov, a Shelepin protégé from their commonly shared *Komsomol* days, fed the flames cheerfully. All four were eventually demoted or transferred: Stepakov and Rumyantsev in 1965; Stepanov in 1966; Goryunov in 1967. But while the debate lasted Kremlin watchers were treated to some of the most acrimonious polemics in Soviet history.

The first compromise had been reached on the basis of the Mazurov–Ustinov exchange during the March 1965 Central Committee plenum from which Brezhnev also emerged considerably strengthened because of the sweeping agricultural reform program he had presented.

This armistice might have lasted a while had Kosygin not pressed for his economic reform to which Brezhnev and the Party's orthodox ideologues objected so strenuously. The delicate balance, arrived at in March, was soon threatened. On 17 May, Stepanov, undoubtedly with Brezhnev's and Suslov's blessings, precipitated a new crisis.

Eschewing his own platform, *Kommunist*, Stepanov turned to the pages of *Pravda* that day with a blistering, albeit esoterically worded, attack on Kosygin, the Government and the reformers whose possible triumph he equated with the advent of "goulash communism" and the *Götterdammerung* of Marxism-Leninism.

The next day Moscow's political climate was tempestuous.

Both Brezhnev and Kosygin seemed to have disappeared. Kosygin failed to attend a reception in the Kremlin for the Bulgarian head of state. Brezhnev was absent from a reception which an Algerian FLN delegation gave in *his* honor.

Precisely what happened on 18 May 1965 remains a mystery. But we do know that the crisis triggered a long hot summer in the Soviet leadership. On 21 May *Izvestia*'s Stepakov replied to Stepanov with an acridly worded and barely disguised attack on Brezhnev. "An engineering diploma is not everything," said *Izvestia*. "To be a leader takes more than having special knowledge of this or that field of technology or economics. The diploma must be supplemented by a talent for organization, by a correct understanding of the leader's political role and by an ability to motivate people . . ."

From that date Brezhnev declined in the protocol rating as Kosygin rose. During his speeches Kosygin was given "stormy" ovations – the first time since Khrushchev's days that any member of the new leadership had received this high protocolic accolade in a printed text of one of his addresses. On one occasion he was even identified as heading a delegation of the Central Committee *with* Brezhnev. To have him head a *party* delegation jointly with the first secretary was like appointing a co-adjutor to the bishop, or worse.

No specific incident or event explains Brezhnev's political recovery. Perhaps it was Kosygin's preoccupation with the mechanics of the reform experiment or his growing attention to foreign affairs. But by the time the Central Committee met in September 1965 to approve Kosygin's reform scheme, Brezhnev's position had improved sufficiently to allow the conflict to be resolved.

That plenum was a compromise in every respect. The reform was adopted in modified form, the centralized state management system re-established and Kosygin acknowledged its master, thus assuring the reform's ultimate failure. But Brezhnev's position was also strengthened. The role of the Party in all other areas besides the economy was reaffirmed and even in economic matters the Party had reserved the right of general supervision which, in practice, eventually led to day-to-day interference. Moreover, three more Brezhnevites entered the top echelon of the Government as deputy prime ministers: Venyamin

Dymshits; Nikolai Tikhonov, the Dnepropetrovsk engineer who had been director of the Southern Tube Mill in Nikopol from 1947–50, and Mikhail Yefremov, former first secretary of Gorky *oblast*, with whom Brezhnev had formed an association in the late 1950s.

Although the Brezhnev-Kosygin strife had been allayed, Brezhnev's position was by no means secure. First he would have to deal with other challengers: Podgorny and Shelepin.

Within days of Khrushchev's fall it was evident that if Brezhnev expected to establish his authority as the first secretary he would face a conflict not only with Kosygin but with Podgorny as well. In a sense Podgorny, who looked like a younger, somewhat thinner version of Khrushchev, posed the far greater threat. Not only had Khrushchev's fall made him, *de facto*, the Party's second secretary, but since Brezhnev's initial authority was very weak, Podgorny's position *vis-à-vis* the new party leader was unusually strong. Podgorny instantly took advantage of that strength.

During the Red Square parade for the cosmonauts Podgorny was master-of-ceremonies. Subsequently he participated in the talks with Chou En-lai. During the November Central Committee plenum it was Podgorny, not Brezhnev, who commanded the stage. He was the *rapporteur* and spoke chiefly about the abolition of the nationwide network of twin party units for industry and agriculture and the Party's reorganization.

That plenum called for local party elections to choose new leaders of single committees in scores of *oblasts* that had been affected by Khrushchev's split. Podgorny, assisted by his confederate Vitaly N. Titov, played a vital role in the selection of candidates for the reunified *oblast* committees.

Podgorny, who had for many years been identified as an advocate of more consumer goods production, also seemed to be forging strong links with Kosygin. In fact, Moscow sources at the time were speaking of a Kosygin-Podgorny axis in the leadership, and that may have been Podgorny's fatal miscalculation.

Brezhnev's first countermove was Titov's transfer to Kazakhstan. Meanwhile, Brezhnev also began chipping away at Podgorny's own Ukrainian apparatus.

In May 1965, it seems Podgorny overstepped himself. Four

days after Stepanov's *Pravda* article attacking the reformers, Podgorny delivered a most extraordinary speech in Baku, advocating both economic reform and more consumer goods production.

"There was a time," Podgorny said, "when the Soviet people deliberately accepted certain material restrictions in the interests of the priority development of heavy industry and the strengthening of our defense capacity. This was fully justified . . . But now with each passing year our social wealth is multiplying and the necessary conditions are being created to satisfy the ever-growing cultural and domestic ambitions of the working people." In another passage of the same address he made a strong pitch for adoption of the principle of "profitability in industrial and agricultural production".

Brezhnev's position was too weak to argue with Podgorny who had so forcefully and dramatically come down on the side of Kosygin and the reformers. But Suslov could, and did, replying sharply to Podgorny's theses during a speech he delivered in Sofia. The day the text of Suslov's speech was published in *Pravda*, Podgorny was "confined to his house on doctors' orders". His illness, which had all the signs of being political rather than medical in nature, lasted almost two months.

He never recuperated fully. On 9 December 1965 Podgorny was "promoted" to the "presidency" of the USSR, replacing Brezhnev's own successor in that office, Anastas Mikoyan, who retired, somewhat reluctantly, from active political life. Podgorny has been chief of state ever since, losing his Central Committee secretaryship four months later at the XXIIIrd Party Congress. As Brezhnev knew from bitter personal experience, the "presidency" is far removed from the levers of power. Podgorny had been neutralized. His age – three years older than Brezhnev – was a further guarantee that the erstwhile co-heir would not return to challenge the pre-eminence of the Party's new leader.

At the same time that Podgorny was "elevated", Alexander Shelepin also lost one of his most important political feathers – his deputy premiership and the Party-State Control Committee of which he was chairman.

No one's political star had risen so quickly after Khrushchev's fall nor was to fall so steadily as that of Shelepin. Then (and still) the youngest member of the Presidium, Shelepin had had a brilliant career. He had joined the Party in 1940 at the age of twenty-two and while completing his studies at Moscow's Institute of History, Philosophy and Literature, specialized in *Komsomol* work, moving up to become head of that organization, as well as a full member of the Central Committee under Stalin in 1952. In 1954 he directed the mobilization of hundreds of thousands of *Komsomoly* to plow the virgin lands. He did so well that in 1958 Khrushchev appointed him chief of the KGB. In 1961 Khrushchev rewarded Shelepin with a party secretaryship and the following year with a post as a deputy premier. After Khrushchev's fall Shelepin was also vaulted into the Presidium.

Shelepin's most important power base – besides the clique of former *Komsomol* and KGB associates whom he had placed into important positions – was the Party-State Control Committee. Established in 1962, as part of the reorganization into agricultural and industrial committees, this powerful and mysterious institution, theoretically at least, had the authority to remove both state and party officials from their posts.

In effect Shelepin had a hand in every phase of the nation's life and with so many strings in his grasp he was obviously too dangerous not only for Brezhnev but for others in the Presidium as well. Nor was his position enhanced by persistent rumors on the Moscow grapevine and the speculative hints in the foreign press about his promising future and the prospects of his supplanting Brezhnev some day.

In fact, from the time he entered the Presidium there were frequent little signs – a misplaced mention in *Pravda*, a too low ranking send-off or airport reception for a trip abroad – that his peers were according him less than equal status, treating him somewhat as an upstart and intruder. There was nothing brutal about it, no frontal attack on Shelepin himself, but the signs of a contest for power between him and Brezhnev were unmistakable.

In December 1965 Brezhnev arranged Shelepin's first demotion. The Party-State Control Committee was abolished and Shelepin lost his deputy premiership in order to "concentrate on his work" in the Secretariat. Both were major amputations. Shelepin was out of the government apparatus entirely. The semi-independent organization which had been supervised by neither the Party nor the Government, only by Shelepin, no longer existed.

There was considerable speculation at the time whether Shelepin was not being groomed to replace Podgorny in the Secretariat. But Brezhnev obviously had no intention of permitting so young, energetic and ambitious a man as Shelepin to move into that crucial position. On the other hand, Shelepin was too powerful to be ousted entirely and too obviously talented to be kept idle. He was sent on a number of diplomatic missions – to Hanoi to improve relations with Ho Chi Minh, to Cairo to coordinate policies with Nasser. Brezhnev would need almost two more years before he could fully neutralize this challenger.

But the December 1965 events had been decisive. Leonid Brezhnev's position was consolidated. The XXIIIrd Party Congress, for which he was already preparing, was to become little more than a forum for the ratification of his new power.

That congress, which opened on 29 March and lasted until 8 April 1966, has left a more evanescent impression on Soviet history and the history of the CPSU than, perhaps, any other conclave. Retrospectively, it seems to have been held for only one reason: the party statutes required it. Unlike many other congresses, since the first one was held in Minsk in 1898, it set no new directions; it neither raised nor settled any great ideological questions. Neither Khrushchev's fall nor the new leadership's policy of re-Stalinization were discussed. Anything and everything of substance was taboo.

It was a long, dull affair which Brezhnev opened with a long, dull accountancy report that lasted nearly eight hours: shorter than some of Khrushchev's speeches had been, to be sure, but not a fraction as much fun. It confirmed what most of the 4,260 delegates probably knew: on a platform Leonid Brezhnev is a crashing bore. The expression "businesslike", one of his favorites, recurred frequently. But there were no jokes.

Brezhnev's only play for popularity was a welfare package which included an increase in the minimum wage schedule, higher old-age pensions, a reduction in income taxes and a proposal to introduce a five-day work week.

The Central Committee which the congress electeɯ larger than any in the Party's history: 195 full members, ɯ whom more than two dozen were Brezhnev clients and confederates of long standing; 165 alternates. Changes at the top were minimal. Dinmukhamed Kunayev entered the Presidium as an alternate member; so did Pyotr Masherov, Mazurov's successor as party leader of Byelorussia. Arvid Pelshe, the aging party leader of Latvia, was named a full member of the Presidium and elected chairman of the Party-State Control Committee. But the only development of any real significance was the appointment of Andrei Kirilenko as a Central Committee secretary in addition to his post as a full Presidium member.

It was all humdrum. Brezhnev and his team had a remarkable way of running affairs as if they had done so for decades. History had been swept under the wall-to-wall carpeting of the Kremlin Palace of Congresses. Khrushchev, so dominating a figure in that same auditorium four years earlier, had ceased to exist.

In fact, if anything made the XXIIIrd Party Congress notable, other than the fact it was even held, then it was that the Presidium was renamed the Politburo and Leonid Brezhnev was henceforth known as the Secretary-General.

The title, so reminiscent of the Stalin era, was ominous. Of course, Brezhnev was no Stalin. But it was a sign of his growing authority and power in the collective – power that his supporters soon sought to broaden and his detractors attempted to circumscribe. By July a barrier of sorts had been raised to Brezhnev's ambitions.

An esoterically worded article in *Pravda*, entitled "Collegiality and Responsibility", hinted at strong opposition to Brezhnev's growing power. "The collegial spirit," said the article, "asserts itself when respect for authority does not go beyond reasonable limits and when the secretaries of party committees have the tact, caution and self-critical spirit which are necessary for the collective exchange of opinions . . . The secretary of a party committee is not its *nachalnik* – its chief – he is not invested with the right to give orders. He is merely the senior man in the collective leadership. True, a greater responsibility rests upon him, but his rights are on a par with those of the other members of the committee."

Despite such hints and admonitions, Brezhnev was acting more and more like a *nachalnik,* broadening his power base and gathering ever more strings in his hands.

True, Kosygin was the man in the public eye, especially abroad. His adroit handling of the Indian-Pakistani conflict at the January 1966 Tashkent meeting between Ayub Khan and Lal Bahadur Shastri had established his reputation as a skilful diplomat. But even then foreigners sensed that Brezhnev was the man in command. In June, when President Charles de Gaulle visited the USSR, Kosygin and Podgorny shared the limelight, but it was Brezhnev – while impressing the French leader with his seeming rigidity – who did almost all the negotiating.

The dramatic change in Brezhnev's public image was to come six months later: on his sixtieth birthday, when the new personality cult was born.

As a birthday present he was awarded a Hero of the Soviet Union medal, just as Khrushchev had been honored on his seventieth birthday in April 1964. The official joint message from the Central Committee, Supreme Soviet and Council of Ministers saluted him as "an outstanding" leader, listed his singular contributions to the framing of domestic policies and praised the sterling qualities of his character.

Pinning the award on Brezhnev's immaculately-tailored dark-blue suit, Nikolai Podgorny said:

". . . Over half your life, more than thirty-five years, has been spent in the ranks of our glorious Communist Party. Everywhere and always you have been in its fighting ranks . . . You have traveled a wonderful path: from rank-and-file fitter to the high position of Secretary-General . . . Wherever you have been, no matter what section the Party has asked you to lead . . . you have always remained staunchly loyal to the Party and the people . . ."

Then, the new gold star gleaming brightly on his chest, Brezhnev went to the Supreme Soviet chamber in the Great Kremlin Palace where the USSR's parliament was in session for its annual budget session. All eyes were on him as he emerged from the left wing of the stage. As he strode toward his seat in the Presidium box, the 1,517 deputies rose and applauded him thunderously.

Ivan Spiridonov, the erstwhile Kozlov client who had made

the motion to remove Stalin's body from the mausoleum at the XXIInd Party Congress in 1961, was presiding over the meeting. He interrupted the session to praise Brezhnev in a manner reminiscent of the Stalin and Khrushchev eras.

Addressing him as "Dear Leonid Ilyich," Spiridonov, praised Brezhnev's "efficiency", "modesty", "consideration", "thoughtfulness" and "irreconcilable stand in the struggle for the purity of Marxist-Leninist theory". Again the deputies thundered their approval. Brezhnev replied with that characteristic public modesty which belies his ambitions.

"At such a stirring moment," he said, "it is difficult to find suitable words with which to express my gratitude . . . I attribute everything said about me . . . to the great Leninist Party which has brought me up and whose son I have regarded myself to be for over thirty years . . . I consider this high appreciation of my work and all the warm feelings expressed to me . . . not only an appreciation of my personal efforts in the past but also appreciation in advance, a token of great confidence in the future, a confidence which I shall try to justify . . . I pledge to dedicate the rest of my life to tireless work for our Party and the Soviet people . . ."

Brezhnev's birthday and the award had fallen on a Monday when Soviet papers, with the exception of *Pravda*, are not published. But on that Monday they came out: with special editions containing mainly news of his birthday celebration, the award, biographical material and a portrait.

Compared with the crawling, self-abasement of the Soviet leaders on Stalin's birthday or the fulsome praise traditionally lavished upon Khrushchev on such occasions, this was all but a whisper of a cult. But it was a cult nevertheless.

However, as Brezhnev himself knew, no personality cult, whether whispered or shouted, means anything unless one has the power that accompanies it. He had already accomplished much in this connection, more or less reasserting the Party's primacy over the Government, shunting aside Podgorny, clipping Shelepin's wings, slipping his friends and supporters into the Politburo, Secretariat and Central Committee apparatus.

But two prerequisites for unchallenged authority thus far eluded him: control of the police and the armed forces.

Khrushchev, in his drive against the old Stalinist order and in his effort at centralization, had disbanded Beria's dread ministry of interior and had placed the *milits*, that is the uniformed police, under the jurisdiction of the fifteen republican governments. In July 1966 Brezhnev renationalized it under a new USSR ministry for protection of public order which, in December 1968, was given its present title, ominously reminiscent of the Stalin era: ministry of interior.

For nearly two months that new ministry remained without a minister. Finally, Brezhnev succeeded in appointing his friend and protégé, Nikolai Shchelokov, to the job.

The uniformed police, however, represents only a portion – and the least important one – of the security establishment and it was Shelepin, through his protégé Vladimir Semichastny, who continued to control the more powerful one: the Committee for State Security, the KGB. Brezhnev needed almost another year – until May 1967 – before he could strike at this vital pillar of Shelepin's might. Semichastny was made a deputy prime minister of the Ukraine and Yuri Andropov became the USSR's new secret police chief.

Andropov, while a friend, could not be described as a Brezhnev client. If anything, he is Suslov's protégé. Recognizing this, Brezhnev surrounded Andropov with loyal deputies and assistants: Semen K. Tsvigun; Viktor M. Chebrikov, former first secretary of Dnepropetrovsk city committee; Colonel General Georgy K. Tsinev, a 1934 graduate of the Dnepropetrovsk metallurgical institute. Tsvigun is the KGB's *first* deputy chairman, Chebrikov and Tsinev are both ordinary deputy chairmen.

There remained the armed forces. Brezhnev, as we have seen, had far-reaching contacts in the military establishment dating from both his wartime days and his brief post-Stalin assignment as chief political commissar of the navy. He had, moreover, enhanced his standing with the marshals and admirals because of the substantial increase in the military budget allocated for 1967. But Brezhnev could not yet claim a major appointment in the military hierarchy for himself. The opportunity arose with Defense Minister Rodion Malinovsky's death on 31 March 1967 and Marshal Andrei Grechko's appointment as his successor twelve days later.

The circumstances surrounding Grechko's appointment as defense minister following Malinovsky's death have been the subject of some very peculiar, persistent rumors. Barrel-chested, usually scowling, Malinovsky had been ill with cancer for months and during this time Grechko was *de facto* chief of Soviet armed forces. It was assumed, as a matter of course, that he would be chosen to succeed Malinovsky. But when Malinovsky died there was a twelve-day hiatus before Grechko's appointment was announced.

The delay, while not inordinate by Soviet bureaucratic criteria, was long enough to set tongues wagging and Moscow's rumor mill into a spin. Some of those rumors may have originated with the KGB's quasi-journalists who feed foreign correspondents with bits of information. The majority probably began on the intramural diplomatic cocktail party circuit. They hinted that the Politburo was trying to block Grechko's appointment and seeking to reassert party supremacy over the military by appointing a civilian, a Soviet "McNamarasky" – Dmitry Ustinov – to the post.

As with so many other Moscow rumors, this story was soon spread as fact by many journalists and accepted by some Sovietologists. It is repeated as fact whenever the discussion turns to the power question between the Party and the generals. But rumor is all it ever was and there has never been a shred of evidence to substantiate it.

Certainly Grechko was Brezhnev's choice and even if he had not been it seems doubtful that a Politburo majority could have been found for Ustinov. If there was a debate over Grechko's appointment, then most likely it was in the defense establishment itself. And if there was an alternative to Grechko, then the only conceivable one could have been Marshal Nikolai Krylov, the commander of strategic missile forces. The debate, if there was one, centered on a question as crucial in Moscow as it was in the Pentagon: conventional versus rocket warfare. Krylov was the main spokesman for the latter, Grechko had taken no significant stand.

Whatever the truth about the rumors or the alleged debates, on 12 April 1967 Leonid Brezhnev could finally count on a reliable ally on Frunze Street. His wartime comrade-in-arms, Andrei Grechko, was confirmed as defense minister.

One problem remained: Shelepin. The débâcle of the Six-Day War in the Middle East solved it for Brezhnev. Shelepin and what remained of his entourage became the scapegoats of the Soviet adventure in the Mediterranean. Brezhnev's own role in encouraging Nasser and the Syrians remains obscure. Suffice it to say that the extension of Russian influence into the Mediterranean had already been a dream of the tsars and Brezhnev dreamed it no less ardently than any other Soviet ruler. In the end, it was Kosygin who emerged from the crisis as the intelligent manager and diplomat who met with Lyndon Johnson to assure that there would be no escalation and no confrontation. Shelepin, whose responsibility for the Middle East miscalculation was neither more nor less than Brezhnev's or Kosygin's, paid the price.

His protégé, Nikolai Yegorichev, the flamboyant first secretary of the Moscow City Party committee, was summarily relieved. Yegorichev's fall was widely reported to have stemmed from his outspoken opposition to Politburo policy on the Middle East. What has never been explained, however, is whether Yegorichev was a hard-liner urging stiffer Soviet action or a soft-liner demanding explanations as to how the Kremlin had stumbled into the Arab-Israeli cauldron to begin with. Nor does it really matter. The fact is that his demotion removed the last of Shelepin's props.

Viktor Grishin, a candidate member of the Politburo, was moved from the chairmanship of the USSR council of trade unions to replace Yegorichev as Moscow party chief. Two weeks later, in July, Shelepin was appointed to replace Grishin in the prestigious but politically meaningless trade union post. In September the last of Shelepin's political feathers was plucked: he lost his secretaryship as well. To this day he remains a member of the Politburo, but his power base has been eroded.

At last Brezhnev could devote himself to what was to be his greatest show: the fiftieth anniversary celebration of the October Revolution in November 1967. He dominated the festivities: a four-hour speech in Moscow; a key address in Leningrad; a military parade through Red Square with an arsenal of new missiles, "red beret" units of paratroopers and "black-beret" marines, myriad banners, portraits, slogans and countless flower-bedecked floats; spectacular fireworks, and five days of receptions, banquets and heavy drinking.

Only foreigners and a few critical insiders seemed to take note of the few sour notes in the fanfare of jubilation: a fifty-part television serial on the history of the USSR that mentioned and showed Stalin often but devoted not a word nor a fleeting shot to Khrushchev; an Order of Lenin award to the judge who had sentenced Yuli Daniel to five and Andrei Sinyavsky to seven years in a concentration camp.

If that in any way touched Brezhnev he gave no sign of it. He basked in the publicity. And why not? Back in 1931 when he had first entered that "élite of the new Russia", the Party, he could not have dreamed that thirty-six years later he would be not only its leader but the ringmaster on so momentous an occasion.

CHAPTER XIV

Invasions and Doctrines

While a skeptical world evaluated Nikita Khrushchev's successors in October 1964, Soviet officials hastened to reassure foreign observers in Moscow that they could expect some tangible improvements from the new leadership. What might those improvements be? Various informants disclosed privately that the new chiefs would probably take pains to undo the damage Khrushchev had done in the Communist world with his bullying, prodding and interfering tactics. The new men would recognize the rights of other Communist parties to handle their own affairs and determine their own policies, even if these did not always conform with Moscow's.

"Perhaps," one Soviet source told a Western correspondent, "we will listen a little more to what they have to say and perhaps even take some of their advice."

Actually Leonid Brezhnev and Mikhail Suslov had other plans in mind. They were determined to restore the unity of, and Soviet hegemony over, the world Communist movement. But history, abetted by their own clumsiness, was against them. True, Brezhnev *has* restored a measure of Soviet hegemony, but only through the brute force of arms and the formulation of a doctrine that justifies the use of force again. Underneath this veneer of hegemony imposed by tanks and guns, the Communist world is more divided than ever.

The essence of Brezhnev's dilemma is the dispute over what unity of the movement really means and what the role of the Soviet Union, the world's first Communist country, should be. The origins of that debate date from the founding of the Comintern in 1919 which its first Secretary-General, Grigory Zinoviev, blatantly described as "a single Communist Party having branches in different countries".

From its inception the Comintern's policies were determined largely by the domestic and foreign requirements of the Soviet Union. It became an *ex officio* instrument of Soviet power in which the Soviet Party dominated all others.

As Manuel Gomez, a Mexican Communist and delegate to numerous Comintern congresses once complained: "no matter how strong [the other parties] might be at home, no matter how popular their leaders might be, they knew they had no chance if the Russian Party was opposed to them."

Although the Comintern and its successor, the Cominform, have long ceased to exist, the inherent conflict between Moscow and the other Communist parties of the world prevails.

That conflict sharpened after World War Two when the Communists of Eastern Europe, North Korea, China and, eventually, North Vietnam, came to power. Moscow, which had created most of these Communist states, regarded them not as members of a commonwealth or alliance but as the satellites and buffers of a new empire.

During Stalin's lifetime Soviet hegemony over this satellite world was challenged only once: by Yugoslavia's Tito. Yugoslavia's excommunication from the Cominform in June 1948 failed to solve the problem, however. On the contrary, Tito's "heresy" unleashed forces of self-determination and desires for independence to which the Stalin regime had only one response: repression.

Although Khrushchev sought reconciliation with Tito after Stalin's death, the centrifugal forces within the Communist world refused to disappear. Indeed, Khrushchev inadvertently encouraged them with his "secret speech" at the XXth Party Congress in 1956, adding ideological factors to what had been largely nationalistic currents. By disputing Stalin's infallibility, Khrushchev himself challenged Russia's role as the model for communism and revolution and the very assumption that a model was needed.

In November 1957 delegations from sixty-four parties met in Moscow to frame a new general line that would reflect the changes brought about by the Polish and Hungarian uprisings. Ironically, it was largely because of Chinese pressure that the 1957 "Moscow Declaration" emphasized not merely unity and the importance of "proletarian internationalism" but the

Soviet Party's leading role in the movement: principles that haunt Peking today.

Soon, however, disagreements between Peking and Moscow grew, leading to the Sino-Soviet rift and to the formation of two wings within the movement, one led by Moscow, the other looking towards China for support, as well as to the emergence of so-called "neutrals" and "independents". As the debates became more acrimonious Khrushchev made several efforts to hold yet another conference to resolve the dispute. Finally eighty-one parties convened in Moscow in November 1960.

The basic line of division at that conclave was the Sino-Soviet schism, although there were other divisive issues. Some of the Latin-American and Asian parties objected to policy on the anti-colonial struggle. The more orthodox East European leaders demanded a tougher condemnation of Yugoslav revisionism. Albania's Enver Hoxha, who supported the Chinese on most issues, stooped to personal vilification of Khrushchev. After more than a month of squabbling the conference produced a declaration of common principles which accomplished nothing except papering over the cracks.

In the half year before his "resignation" Khrushchev devoted much energy to whipping up fraternal support for what was intended, essentially, as a showdown conference with Peking. His proposal was anything but popular. The pro-Soviet front had broken. Increasingly, other parties–notably the Romanian, Italian, Yugoslav, British, Swedish and Dutch – objected to the principle of excommunication and displayed extreme reluctance to be drawn into public ostracism of any other party on the logical premise that attacks in which they might engage could, in time, be turned against them.

Nevertheless, by the end of July 1964, Khrushchev had committed himself and the prestige of the CPSU: a preparatory committee for the conference would meet in Moscow on 15 December regardless of the "refusal of this or that party to join in this collective work".

Two events intervened to postpone that 15 December meeting: Khrushchev's fall and the new leadership's desire to explore the possibilities of compromise with Peking.

The failure to reach an accommodation with China persuaded Brezhnev and Suslov to reschedule the 15 December conclave for 1 March 1965. Of the 26 parties originally invited, 19 attended the consultations in Moscow. Differences of opinion among them were so great, however, that the meeting did more to focus on disagreement and Moscow's dwindling influence than any promise of unity.

Brezhnev and Suslov refused to stop trying, though. Their personal prestige, especially Brezhnev's, became wedded to the idea of another world Communist conference. Finally invitations were issued to the 81 parties which had attended Khrushchev's November 1960 conclave to come to a preparatory world meeting in Budapest in February 1968.

Of those 81 only 67 parties showed up – reluctantly – in the Hungarian capital for a meeting so disrupted by dissension that it bordered on anarchy. Not only did the Romanian delegation stage a dramatic walkout, but the participants failed to agree on a common policy toward China or West Germany or even on whom to blame for the Middle East crisis.

Nevertheless, the delegates to that preparatory meeting *did* reach a tentative decision to hold a full-scale world conference in November 1968. Eventually that conclave was held, albeit with an eight months' delay, in June 1969. But before it took place the Communist movement was to be rocked by the severest convulsion and the most naked display of Soviet power in its history and Leonid Brezhnev was to pass through the darkest hours of his political life: the invasion of Czechoslavakia.

Brezhnev's Czechoslovak misadventure began on 8 December 1967 when he arrived in Prague at the urgent invitation of Antonin Novotny, Czechoslovakia's president and Communist party chief.

Novotny, an orthodox Stalinist who had come to power shortly after Stalin's death, was the political embodiment of history at a standstill. He had never learned to abandon the harsh manners and intrigues of the Stalin years or to deal with the realities of the 1960s. When the country demanded economic reforms, he hedged. When the intellectual community insisted on greater freedom from the strictures of the past, he repressed. In the end he alienated everyone and became the victim of those forces which he had failed to control or guide.

Three times since 1953 Novotny's fall from power had been

imminent. On each occasion he had grudgingly loosened the dictatorial reins lightly and made just enough concessions to stave off political disaster. But it was always too little and too late. In the autumn of 1967 he faced his fourth and final emergency.

His deliberate subversion of Czechoslovakia's half-hearted economic reform had placed the country in a stranglehold and brought it to the precipice of economic chaos. The intelligentsia and the students were in ferment. The traditional animosities between Czechs and Slovaks (whose party leader was Alexander Dubcek) had reached a degree of ferocity which threatened the very fabric of the bi-national state.

The crisis had been building up since the summer and reached a climax in December when Novotny found eight of the Party Presidium's eleven members arrayed against him and demanding his resignation as first secretary. In desperation he called upon Brezhnev for help: a grave mistake.

Once before, in 1963, Brezhnev had rushed to Prague – at Khrushchev's bidding – to assist Novotny in a political bind. Clapping him on the shoulder and hailing him as "a loyal son of the Czechoslovak people and an indefatigable fighter for Communism", Brezhnev had helped Novotny ride out that storm. But it was to Khrushchev, not Brezhnev, that Novotny expressed his gratitude. To Novotny, "Number Two" men like Brezhnev simply did not count. Brezhnev, naturally, was piqued.

Novotny's expression of support for Khrushchev and his opposition to Brezhnev in October 1964 caused relations to deteriorate.

On 8 December 1967, when Novotny was fighting with his back to the wall, Brezhnev flew to Prague as requested, but he refused to play. He had never really liked Novotny. Moreover, it was evident, even to Brezhnev, that the country he had helped to liberate during World War Two was ripe for a change in leadership. Brezhnev talked to Novotny, Dubcek and some of the other protagonists and according to some unconfirmed reports even tried to sway several of the wavering votes towards Novotny. But that was the extent of his commitment. Without even attending the formal dinner which Novotny had prepared for him, Brezhnev left again for Moscow, telling the Czechoslovak leaders *"eto vashe delo* – this is your affair."

Novotny is said to have remarked bitterly that he would have been better off without Brezhnev's presence. Indeed he would have been, for Brezhnev's visit virtually put the Kremlin's stamp of approval on Novotny's fall. The crisis, interrupted by Christmas and New Year, simmered on for another month until 5 January 1968 when Alexander Dubcek was named first secretary of the Czechoslovak Communist Party.

Dubcek was not an unknown quantity to Brezhnev. They had known each other at least since 1963 when Brezhnev, on his rescue mission to Novotny, had also flown to Bratislava, to call on Dubcek, then party leader of Slovakia. Both had slapped each other's backs profusely and Dubcek had promised Brezhnev that "our people fully realize the meaning of friendship and cooperation with the Soviet Union." In Brezhnev's eyes Dubcek had an almost perfect pedigree. The son of proletarian parents, brought up and educated in the USSR, a graduate of Moscow's Higher Party School, a loyal *apparatchik*, a man whose regard for Russia had always been unconditional, he seemed in many ways more Soviet than Czechoslovak.

Indeed, the first month or two of Dubcek's stewardship really gave Brezhnev no cause for concern. At the end of January when Dubcek flew to Moscow for a meeting with Brezhnev and other Soviet leaders the communiqué reported "full identity of views on all questions discussed". Brezhnev's confidence could not have been seriously shaken even when Dubcek reneged on his promise that no further action would be taken against Novotny. After all, the man elected in March to replace Novotny as president of Czechoslovakia was none other than Brezhnev's old comrade-in-arms, Ludvik Svoboda.

If anyone objected to Dubcek during the initial period of his era it was East Germany's Walter Ulbricht who, alone among Communist leaders, had refused to meet with or pay his respects to the new Czechoslovak party chief.

With the preparatory world Communist meeting scheduled to convene in Budapest on 28 February 1968, Brezhnev was anxious to avoid a Prague-Berlin rift and devised a convenient venue for bringing Ulbricht and Dubcek together without loss of face for either man. All the Communist leaders would come to Prague on 25 February to help celebrate the twentieth anniversary of Communist power in Czechoslovakia.

During his main address in the Hradčin Castle's Spanish Hall that day, Dubcek took pains to reassure both Ulbricht and Brezhnev. Looking hard at Brezhnev, he pledged Czechoslovakia's eternal loyalty to the "community of socialist countries". Then, turning to Ulbricht whom he singled out by name, Dubcek promised Czechoslovakia's support of the GDR and "constant opposition to revanchism in West Germany". Both were policies to which Dubcek would adhere unswervingly despite subsequent Soviet insinuations to the contrary. But to Brezhnev's visible consternation, Dubcek also unveiled a domestic policy of reform and liberalization: "Communism with a human face", as it came to be known.

It was this policy of domestic liberalization, and it alone, which eventually induced Brezhnev to crush the frail flower of the "Prague Spring". Had it been allowed to flourish, its spores of democratization would have pollinated the entire Communist bloc, especially the Soviet Union, ultimately breaking the monopoly of power on which Brezhnev's leadership depended. Brezhnev recognized this danger at an early point and himself circumscribed the nature of the dispute with Dubcek.

In his 25 February speech Dubcek had warned that "to lead the masses does not mean to boss them about . . . The present effort for democratization," he said, "should inevitably include the restoration of true dignity to all those who served the country and socialism . . . All wrong-doings must be put right . . . The class aspect in the traditional sense of the word is on the wane and the sharp international struggle between the classes is withering . . . Democratic centralism in the Party and in the State is necessary, but its nature and application must be reconsidered."

To Brezhnev this was patent heresy and one month later, speaking at the Moscow City Party conference, on 29 March, he replied in the strongest terms, simultaneously laying down an ideological line to which he has adhered ever since.

"The Communist Party," said Brezhnev, "is a party of people who not only think as one but act as one . . . Experience has taught incontrovertibly that the Party needs firm, conscientious discipline both when it leads the masses to revolution and when, at the head of the masses, it fights for the creation of a socialist society . . .

"An acute ideological struggle is now in progress. The front line of this struggle, its watershed so to speak, lies between socialism and capitalism . . . Imperialism has attempted to weaken the ideological-political unity of the working people in the socialist countries. It banks mainly on nationalist and revisionist elements. To put it briefly, the ideological struggle in our times is the sharpest front of the class struggle. In it there can be no political indifference, passivity or neutrality with respect to the aims pursued by the enemy."

Then addressing domestic reformers and dissenters who were soon to inscribe Dubcekism on their banner of protest, Brezhnev said: "Anti-Soviet organizations created by the imperialists are looking for morally unstable, weak and politically immature people. Enmeshed in their traps are persons prone to self-advertisement and ready to 'assert' themselves as loudly as possible – not by working for the good of the country but by any politically dubious means . . . These renegades cannot count on remaining unpunished."

Every aspect of the Czechoslovak reform program posed a challenge to Brezhnev's power structure: press freedom and the abolition of censorship; the cultural and artistic thaw; Ota Sik's concept of a socialist market economy; Czech-Slovak federalization; the enhanced role of parliament; freedom of movement; rehabilitation of the victims of Stalinism; investigation and possible prosecution of Stalinist crimes; popularization of the Party's image, and the program for inner-party democracy. It was to counter these threats that the Soviet leadership ultimately opted for armed intervention.

Armed action against Prague had arisen as a possibility at an early stage of the crisis. The military maneuvers in and around Czechoslovakia during the spring and summer of 1968 were a clear sign of that. But Brezhnev obviously sought other solutions first because he knew that the price of invasion would be high. The world Communist conference to which he had devoted so much energy and on which he placed such hopes would be jeopardized. East-West *détente*, only recently resuscitated by President Johnson's decision to halt the bombing of North Vietnam, might be deferred for years. Yet Brezhnev definitely desired both a demonstration of Communist unity and some accommodation with the US, if only to alleviate some of his other problems: China, military spending and an increasingly troubled and lethargic domestic civilian economy.

Moreover, Tito had been warning him not to interfere. So had Italy's Luigi Longo. Romania's Nicolae Ceausescu who had ordered the walkout of his delegation from the Budapest meeting had abstained from attending any of the conferences dealing with Czechoslovakia. The Hungarian example of 1956 was too recent to be forgotten and Janos Kadar, the chief moderate during the Czechoslovak crisis, was on hand frequently enough to remind Brezhnev of it. Brezhnev had no particular desire to become history's second Khrushchev. In June, for example, he tearfully told Josef Zednik, the deputy chairman of the Czechoslovak National Assembly, that the USSR had no intention of using force or interfering in Czechoslovakia's internal affairs. A variety of pressing considerations obviously stipulated restraint.

On the other hand, Brezhnev was keenly conscious of the growing danger of the Czechoslovak experiment. Moreover, he was under mounting pressure from domestic critics as well as such foreign militants as Ulbricht and Wladyslaw Gomulka to do something and to do it quickly.

Preferring, as usual, to postpone and procrastinate, Brezhnev continued to weigh the various dangers and alternatives while seeking to influence events in Prague through means less drastic than invasion: persuasion, intimidation and incessant sabre-rattling.

The final attempt at "peaceful measures" was the historic meeting at Cierna-nad-Tissou between nine of the Soviet Politburo's eleven members and the entire Czechoslovak Party Presidium. Brezhnev's objective was to split the Czechoslovak leadership and bring Dubcek down. Failing that, he hoped to wrest concessions from Dubcek.

The conference began on a discordant note the minute Brezhnev's special train of fifteen bullet-proof cars pulled into the station of the little Soviet-Czechoslovak border town. As Dubcek climbed aboard to welcome him, Brezhnev looked out grimly at the army of newsmen and photographers who had come to record the event. He was in no mood to practice political blackmail in the public spotlight and upbraided Dubcek for not having kept the venue secret. Bareheaded and hardly smiling, Brezhnev stepped down on the platform, shook hands coolly with the assembled Czechoslovak leaders and reserved the traditional embrace and kiss for one man: Ludvik Svoboda.

The four-day meeting, from 29 July to 1 August, was punctuated by table-pounding, shouted insults and a feigned Brezhnev illness whose purpose, apparently, was to have a private meeting with the intransigent Dubcek and hammer out the compromise in which Dubcek gave general assurances designed to assuage the Soviets. Among these were vague promises to curb freedom of the press and halt the headlong pace toward political and economic reform.

These concessions were reaffirmed and codified at the six-power conference held in Bratislava immediately following the Cierna meeting. And in Bratislava Brezhnev seemed transformed. He was as jovial and good-humored as he had been glum and menacing at Cierna. He gave an impromptu trainside interview to Slovak television, smiled and waved and even took time out to visit and weep over the graves of fallen wartime comrades. The crisis seemed over.

But within a few days it became evident that Dubcek was either incapable of fulfilling his promises or had interpreted them in a different way from Brezhnev, feeling he had made no concessions of substance.

It is difficult to ascertain what single factor, if any, persuaded the Soviet leaders to invade during the night of 20 August. One, undoubtedly, was the 10 August publication of the draft of the new Czechoslovak Party statutes to be presented at a special party congress scheduled to convene on 19 September. The draft provided, among other things, for election of party officials by secret ballot, a practice which would jeopardize the entire hierarchical structure if adopted in the USSR. It also placed limitations on tenure of party office and imposed restrictions on the concentration of powers. Most heretical of all, it redefined a canon of "democratic centralism" to allow continued propagation of minority views *after* a policy decision had been taken. The planned congress, moreover, would be certain to elect a majority of liberals and reformers to a new Czechoslovak central committee, thus putting a further stamp of legitimacy and irreversibility on the nine-months-old Dubcek regime.

To prevent that congress from approving the draft and making such far-reaching decisions, the Soviets would have to intervene before that congress convened.

Numerous theories, all based on conjecture and unconfirmable rumors, have been advanced on how it happened. According to one, a junta of marshals and generals recalled Brezhnev, Podgorny, and Kosygin, all of whom were vacationing, and confronted them with an ultimatum: invade or else. Another version holds that the Central Committee convened itself, decided to invade and presented the Politburo with a *fait accompli*. But except for a few additional Chaika limousines parked outside the Central Committee building one early August afternoon, there is no sign that the Central Committee even met between 17 July and October 1968. A third version blames Walter Ulbricht who, after a tense and acrimonious meeting with Dubcek in Karlovy Vary on 12 August, pushed Brezhnev over the brink. Ulbricht, as Communism's senior statesman, was undeniably influential in Moscow in those days: but not that influential.

Precisely when and where the decision was reached also remains a mystery. In all likelihood it was taken in Moscow between 14 and 18 August. Brezhnev and Podgorny were both on the Black Sea coast and met there with Kadar on the 14th. But by the 15th they are believed to have returned to Moscow. On that day, moreover, Marshal Grechko and General Yepishev arrived in the GDR to inspect the Soviet forces massed there. On the 16th Soviet press attacks on the Czechoslovak leadership resumed, after a two-week pause, although they did not assume a really menacing tone until the 18th.

There are almost as many theories about how the Politburo divided and voted in the crucial session as there are theorists proposing them. The trouble with all of these is that one theorist's doves are another's hawks. In fact, no one but the Politburo members and their closest staff aides know and all the theories are merely based on rumors and conjecture. Certain assumptions, however, can be made. Pyotr Shelest, who had been outspokenly militant from the outset and as party chief of the Ukraine was closest to the "source of danger", undoubtedly argued passionately for intervention. Mikhail Suslov, who feared for the future of the world Communist conference and who is known to have opposed the Hungarian intervention in 1956, probably dragged his heels. Leonid Brezhnev, in all likelihood, remained in character by wavering until the last possible moment.

From a military viewpoint the invasion was executed brilliantly. Politically it was a fiasco. Czechoslovak popular resistance and allegiance to Dubcek far exceeded anything Soviet advisers and diplomats had led Moscow to expect. The plan had called for installation of a conservative quisling leadership to replace Dubcek, Prime Minister Oldrich Cernik and National Assembly Chairman Josef Smrkovsky. But it was bungled. Dubcek, Cernik and Smrkovsky were kidnapped by the KGB and spirited to Moscow, presumably for secret execution. However the quislings failed to take power, largely because of the integrity and steadfastness of President Svoboda who refused to appoint a new government.

Brezhnev was in a quandary. What had been conceived as a quick surgical incision and disguised as a call from loyal Communists to help unseat a clique of counter-revolutionaries and traitors, was suddenly a bungled and massively aggressive interference by an imperialist power in the internal affairs of a defenseless little neighbor. The Soviet press, on cue, had labeled Dubcek and other reformers as accomplices of the "counter-revolution", yet within a few days Brezhnev would be forced to negotiate with them and ratify their continuation in office.

Those "negotiations" began with Svoboda's arrival in Moscow on Friday afternoon, 23 August. Brezhnev received him with all the honors due to a visiting head of state. Invader and invaded greeted each other at Vnukovo Airport as if nothing had transpired: red carpet, 21-gun salute, honor guard, national anthems and the traditional ride down Leninsky Prospekt to the Kremlin in a black ZIL convertible from which Svoboda, Brezhnev, Podgorny and Kosygin waved weakly and smiled wanly at a quickly assembled rent-a-crowd. That Brezhnev was able to carry it off with such aplomb is certainly a mark of his political toughness. That Svoboda succeeded in maintaining the façade – at least as far as the Kremlin wall – is a sign of his stature.

But as soon as they were inside the ancient Muscovite fortress, the masks fell.

According to one reliable but unconfirmed Czechoslovak report, Svoboda started out calmly enough but was soon arguing heatedly with Brezhnev. He insisted on seeing Dubcek, Cernik and Smrkovsky and demanded their release. When Brezhnev refused, Svoboda threw his Hero of the Soviet Union medal and other decorations on the conference table, drew out a pistol – the very pistol, as he explained, which Stalin had given him "for our common fight against Hitler" – and threatened to shoot himself. "You can tell the world I killed myself," Svoboda warned Brezhnev, "but no one will believe you."

The tempestuous Brezhnev-Svoboda exchange was punctuated by mutual recriminations and Svoboda's insistence that there was nothing to discuss until he could see the imprisoned member of his government and foreign troops left Czechoslovak soil. The talks continued for several hours until Brezhnev and the other Soviet leaders retired to consult among themselves. Svoboda was assigned an apartment in the Kremlin.

The next morning it was obvious that Brezhnev and his colleagues had changed their tactics. Svoboda was given two hours with Dubcek and the others, who looked considerably the worse for wear. The Soviets wanted to negotiate and had brought the quislings – Drahomir Kolder, Alois Indra and Vasil Bilak, as well as other Czechoslovak leaders, including Gustav Husak, to Moscow. Svoboda still insisted there was nothing to discuss until the troops left.

Finally Brezhnev persuaded him to come to the conference room where practically the entire Czechoslovak Presidium – reformers and conservatives, prisoners and collaborators – were assembled. Brezhnev launched into an hour-long dissertation about socialist brotherhood and mutual assistance which, reportedly, Svoboda interrupted by banging his fist on the table and shouting: "Get on with the negotiations." On another occasion Brezhnev allegedly retorted: "We've already taken care of other little nations, so why not yours, too? As for the intelligentsia, don't worry. In fifty years there'll be a new generation, healthier than this one."

There were many other fist-banging and shouting matches during the "negotiations" which dragged on for three more days. The outcome, of course, was a compromise. The troops would remain, at least until Czechoslovakia had been "normalized" and the reform was all but dead. Yet Dubcek, Cernik and Smrkovsky, their powers admittedly curtailed, returned to Prague as Czechoslovakia's legitimate leaders. At least for a while.

On walls and fences in Prague a slogan had been daubed during those critical first days of the invasion: "Lenin, wake up! Brezhnev's gone mad!"

Had he really? Within a few weeks after the march into Prague the method behind Brezhnev's madness became apparent: it is embodied in the doctrine of "limited sovereignty" of Communist countries, the "Brezhnev doctrine", as it has come to be known.

It had been expressed in rather vague terms in the August Bratislava communiqué, then reiterated more precisely by a Soviet theorist using the pseudonym Sergei Kovalev, in a 26 September article in *Pravda*.

"There is no doubt," he wrote, "that the peoples of the socialist countries and the Communist parties have and must have freedom to determine their country's path of development. However, any decision of theirs must damage neither socialism in their own country nor the fundamental interests of other socialist countries, nor the worldwide workers' movement . . . This means that every Communist Party is responsible not only to its own people but also to all the socialist countries and to the entire Communist movement . . ."

In November, at the Polish Party Congress, Brezhnev formulated that doctrine more emphatically, underlining the "qualified sovereignty" of Communist countries and the USSR's obligation to intervene where "socialism is imperiled". In view of the fact that Moscow considers its own "model" of Communism as the only acceptable one, it follows naturally that Communism is "imperiled" whenever there is a deviation from the Soviet path.

Would Brezhnev, if he could, apply his doctrine to China?

In 1969, after Sino-Soviet relations had deteriorated to the point of open mini-warfare on the Ussuri River with scores of dead and wounded on each side, it certainly seemed that way. The evidence is persuasive that a pre-emptive military strike at Chinese nuclear installations was seriously under consideration in the late summer or early fall of that year. That threat apparently persuaded Chou En-lai to meet with Kosygin, after Ho Chi Minh's funeral, in September 1969 and open the Sino-Soviet river talks which augured the first thaw in a decade of frozen Russo-Chinese relations. But at the time of writing those talks are still going on, in fits and starts. By the summer of 1973, however, Brezhnev had concluded that they were accomplishing little. "We were doing all we could to normalize Soviet-Chinese relations," he said during a speech at Alma Ata in August. "But unfortunately it was impossible to make a significant advance on this." The fault, he added, lay entirely with the Chinese leadership "which is based on rabid anti-Sovietism and subversive activity against the Socialist countries."

China is not Czechoslovakia, of course, and the hesitancy of Brezhnev's policy toward Peking is dictated by China's growing strength and obvious retaliatory capability. Moreover, Brezhnev and his advisors have learned a few lessons from the Czechoslovak experience.

Brezhnev has not shrunk from applying pressure, of course. Massive pressure, if one considers that Soviet troop strength in Central Asia and the Soviet Far East has nearly tripled since 1969 and that fifty Soviet divisions now are massed along the border with China.

But since the invasion of Czechoslovakia, Brezhnev has also displayed more finesse and versatility in dealing with Peking, indisputably his primary foreign policy and ideological problem. In late 1969 and early 1970 Soviet sources were bluntly telling Western diplomats and newsmen in Moscow that Kremlin policy banked on a change of leadership in China. To judge from the Chinese description of the abortive Lin Piao plot against Mao in September 1971, the Kremlin was not merely relying on fate but was actively encouraging such a change.

Brezhnev has also picked up where he and Kosygin had left

off in 1966 by pursuing the extension of Soviet influence in China's Asian backyard, especially in India, Bangladesh and Japan. One of Brezhnev's goals seems to be the creation of some type of Asian collective security pact directed against Peking. He first broached the idea in the summer of 1969, several months after the Ussuri fighting, then dusted it off once more four years later in July 1973. One factor prompting this renewed endeavor was the Sino-American *rapprochement* which gave Brezhnev and every other Russian nightmares about encirclement.

China, of course, is one of the principal considerations behind Brezhnev's *Westpolitik*. And it was the spectre of growing Chinese influence in the Balkans in the summer of 1971 that triggered Soviet sabre-rattling against Romania and Yugoslavia and a virulent press campaign which accused Bucharest, Belgrade and Tirana of forming an "anti-Soviet axis".

That July-August 1971 crisis, precipitated by Ceausescu's return from a triumphal tour of China, a $244 million Chinese credit line, and Peking's promises of military assistance to Romania in case of attack, was ominously reminiscent of the Czechoslovak events in 1968: military maneuvers along Romania's borders and a torrent of polemics. However, Brezhnev was persuaded that action or continuing massive pressure on Romania – and by extension Yugoslavia – would be counter-productive. The campaign threatened to discredit his *Westpolitik* and to diminish prospects for a European security conference which, in the long run offered a better counterbalance to Peking than action against Romania. The mini-crisis was defused. But that does not mean that Soviet-Romanian disagreements have been settled. For nearly a decade now Romania has endeavored to carve out a greater measure of independence from Moscow by exploiting the USSR's fear of Peking. How long Brezhnev will tolerate this remains to be seen; it seems unlikely, however, that he will play the Czechoslovak card again.

On balance it certainly appeared initially that the price Brezhnev had paid for the invasion was painfully high. The pro-Russian sentiments of the Czechs and Slovaks, nurtured over centuries, had been destroyed overnight. The entire world condemned the invasion in the strongest terms. The USSR's image as the champion of peace and paragon of anti-imperialism had been shattered. Romania and Yugoslavia, convinced they were next on Moscow's liquidation list, had begun to mobilize their armies. East-West *détente* had to be put into the deep freeze again. The Communist movement was in shambles and, to some extent, has not recovered yet from the shock of the invasion.

But despite the high price, the invasion had served its purpose. The Prague reform with all its apparent "dangers" had been contained and by April 1969 Dubcek, its architect and chief spokesman, would be removed from power. Moreover, as Brezhnev soon discovered, or perhaps had suspected all along, world public opinion has a remarkably short memory and the realities of big power politics dictate their own rules.

Although *détente* had been deep frozen, it was thawed out again – after a respectable "period of mourning" for Czechoslovakia. Indeed, the invasion actually provided a new basis for Soviet-American relations. For the first time since World War Two, Washington was prepared to recognize Moscow's stated claim to its own sphere of influence, to its own empire.

Brezhnev and Suslov even got their coveted world Communist conference, though in June 1969 it was, admittedly, a tarnished and battered prize which they collected.

To induce other parties to come to Moscow, Brezhnev and Suslov had agreed to reduce the discussion to the lowest common denominator on which all could find accord. Even that was occasionally not low enough. Under pressure from the Italian and Romanian Communist Parties, they had also acceded to an open information policy for the conference itself. Detailed daily summaries of all speeches were issued and, as the ground rules stipulated, were published verbatim in *Pravda* and other Soviet papers. Soviet readers were exposed to extremely critical views of the invasion and Kremlin policies. In fact, some of what *Pravda* was forced to publish was as censorious of the Kremlin as articles that had appeared in *samizdat* form by political dissenters.

Only 75 of the world's 111 parties attended. Noticeably missing were five of the ruling ones: Yugoslavia, Albania, China, North Korea and North Vietnam. Even Cuba sent merely an observer delegation. Of the 75 that did attend, many were minuscule groups from dwarf countries such as San Marino and Lesotho. Others were minority wings of parties that had split over the schism in the Communist world. A half dozen were illegal parties whose émigre delegates lived within a subway ride of the Kremlin's ornate Georgyevsky Hall where the conference took place. Others were so captive and dependent that their leaders would report punctually for their own liquidation if Moscow ordained it.

In the end, only 61 parties agreed to ratify the basic conference resolution without equivocation. Five refused to sign it at all, nine others initialed only certain sections of the document, and those with grave reservations.

Nevertheless, the fact that the conference was even held was a victory in which Brezhnev seemed to rejoice. He gave a long speech – almost four hours – and like most of his speeches it was painfully dull and offered little that had not been said before. Even some of the top Kremlin leaders appeared bored. As Brezhnev rambled on, punctuating his remarks with a rare gesture or a pause to drink some water, Kosygin cast long, weary glances at the ornately stuccoed ceiling and Shelest spent almost the entire time rubbing his bald dome. At public ceremonies, such as a gala concert for the delegates in the Kremlin Palace of Congresses, Brezhnev deliberately snubbed foreign comrades whose policies disagreed with his: notably Romania's Ceausescu and Italy's Enrico Berlinguer. And yet, it was a personal triumph. Leonid Brezhnev was at last on stage, in the international limelight.

Just as the XXIIIrd Party Congress had been a watershed of his domestic career, so the world conference became a turning point of his international role. Communist unity was just as evanescent a goal as ever, but Brezhnev had emerged from the conference with his prestige enhanced.

CHAPTER XV

Struggle for Supremacy

22 January 1969 was one of those days when Moscow looked as it does in travelogues: bright, clear and bitterly cold. The thermometer stood at eight degrees below zero. Snow drifts sparkled in the noon sunshine and hoary frost filigreed the birch groves around Vnukovo Airport where the newest space heroes – Vladimir Shatalov, Boris Volynov, Yevgeny Khrunov and Aleksei Yeliseyev – were about to land for the traditional gala reception.

The scenario was familiar: a crowd of Muscovites swinging little red flags and portraits of the four space men; the heroes' wives and children; foreign diplomats and military attachés; Leonid Brezhnev, Nikolai Podgorny, First Deputy Premier Dmitry Polyansky and lesser officials; a delegation of other cosmonauts including Valentina Nikolayeva-Tereshkova, her husband Andrian Nikolayev, Aleksei Leonov and Major General Georgy Beregovoi, a handsome, dark-haired man whose heavy black eyebrows lend him a striking facial resemblance to Brezhnev.

The ceremony – Brezhnev's fourth since Khrushchev's fall – was almost routine: the solemn strains of the "Airmen's March" as the men, who had performed the first Soviet docking maneuver strode smartly along the red carpet from their silvery Ilyushin-18 to the reviewing stand; their snappy salutes; Shatalov's crisply-worded "mission accomplished"; the enthusiastic embraces and the kisses; the handshakes and short welcoming remarks. Then everyone headed through the VIP building to a fleet of waiting black ZILs and Chaikas for the traditional 20-mile parade to the Kremlin and a formal reception.

It must have been at about this moment that Soviet Army Engineer Lieutenant Ilyin, 21, – absent-without-leave from his unit in Leningrad, wearing a police captain's uniform borrowed from a relative, two pistols secreted in his pockets – slipped past security guards, who probably assumed he was a policeman on duty, and took up position inside the archway of the Kremlin's medieval Borovitsky Tower. There he waited.

When the motorcade reached the Moskva River it halted. The cosmonauts left their limousine to get into an open-topped convertible for the short remaining ride across the Kameny Bridge into the Kremlin. The parade order also changed. The car carrying Brezhnev, Podgorny and, presumably, Polyansky, left the column and sped ahead into the Kremlin so that the leaders would be in the Palace of Congresses to greet the heroes as they arrived. Into second place, right behind the convertible, where Brezhnev's car should have been, went the ZIL-111 carrying Valentina Tereshkova, Nikolayev, Leonov and Beregovoi. Then the convoy started again.

As the convertible, flanked by police motorcycles, reached the Kremlin, it slowed to negotiate the sharp turn and steep, cobblestoned incline that passes through the Borovitsky Gate. A few yards behind it – with Beregovoi, his dark wavy hair and heavy black eyebrows faintly outlined through the frost-fogged side windows – came the ZIL limousine. As it passed through the archway, Ilyin, brandishing both pistols, fired six shots, injuring one of the outriders, fatally wounding the chauffeur and spraying slivers of bullet-proof glass on the passengers. Within seconds KGB guards clubbed him unconscious and dragged him away – too soon to crack and swallow the cyanide capsules he reportedly had with him. Only a handful of people had witnessed the incident – from a distance – but news of it spread quickly through Moscow.

No one doubted that Brezhnev had been the intended victim. The evidence, though circumstantial, is persuasive: the resemblance between Brezhnev and Beregovoi, especially behind glass fogged or frosted in the extreme cold and the limousine's position – in Brezhnev's traditional second place – in the motorcade. Moreover, why would anyone want to assassinate popular cosmonauts?

Predictably, foreign ministry officials immediately told Western correspondents and diplomats that Ilyin was insane.

Fourteen months later the Soviet supreme court, without public trial, ordered him confined indefinitely to a psychiatric hospital of a "special type" for compulsory treatment. As the cases of numerous political dissenters currently serving open-ended terms in similar psychiatric penitentiaries attest, such commitments are based on spurious findings.

Ilyin, reportedly a veteran of the Czechoslovak occupation forces, was probably a political dissident. According to one report, when he was questioned personally by Yuri Andropov, the KGB chief, Ilyin replied that he had fired "to wake up Russia".

Sane or insane, Ilyin's "provocation", as Tass had called the shooting in an eight-line dispatch more than twenty-six hours afterwards, signalled the start of one of Brezhnev's most critical periods as party leader.

Ilyin was not alone in his opposition to Brezhnev or the Czechoslovak invasion. The objections emanated from the intellectuals who identified with Prague's cause, from hard-liners who had disapproved of Brezhnev's equivocation and from generals who felt strongly that the politicians had bungled a masterfully executed military operation.

To a degree Western reporting – based on rumors, speculation, wishful thinking, misleading leaks and fertile imagination – presented an exaggerated and distorted picture of the extent of that opposition. But that is understandable when correspondents and diplomats are forced to operate in an information vacuum. Facts were harder than ever to come by in Moscow in those days.

When Kosygin went on his long-overdue vacation in December 1968 and Soviet officialdom declined to explain his seven-week absence, it was hinted that he had become the scapegoat for whatever had gone awry in Prague. No sooner had Kosygin returned to work in February, than speculation focused on Brezhnev whose imminent fall was predicted by "usually reliable" sources in nearly every East European capital.

But not everything was imagination. There was no doubt about the smoke, the difficulty lay in locating the fire which, as is usually the case in Moscow, was hidden by esoteric language. Brezhnev was, indeed, facing resistance. The objection, however, was less to what he had done than to the style in which he had acted.

More than two months had passed after the intervention in Prague before Brezhnev condescended to obtain the Central Committee's retroactive approval for it. Even then, to judge from the communiqué of that 31 October–1 November plenum, Czechoslovakia was treated as an incidental point on the agenda. Agricultural matters seemed to be a more important subject at that meeting.

Soon theoretical magazines such as *Kommunist Estonii*, began hinting that the Party needed more collectivity of leadership, more consultation on vital questions. Discreetly referring to Lenin's exemplary style of leadership, the December issue of that Estonian Party journal said.

"Lenin adhered to the principle that if a question concerns the interests of the whole Party then he cannot decide personally for the Party or in the name of the Party . . . Under Lenin there was always a businesslike and entirely free atmosphere of collective decision . . ."

Then a much more influential journal, *Partiinaya Zhizn* (Party Life), took up the issue of collective leadership. In its first issue in February 1969 a Shelepin protégé, who had tangled with Brezhnev once before, argued sharply that "glorification of any one person . . . undermines the very basis of party democracy."

The question of Brezhnev's "glorification" might have evoked even sharper criticism and exchanges had other, more pressing events not relegated it to the background: the outbreak of fighting between Chinese and Soviet troops on Damansky Island; the second Czechoslovak crisis; the world Communist conference and the deteriorating domestic economic situation.

Specific responsibility – who fired first, who provoked whom – for the bloody battle on Damansky, or Chenpao as the Chinese call the little islet in the Ussuri, may never be assigned. But that armed confrontation was obviously a consequence of the Czechoslovak invasion. Peking, just emerging from the "cultural revolution", had recognized the danger in the Soviet march on Prague and the implicit threat of Brezhnev's doctrine of limited sovereignty. It was prepared for a showdown.

In previous years there had been hundreds if not thousands

of incidents along the 4,000-mile boundary between the USSR and China; none, however, had matched in ferocity and casualties the fighting on Damansky on 2 March 1969. Two weeks later a second, even fiercer battle with armor, artillery and regiment-sized units broke out on the frozen river. For Brezhnev, as for most Russians who know their history and in whose psyche the two centuries of Tartar occupation remain permanently inscribed, those battles raised the spectre of an ancient fear: the yellow Mongol terror. Inadvertently, those Ussuri engagements changed the course of history.

One day after the second Ussuri battle Brezhnev, accompanied by Kosygin, Marshal Grechko and Foreign Minister Andrei Gromyko, arrived in Budapest for a previously scheduled Warsaw Pact summit meeting. The conference had originally been called to discuss the Pact's military command structure and integration, to which Romania seemed implacably opposed. But as the talks got started, it became apparent that the lingering issue of integration was far from Brezhnev's thoughts.

As one participant told the *Washington Post*'s Anatole Shub: "Brezhnev's face was red and he did not look well. He was nervous and impatient. His temper flared and he pounded on the table. He had only one thing on his mind – and that was China."

Of course, China was never mentioned in the formal communiqué, but it had obviously loomed as the major issue, setting the scene for a new departure in Soviet diplomacy. The communiqué was noteworthy for its perceptibly softer tone towards West Germany and the United States. But the most significant development was a resolution calling for a European security conference. The idea of such a conference was hardly new. The Soviet Union had raised it on previous occasions. But now there was a certain urgency and credibility to the Soviet appeal. It was at that Budapest conference that Brezhnev's *Westpolitik* was conceived.

Before it could hatch and mature, however, a variety of other problems had to be solved and a new crisis overcome. The first of these was Czechoslovakia.

Although the invasion had stifled the reform, the reformers had remained in office and, to the bewilderment of the West and the consternation of Brezhnev's hard-line detractors at home, the Kremlin had been forced to reach an uneasy truce with them. At 9 p.m. on 28 March, ten days after the Budapest conference at which Dubcek had presided as chairman, that truce was broken. The *casus belli* was Czechoslovakia's four-to-three triumph over the USSR in the world ice hockey championship in Stockholm.

Six million Czechoslovak hockey enthusiasts had watched the game on television and within minutes of the final whistle thousands of ecstatic, singing and chanting youths converged on Prague's Wenceslas Square to gloat over the victory and give vent to their pent-up hatred of the Russians. They converged on the offices of Aeroflot, the Soviet airline. Someone threw a brick. Then another. With the plate-glass windows smashed, the mob barged in, ripped out the furnishings and set them afire in the street.

That pillage ended Dubcek's leadership. To Brezhnev and his colleagues it was conclusive evidence that Dubcek had failed to "normalize" the country. Soviet Deputy Foreign Minister Vladimir Semyonov, believed by some kremlinologists to be the real architect of the Brezhnev doctrine and the author of the pseudonymously written 26 September 1968 *Pravda* article on limited sovereignty, arrived in Prague on 30 March to deliver an ultimatum.

As William Shawcross described the events in his biography of Dubcek, Semyonov told Dubcek and President Svoboda that unless they could preserve order with their own troops, which seemed unlikely, the Soviet Army would have to intervene again. The next day, to underscore the threat, Grechko arrived. He authorized his occupation troops, by then quartered in barracks discreetly away from the main population centers, to shoot in self-defense and empowered them to impose martial law and take preventive action in case of further disturbances.

On 1 April, Semyonov, accompanied by Grechko, presented Svoboda with a letter from Brezhnev which demanded Dubcek's dismissal and replacement by either Vasil Bilak, a hard-liner, or Lubomir Strougal, a conservative. As a "temporary solution" Brezhnev also proposed a military government which could be headed by Svoboda. Grechko, menacingly, filled in some imaginatively lurid details such as the prospect of a Soviet re-occupation of the main cities. Svoboda begged for time to consider, while rejecting outright the proposal of military rule. Later that day Brezhnev and Dubcek reportedly talked on the phone and another brief compromise was worked out. Brezhnev gave Dubcek time to resign before making good his threat to send the troops back into Prague.

Ten more days passed without any apparent action and on 11 April Brezhnev summoned the Czechoslovak ambassador in Moscow, Vladimir Koucky, and instructed him to tell Svoboda that Soviet patience was wearing thin. If the Czechoslovaks could not get rid of Dubcek then the Soviets would do it for them.

Dubcek finally resigned on 17 April and Dr Gustav Husak – a compromise between liberal hopes and the Kremlin's demands for a hard-line leader such as Strougal, Bilak or Alois Indra – was named to replace him as first secretary of the Czechoslovak Communist Party.

Czechoslovakia had at last been "normalized". But oddly, some Western and East European observers "credited" Grechko with this "achievement", raising widespread speculation about whether the Praetorian guard had taken *de facto* control of the Kremlin. It had not, though there were some odd signs that at least justified the question.

No sooner had Grechko "succeeded" in Prague where diplomats and politicians had "failed", than he scurried off to East Berlin to meet as an equal with East Germany's and Poland's party chiefs Walter Ulbricht and Wladyslaw Gomulka.

Back in Moscow, meanwhile, General Yepishev delivered himself of a sabre-rattling dissertation that seemed to contradict the tones of *détente* struck at the Warsaw Pact meeting in Budapest. Writing in *Kommunist*, he charged the "imperialists" with "hypocritically preparing for a new world war". *Kommunist* was barely off the presses when *Partiinaya Zhizn* opened its pages to Marshal Matvey Zakharov, the chief of the general staff and first deputy defense minister, who wrote about "justified wars of revolution and liberation to defend the socialist fatherland".

Unquestionably Brezhnev's debt to the military leadership had grown in connection with the Czechoslovak intervention and the threat of war with China made him more dependent on the brass. It was also logical for the military-industrial establishment to join forces with hawkish ideologists in opposition to the embryonic *Westpolitik*, to the conciliatory attitude toward the United States which had been heralded only a few days after Nixon's inauguration, and to the impending strategic arms control negotiations.

The signs and currents, however, were overrated. The importance ascribed to them in the spring of 1969 failed to take into account Brezhnev's own ascendancy or his close personal links with the very marshals and generals suspected of challenging civilian authority. Moreover, Western observers expressed an almost obstinate tendency to underestimate the grave economic and technological pressures facing the Soviet leadership.

During the last week of April 1969, under circumstances which remain obscure, Brezhnev provided the symbolic reminder of the primacy of political leadership. The traditional military portion of the May Day parade in Red Square was canceled – literally at the last moment, for the rockets and other hardware had already been moved to the suburban staging areas where preliminary rehearsals usually took place. There has been no martial display on May Days since then. And instead of the defense minister, Brezhnev delivered the key address from the Mausoleum.

There was to be one more curious incident that year. In March 1965, when he had promulgated his agricultural reform, Brezhnev had also promised that a new charter for collective farms would be drafted and presented for ratification to a nationwide *kolkhoz* congress, the first since 1935. More than four years passed before the draft was ready. The long-awaited congress finally convened in November 1969. The charter proposal fell considerably short of what agricultural reformers and liberals had expected. Nevertheless it was adopted with due fanfare. On 30 November, when *Pravda* published the joint Party-Government resolution to endorse the charter, it was signed on one side by "A. Kosygin, Chairman of the Council of Ministers," on the other by "L. Brezhnev, Secretary of the Central Committee."

Secretary? *Just* Secretary? Not Secretary-General? To

observers conscious of the importance Soviet officialdom attaches to protocol and the full use of titles, it seemed a strange way to identify the party leader. Such omissions usually imply serious political difficulties. This was clearly neither an accident nor a typographical error, for the omission was not only repeated in other Soviet papers but in Novosti's English translation of the text several days later.

No satisfactory explanation has ever been offered. Was Brezhnev in political trouble or being admonished in some oblique fashion by a powerful faction opposed to him? Perhaps. But on what issue?

The blandness of the *kolkhoz* congress itself and the lack of striking new directions in the *kolkhoz* charter obviously had disappointed some influential people, including Gennady Voronov, then a Politburo member and the prime minister of the Russian Federation, who for some time had been identified with agricultural reform ideas which were too innovative and too heretical for the majority of the ruling establishment. But people such as Voronov lacked the political muscle to effect a significant editorial change in *Pravda*.

Possibly Brezhnev's incipient cult was under attack. He had played a dominant role in the world Communist conference in June. The 1970 *Soviet Soldiers' Calendar*, cleared for printing in mid-September 1969, for the first time included a compilation of several pages of Brezhnev quotations. Most important, perhaps, a two-volume edition of his 1964–1969 speeches and articles had just been published – as a trial balloon, of course – in Bulgaria and was receiving eulogistic reviews. Was some group or someone – for example Suslov, the guardian of the holy grail of collectivity – warning Brezhnev not to go too far?

The crisis, assuming there had been one, was brief. The next time Brezhnev's name appeared in the press it was with full title and by mid-December he was incontrovertibly on the offensive. The sluggish economy was his target and Kosygin's government administration and the floundering economic reform became his whipping boys.

As 1969 moved to a close it was evident that the Soviet economy was in serious straits. The year would end as one of the most disappointing in peacetime history. Instead of increasing as planned by 6.1 percent, gross agricultural production had actually declined by 3 percent. Gross industrial output had improved by only 7 percent, the worst peacetime rate since 1928. National income had grown by only 6.1 instead of the targeted 6.5 percent. Later productivity, instead of improving at the planned rate of 5.9 percent, had grown by only 4.4 – the lowest since the year of Khrushchev's fall and the second worst in a decade. In fact, only wages and purchasing power had grown faster than planned. But with no consumer goods and services to spend it on, money was piling up in savings accounts to cause inflationary pressures and was spent on vodka and drinking binges whose sole effect was rising absenteeism and declining productivity.

Economic performance had been so minimal that virtually all the goals for the 1966–1970 *pyatiletka* – five-year-plan period – had to be revised downward. The target figures for 1970 were correspondingly reduced so that in that important year of the Lenin Centennial it would at least seem as if the Soviet economy had more than fulfilled its quotas.

Actually, complex 1969 weather conditions – a long, cold winter with insufficient snow cover, spring deluges, summer drought and early autumnal rains – had been a significant factor. And adverse weather in the USSR is notorious for its deleterious effect not only on agriculture but virtually every other aspect of the economy, in particular transportation and construction.

But Brezhnev chose to ignore the weather. He blamed Kosygin and the administration instead. During the 15 December Central Committee plenum he delivered a secret speech which was violently critical of the state of the economy and called for draconian, orthodox measures to deal with it. The text of that address was never made public but the gist of it was disclosed in a 13 January 1970 *Pravda* editorial.

Virtually throwing the economic reform into the dustbin of history, Brezhnev eschewed material incentives and called for more "moral stimulants", propaganda and appeals to patriotism to reinvigorate the sluggish economy. He insisted on reinforcement of discipline and a tightening of screws on labor, management and the ministerial administration. He called for tough repressive measures against slackers, absentees, drifters and drinkers. Total prohibition was under consideration but finally jettisoned in favor of a price increase on alcohol and restrictions on hours and points of sale. Even the long-abandoned but hatefully-remembered *subbotnik* – an annual day of work without pay – was reinstated. Ignoring the pleas of the reformers who argued that compromises and party meddling had prevented effective implementation of the reform, Brezhnev resorted to time-worn remedies: reinforcement of the Party's role in enterprises, tighter controls, threats, exhortations, penalties and shuffling of officials.

It was, in short, a Brezhnev declaration of war on Kosygin and a bid for supreme power. As resistance to Brezhnev took shape, strange things started to happen. The "mini-crisis" of 1970 began.

For the next seven months the Soviet scene was a turbulent, confusing secret political battle set against two important events – the Lenin Centennial celebration in April and the Supreme Soviet election in June – and one even more important non-event – the XXIVth Party Congress which, by law, should have been held in March 1970 but was actually postponed a year until April 1971.

The first two months of 1970 – except for the new economic discipline drive – were relatively quiet. The most noteworthy incident was an 8 January speech by Vasily Tolstikov, the Leningrad Party chief, who seemed to be contradicting Brezhnev about the timing of the Party Congress. Until then it had more or less been assumed that the conclave would take place in 1970, albeit later in the year. But Tolstikov described 1970 as the year of "the Party's *preparation for* its regular XXIVth Congress".

It was also in January that the first *Soviet* review of the trial-balloon Bulgarian edition of Brezhnev's speeches appeared and that Brezhnev's birthdate began to change – from 19 December 1906 to 1 January 1907 – on some of the 1971 calendars then being printed. Two calendars cleared for publication by the censors that month contained the new date.

In March Brezhnev began flying solo. *Pravda* reported that he had held a "consultative" meeting with a group of "technical ministers" from the fifteen Soviet republics to discuss agriculture. That was a conspicuous incursion on Kosygin's area of responsibility.

Then, unaccompanied by any other Politburo member or government leader with the exception of Marshal Grechko, Brezhnev journeyed to Minsk to review the military maneuvers being staged in Byelorussia.

On 1 April, accompanied only by his friend and client Vladimir Shcherbitsky and Marshal Zakharov, Brezhnev traveled to Budapest for the twenty-fifth anniversary of Hungary's World War Two liberation. That same day Kosygin, Podgorny, Suslov, Shelepin and Polyansky seemed to vanish from public view and mention in the media.

Simultaneously there were reports – all eventually confirmed – of high-level demotions in the propaganda and media field. Vladimir Stepakov, the former editor-in-chief of *Izvestia*, a Kosygin man, who had taken such an outspoken view during the economic reform debates in 1965, was dismissed as head of the Central Committee's department of propaganda and agitation and named ambassador-designate to Peking. Nikolai Mikhailov, Shelepin's predecessor (from 1938 to 1952) as first secretary of the *Komsomol*, was relieved as chairman of the State Committee on the Press. Another Shelepin associate, Nikolai Mesyatsev, was sacked as chairman of the State Committee for Radio and TV. Aleksei Romanov, chairman of the State Committee on Cinematography, was retired.

Then Podgorny canceled a scheduled state visit to Japan because of a "fever and cold". Kosygin was listed as in hospital suffering from post-influenza complications. Shelepin, Suslov and Polyansky were also reported ill.

When Brezhnev returned from Budapest on 6 April only three Politburo members – Kirilenko, Mazurov and Voronov – remained on duty in Moscow to greet him at the Kievsky railway station where security precautions struck correspondents as exceptionally tight. Ignoring a small crowd of onlookers kept at bay across the street from the VIP exit, Brezhnev fled into his Rolls-Royce and was whisked off in the direction of the Kremlin.

On 10 April Shelepin, looking very haggard, reappeared and participated, with Kirilenko, Mazurov and Voronov, in the annual Cosmonauts' Day festivities.

On 11 April, tucked away amid the usual reports on the activities of local party organizations, *Pravda* published a tiny item announcing the transfer of two provincial *apparatchiki* – Leonid Yefremov and Tikhon Sokolov, both associates of Brezhnev – to crucial senior government posts. Sokolov was named first deputy chairman of Gosplan, the State Planning Commission; Yefremov first deputy chairman of the important State Committee on Science and Technology where he became senior to Kosygin's son-in-law Dzherman Gvishiani.

On 13 and 14 April an even stranger event took place. Brezhnev went to Kharkov to present Orders of Lenin – usually a ceremonial government or state function – to a tractor plant and the city. His performance, by any criterion, was singular. Not only did he plant two kisses on the cheeks of a buxom blond assembly-line worker with such enthusiasm that she pushed him back in embarrassment, but he delivered two major speeches – one on domestic, the other on world affairs – which were telecast live to a nationwide audience. The foreign affairs speech was a reiteration of his new policy and intended to transmit unmistakable signals to Washington. The domestic address reaffirmed his tough new economic and ideological line. It was also marked by two important statements: The Party Congress *would be held* that year, he said. Moreover, he contended, Soviet society had reached the point where "old methods" no longer served to deal with problems. He called for "a new approach" to the economy.

The following day other members of the leadership began reappearing and looked none the worse for their bouts with fevers, influenza and lung congestion. Only Shelepin seemed wan and drawn when he and Brezhnev met in Ulyanovsk, Lenin's birthplace, to unveil a sprawling new memorial complex. Just before Brezhnev launched into his third major TV address of the week, the cameras zoomed in pointedly as he and Shelepin hugged and kissed each other.

On 21 April the world's Communist leaders converged on Moscow to celebrate Lenin's 100th birthday. At a commemorative ceremony in the Palace of Congresses that evening, the entire Kremlin leadership was back in view and applauded enthusiastically as Brezhnev delivered one of his seemingly endless speeches. He again indicated that the Party Congress would be held that year. He again demanded "intensified development" and "increased productivity of labor in every sphere". Then he issued a crude warning: Lenin's attention, he said, had always focused "on tempering and strengthening the Party's ranks. He regarded factionalism and group action in the Party as the greatest evil, an evil which had to be fought resolutely and relentlessly." Whom was Brezhnev addressing?

Correspondents and diplomats who watched for signs of reaction among the oligarchy found few. Suslov had donned sun-glasses to shield his eyes from the TV-lights. Kosygin looked no glummer than usual. At one point during the long ceremony Voronov and Shelest were even laughing and seemed to be telling each other jokes.

Was the leadership crisis over? Though it seemed that way, it was really just in recess.

By the end of May – at the height of the Supreme Soviet "election campaign", Brezhnev returned to the offensive. *Pravda* reported that he had delivered "major speeches" to both the Soviet and the Russian Federation's councils of ministers, though he is a member of neither. That was a massive intrusion on Kosygin's and Gennady Voronov's preserves. What Brezhnev said was never disclosed, though the impression created was that he had virtually chaired both sessions.

On 12 June, two days before the election, Brezhnev delivered a speech in his own constituency, Moscow's Baumanski District, where he once more asserted that the XXIVth Party Congress would be held that year.

On 2 July, the day a Central Committee plenum convened in Moscow, the London *Evening News* published a highly unusual despatch from its most unusual Moscow correspondent, Viktor Louis. The only Soviet citizen permitted to write freely for a major Western newspaper, Louis is one of Moscow's most mystifying figures. His real role in the Soviet establishment and his reputed connections to the KGB remain subject to interminable speculation. Suffice it to say that whatever his connections, they are good.

Implying that a Kremlin reshuffle was imminent, Louis said: "Rumors that Mr Brezhnev has high blood pressure and that his doctors insist that he should stay home under medical observation are most likely reliable . . . The reshuffle rumors would gain probability today if Mr Brezhnev is unable to attend the plenum of the Central Committee on agriculture. Apart from today's meeting, the next public appearance of Mr Brezhnev is due in Bucharest with a Soviet delegation in a few days, but taking his apparent state of health into account, it is possible the doctors will cancel his visit to Romania."

What was Louis trying to say? That will probably remain his secret. The fact is that Brezhnev *did* attend the Central Committee meeting but that he did bow out of the Bucharest affair, pleading a "catarrhal ailment" and sent Kosygin and Suslov in his stead.

But the very day Kosygin and Suslov arrived in Bucharest for the long-delayed and twice-postponed signing of a new twenty-year Soviet-Romanian friendship treaty, Leonid Brezhnev went to see a soccer game. Accompanied by Podgorny and the Central African Republic's President Jean Bokassa, Brezhnev sat in the VIP box of Lenin Stadium to see his favorites, Kiev Dynamo, suffer a one-nil defeat at the hands of Moscow Torpedo. Those who watched Brezhnev cheer his team and agonize over their loss knew that he had neither high blood pressure nor catarrh.

What he did have were several hundred members of the Central Committee sitting around in Moscow waiting for yet another – unannounced and previously unscheduled – plenum. It was finally held on 13 July and all it did was to decide that the XXIVth Party Congress would *not* take place in 1970, as Brezhnev had been saying only recently, but in April 1971.

On 14 July, the newly elected Supreme Soviet met for its initial session. The main order of business: Kosygin's re-election as prime minister and the re-constitution of his entire Government with all its more than ninety ministers. At last the "mini-crisis" of 1970 was over.

Three years later sovietologists are still trying to sort out what really happened in those tempestuous days between mid-December 1969 and mid-July 1970. One thing appears certain. The essence of the dispute was between Brezhnev and Kosygin, between Party and Government. It also seems obvious that Brezhnev attempted to reshape the leadership team in a form more desirable to him. That explains why, until the last minute, he wanted the XXIVth Party Congress to take place in 1970, as soon as possible, for that congress was sure to strengthen his political posture. Although he emerged from the crisis with his position enhanced, he had nevertheless suffered a rebuff.

One of the more intriguing and plausible theories holds that Brezhnev's rolling attack against the Government on economic matters had either forced Kosygin into an untenable position by the end of March or persuaded him that there was no point in resisting Brezhnev any longer. Rumors that Kosygin was weary, tired of pulling Brezhnev's domestic and foreign chestnuts from the fire and anxious to resign had circulated persistently in Moscow ever since early 1968.

By mid-April, according to the theory, the question of Kosygin's retirement had more or less been decided. It would be done honorably in July at the first session of the newly elected Supreme Soviet. The regular four-year parliamentary period over, Kosygin's Government would have to submit its formal resignation anyway and his successor could thus be named in a fashion as democratic as any in the West.

In fact, according to this theory, by the middle of April, that is at about the time everyone was returning from their various ailments and illnesses, Kosygin's successor-designate – Dmitry Polyansky -- had more or less been agreed upon. But, so the theory goes, there was opposition to Polyansky from the heavy-industry lobby which considered him too agriculturally oriented. Moreover Polyansky seemed to have some powerful competitors for the prime ministership, one of them probably Brezhnev himself.

Some time between mid-April and late June, according to the theory, the mounting opposition and the emergence of that second candidate threw Polyansky's candidacy into doubt once more. In late June the Politburo probably met to reach a decision and apparently reached deadlock, deciding to refer the question to the Central Committee for a vote. When the Central Committee met on 2–3 July it also reached an impasse. This would explain why Brezhnev missed the Bucharest trip; he was fighting for control over the Government. But Kosygin, who expected to be out of office within a week or so, had nothing to stay in Moscow for. He scurried off to meet with Nicolae Ceausescu. The Moscow discussions about Kosygin's successor probably continued right up to the second Central Committee meeting on 13 July by which time there was no alternative but to ask Kosygin to stay on the job.

All the evidence indicates that Kosygin had not expected to be entrusted with the formation of the new government at the 14 July Supreme Soviet session and was unprepared to start yet another term as prime minister. He took the unprecedented step of not replacing a single member of the Council of Ministers and did not even deliver a major policy statement as he had done upon his re-election as premier four years previously.

This postulated scenario would also help to explain the postponement of the Party Congress. Party rules dictate that whoever is prime minister is responsible for delivering the main economic report at the congress. His name would have to be given on the agenda and it is customary to announce the agenda along with the dates of the congress. Thus no date could be agreed upon until the economic *rapporteur* had been chosen. Only after it was decided that Kosygin would stay on could the congress date be announced. And Kosygin, already counting his retirement benefits, obviously needed some time to prepare for the conclave – at least until early 1971.

Whether this explanation fits the facts only the men in the Kremlin can say. But two things were incontrovertible. Although Brezhnev had fallen far short of one aim – to become prime minister – he had, nonetheless, won a great deal of ground since December 1969. He wasted little time during the next six months in consolidating this advantage. Military historians began publishing detailed, eulogistic accounts of his wartime exploits. His collected speeches – in two volumes – appeared in Russian, went on sale in book shops all over the USSR and were soon reviewed in glowing terms by the party press.

Cautiously he began wetting his toes in diplomatic waters, meeting Willy Brandt who had come to Moscow to sign the Soviet-German renunciation of force treaty in August, and playing the gracious host to French President and Madame Pompidou in October.

On 26 August Brezhnev flew to Alma Ata to help Kunayev celebrate the fiftieth anniversary of Kazakhstan. Then he set out on a two-week tour of the other Central Asian republics. The coverage and size of the headlines increased and the commentaries grew more effusive with each day he was on the road. On six occasions *Pravda* published front-page photographs of Brezhnev – a record unmatched since Khrushchev's times.

He also settled a few political scores. The Chinese had refused *agrément* to Vladimir Stepakov, providing Brezhnev with a perfect opportunity to send a far more dangerous political opponent, Leningrad's Vasily Tolstikov, to Peking as ambassador. Could there have been a more convenient way to neutralize Frol Kozlov's last remaining protégé, a man who was being touted as a rival to Brezhnev's power?

Of course there was some carping, too. Certain theoretical journals continued to emphasize the need for collective leadership. Clearly, too, the calendar gambit had failed. Those approved for printing after the middle of the year gave Brezhnev's real birthdate.

But the remaining doubts about Brezhnev's ascendancy were dispelled a few minutes before midnight on 31 December 1970. For years – as long as anyone could remember – Yuri Levitan, the best-known Soviet announcer, had rung out the old year and ushered in the new by reading a message of greetings from the Party and Government in his inimitable stentorian style. But this time Levitan simply introduced Brezhnev – sitting at a desk, a microphone beside him, a map of the USSR in the background. Precedent was shattered. Never before had the leader of the Party – not Lenin, not Stalin, not Khrushchev – personally delivered New Year's greetings to the country. As millions interrupted their merrymaking and their toasting to listen to Brezhnev address them as "dear compatriots, dear comrades, friends," it was obvious to everyone that he was now really the Soviet Union's new ruler.

CHAPTER XVI

Lenin's Heir

In the Communist world it used to be axiomatic that when Moscow sneezes the other capitals catch cold. But in December 1970, when the inadequate supply and high prices of consumer goods sparked off bloody riots by thousands of Polish shipyard workers and precipitated the sudden fall of Poland's party leader Wladyslaw Gomulka, it was Moscow that came down with congestion.

Leonid Brezhnev's economic austerity program was abandoned almost immediately. The strident demands for greater production efforts and more labor discipline were muted. The party press criticized various technical ministries and administrative agencies for the insufficiency of food and consumer goods. Government officials hastened to deny that price increases of any kind were intended. Trade union representatives were upbraided for failing to pay attention to workers' demands in factories.

Most significantly, however, the draft of the 1971–75 five-year plan, almost ready for public presentation in late December 1970, was held up for drastic revision and a precedent shattering shift of emphasis from traditional producer to consumer priorities.

As recently as the 12 June pre-election rally in Moscow's Baumanski district, Brezhnev had told his constituents: "Work on the five-year plan is continuing and (although) it would be premature to speak of concrete figures and targets, I can assure you that a further important industrial growth is envisaged primarily for those branches that produce the means of production . . ."

When Brezhnev made that prediction the draft of the plan, which Kosygin had once promised to have ready by August 1969, was already many months overdue. The reason for the delay was undoubtedly the sluggishness of the economy and the behind-the-scenes debate over solutions and priorities. Brezhnev's remedy had been moral rearmament. But professional economists, especially the reformers, pleaded for more material incentives. And they did not mean merely more bonuses and bigger paychecks but a quantative and qualitative improvement in the supply of consumer goods. They argued convincingly that no amount of monetary incentive would reinvigorate the economy if workers had nothing or little on which to spend their increasing wages. The alarming rate at which savings had accumulated and millions of rubles had passed down millions of gullets in a national drinking spree was a reflection of the absence of meaningful production stimuli.

The only alternative, perspicacious economists argued, was to keep wage increases at a minimum for a while but improve the flow of consumer goods. Available evidence indicates that by autumn 1970 a compromise had been worked out. The traditional bias favoring heavy industry and producer goods would be maintained, but the consumer goods sector would receive more investment funds and production of consumer goods would be stepped up.

Then came the riots in Poland – a tocsin which even Brezhnev could not help but hear. At the last minute, that is after the December 1970 uprising in Gdansk, the plan was hastily revised with a shift of priorities.

When the plan was finally promulgated – by Brezhnev personally and signed by him alone – on 14 February 1971, it marked a dramatic departure from tradition. For the first time in Soviet history a *pyatiletka* stipulated a faster growth rate for the consumer goods sector (44 to 48 percent) than heavy industry (41 to 45 percent). It called for vast investments in agriculture and those industries manufacturing for general consumption, notably passenger cars and other consumer durables. It declared that the "main task" of the future was "to ensure a significant increase in the material and cultural standard of living".

Six weeks later, in his principal address to the XXIVth Party Congress, Brezhnev reiterated the new line so emphatically that the powerful heavy-industrial and metal-eating lobbies induced *Pravda*'s editors to censor two important passages from the published version of Brezhnev's congress report.

Though taking care to reassure those lobbies that they had not suddenly become the step-children of the nation, Brezhnev paraphrased Lenin to contend that "in the ultimate analysis the manufacture of means of production is necessarily connected with the manufacture of consumer goods because the means of production are made not for their own sake . . ." He left little room for equivocation and demanded a "serious change in the very approach to consumer goods".

Ushering in what he described as a new consumer era, Brezhnev said: "The long years of heroic history when millions of Communists and non-Party people deliberately made sacrifices and underwent privation . . . lie behind us . . . What was explicable and only natural in the past when other tasks stood in the foreground is unacceptable under present conditions."

Brezhnev promised to raise investments in agriculture, he strengthened the role of private plots and stressed the need for quality in food and consumer products. He called for new heights in technological and scientific achievement and emphasized efficiency. Finally, he promised bigger pensions, higher minimum wages and a catalogue of other benefits.

Could this be the same man who fifteen months previously had insisted on tightened labor discipline, stressed the importance of moral stimuli, demanded stringent control and introduced draconian penalties? Some of the statements in his speech sounded identical to those Podgorny had made in his pro-consumer talk six years earlier in Baku.

Brezhnev's metamorphosis may have caused some bewilderment and elicited incredulity, but it was hardly unique. He was not the first politician – Communist and non-Communist – to change his policies and alter his views virtually overnight. Moreover, the Kremlin power struggle has always followed its own peculiar rules. Stalin himself had, on occasion, adopted the policies of his opponents – after he had defeated them. Khrushchev, too, had decided soon after settling scores with Malenkov to spend more money on consumer goods and less on defense.

There may have been skepticism about Brezhnev's

inclinations, but the Party Congress left him shining as the new benefactor of the Soviet common man. It also entrenched him as virtual master of the Party. He did not even trouble to apologize for or seek to explain the illegal one-year postponement of the congress: he simply institutionalized the delay. Cries of "Hear! hear!" resounded through the hall when Brezhnev said: "Many comrades feel that regular congresses of the CPSU should convene not once in four years but once in five." And so it was decided.

Above all the congress engendered a new personality cult. His six-hour-long address – almost equalling Khrushchev's eight-hour record setter – was televised live to the nation. Subsequently, virtually every other speaker – Soviet or foreign – lauded the claimed achievements of the USSR during the preceding three years and effusively mentioned Brezhnev's personal role in them.

Yevgeny Tyazhelnikov, first secretary of the *Komsomol*, managed to refer to Brezhnev eight times in his short talk. So did A. P. Filatov, party leader of Novosibirsk *oblast*. The first secretaries of Latvia and Tadzhikistan and the minister of ferrous metallurgy each gave him seven mentions.

Geidar Aliyev, the former Azerbaidzhani KGB chief who had become that republic's first secretary thanks to Brezhnev's patronage, spoke of the "general love" Brezhnev had gained and the "respect" he had won through "his tireless activity and his constant concern for the welfare of the people". Sharaf Rashidov, the Uzbekistan party chief, recalled warmly that Brezhnev had rushed to Tashkent after the 1966 earthquake and had been "in the forefront when the most important measures of assistance were worked out".

He was praised for his "dedication to principle", "consistency", "profound faith in the peoples' creative strength", "deep scholarliness", "creativity", "enormous organizational activity", "staunch devotion to the Leninist manner", "understanding of the life of the people", "simplicity" and his "humanity".

A milkmaid from the Dawn of Peace *kolkhoz* in Orel *oblast* even told the 5,000 delegates that the "warmth and sincerity" of "Leonid Ilyich's report" had brought "tears of joy and pride to my eyes".

Undeniably the congress was a personal triumph and a tribute to his enhanced prestige. But all the laudations could not conceal that it had failed to provide Brezhnev with the uncontested political power to which he aspires. As so often in his career, he had been forced to compromise. His victory, while considerable, was nonetheless qualified.

Brezhnev's growing influence and authority was most notable in the new Central Committee – 241 full and 155 alternate members – elected by the congress. True, the relative numerical weight of Brezhnev's central and regional party apparatus had diminished somewhat *vis-à-vis* Kosygin's government bureaucracy. But that is merely a superficial calculation which does not take into account the loyalties of the individual Central Committee members. In total strength the Brezhnev group – clients, protégés, patrons, allies, friends and confederates – had increased dramatically, not only in the Central Committee as a whole but among its various professional interest groupings such as the party apparatus, the government bureaucracy, the military contingent and the police and security bloc.

Of the 241 full members at least 30 can be considered Brezhnev clients and fully dependable allies. Many more rank as reliable associates or confederates.

Virtually the entire Dnieper Mafia was elected. The list includes not only such obviously powerful members of the clique as Shcherbitsky, Shchelokov, Kirilenko and three deputy prime ministers, but less influential veterans of the early days like Ivan Grushetsky and Konstantin Grushevoi. Although not every *oblast* party leader in the USSR wins a seat on the Central Committee, the election of Aleksei Vatchenko, present first secretary of Dnepropetrovsk *obkom*, and Ivan Yunak, the former Dnepropetrovsk executive committee chairman who is now party leader of Tula *oblast*, seemed a foregone conclusion. But who would have imagined that even I. L. Furs, currently first secretary of Dneprodzerzhinsk city committee, would be named an alternate member of the Central Committee? Next to party leaders and city secretaries from the three largest metropolises – Moscow, Leningrad and Kiev – Furs is the only municipal party chief in the USSR who belongs to the Central Committee.

Three of Brezhnev's closest aides and advisors – Georgy Pavlov, Georgy Tsukanov and Konstantin Chernenko – were elected full members, a feat not even Khrushchev had accomplished. His foreign policy expert Andrei M. Aleksandrov-Agentov won a seat on the Central Auditing Commission. A fifth Brezhnev advisor, Konstantin Rusakov – not assigned to Brezhnev's personal staff until June 1972 and believed to be responsible for whatever peaceful overtures Brezhnev makes to Peking – was also elected to the Central Committee as a full member at the Party Congress.

Naturally, Andropov, his friendly neighbor and secret police chief, was re-elected. But even Brezhnev's own watchdogs within the KGB won seats. Semyon Tsvigun and Viktor Chebrikov were named alternate members of the Central Committee while G. K. Tsinev was elected to the Party's Central Auditing Commission. Not since Stalin's days had so many senior security officials belonged to "leading party organs".

Brezhnev's achievements were formidable. Death, retirement, old age and political attrition had decimated the ranks of old Khrushchevites, Shelepinites and supporters of Kozlov and Podgorny. Friends of Brezhnev, cronies, clients and confederates were elected in their places, leaving Brezhnev with a favorable balance of power.

But as Brezhnev realized, that favorable power balance would mean little unless he could also change it within the Politburo. There however, he encountered resistance. All members were re-elected. Two more years were to pass before Brezhnev had the power to ease some of his opponents out of the inner circle.

Shelepin, for example, had been weakened and his eroded power base was but a shell of its former self. Yet he remained entrenched in the Politburo and at the time of writing is still in it.

Gennady Voronov, the premier of the Russian Federation, had been at odds with Brezhnev and other conservatives for some time because of his advocacy of the mechanized *zveno* system, a farm version of economic reform, which called for assigning plots of *kolkhoz* land to self-sufficient, cost-accountable teams in agriculture. His standing in the leadership had deteriorated steadily and on his sixtieth birthday, in September 1970, he was even denied the traditional Hero of Socialist Labor award. Yet, he was re-elected to the Politburo. In July 1971 he was demoted from the premiership of the RSFSR and assigned a sinecure, the chairmanship of the People's Control Committee. Even then he remained a full member of the Politburo and held on tenaciously to his seat until April 1973.

Pyotr Shelest had voiced opposition to both Brezhnev's domestic and foreign policies on the eve of the Party Congress. He, too, was to remain a member of the Politburo for another two years.

Unable to muster the necessary forces for a purge of the inner circle, Brezhnev employed an old device successfully tested by Stalin and Khrushchev: he enlarged it. But he was compelled to compromise even in that effort. Of the four additional men elected to the Politburo on the closing day of the XXIVth Party Congress in April 1971, two were his clients: Shcherbitsky and Kunayev. A third, Fyodor Kulakov, the Central Committee secretary for agriculture, was a reliable associate. The fourth, however, Viktor Grishin, party chief of Moscow, was an independent. A Politburo of fifteen members was certainly more unwieldy than one with eleven, but Brezhnev's position within it had improved.

Even more significant than the enhancement of Brezhnev's personal prestige and power at the congress was his new role as peacemaker and architect of Soviet foreign policy. Within a few months after the congress he embarked on a sensational round of personal diplomacy which opened with his private meeting with West German Chancellor Willy Brandt in September 1971.

Soviet-West German *rapprochement* had been sired by the Kremlin's economic dilemma and the putative threat from China. It was conceived together with Brezhnev's *Westpolitik* at the Warsaw Pact meeting in Budapest in March 1969.

Brezhnev's policy had several interrelated objectives: recognition of the European *status quo* and the postwar boundaries, particularly the Oder-Neisse line and the division of Germany; legitimization of Soviet suzerainty over the East European empire of buffer states which Stalin had carved out of the ruins of war; a European security conference whose purpose – besides enhancing the Soviet and diminishing the US role in Europe – would be, primarily, to reduce the military engagement and allow Moscow to transfer troops and material to the eastern frontiers; alleviation of economic pressures by reduced military preparedness as well as through greater access to West European technology and more trade.

Brezhnev was undoubtedly aware that he would have to make substantial concessions, especially on guarantees for West Berlin and regarding the position of East Germany. It was he, after all, who had suddenly decided that he needed Western Europe, not Western Europe which needed the Soviet Union.

He must have realized too that the new course was fraught with dangers. The trauma of the war with Germany, twenty-five years of cold war and propagandistic self-hypnosis had created their own world of suspicions, hatreds, vested interests, national aims and ideological shibboleths which any new policy, no matter how exigent, would have to take into account.

There was bound to be strong opposition in both the USSR and Western Europe from elements who, though ideologically at opposite ends of the pole, thought essentially along the same lines: the military-industrial complex, super patriots, cold warriors, the distrustful and the fearful, the professional haters and the orthodox ideologists. In Eastern Europe Brezhnev would have to reckon with those allies, especially East Germany, who feared that he might sacrifice their interests in favor of his own.

The first tentative feelers to Bonn had been put forth in May 1969 by Wladyslaw Gomulka who suggested a bilateral agreement on the Oder-Neisse frontier. The Polish proposal itself was not strikingly new, but it was significant for its omission of some previously familiar demands such as formal recognition of East Germany, renunciation of all claims to nuclear weapons and retroactive nullification of the 1938 Munich Pact between Hitler and Chamberlain by Bonn.

The offer languished until October 1969. Then Willy Brandt, whose vision of *Ostpolitik* neatly complemented Brezhnev's concept of *Westpolitik*, came to power in Bonn. In December Gromyko and Helmut Allardt, the West German ambassador in Moscow, opened preliminary discussions. In February 1970 the protracted negotiations between Gromyko and Brandt's advisor Egon Bahr began. The result was the Bonn-Moscow reconciliation and non-aggression treaty which Brandt signed in Moscow in August 1970.

Although it was Kosygin who shared the formal limelight with Brandt during the signing ceremony, Brezhnev had been the powerful, driving force behind the treaty and he wanted the world to know it. He stole the show from Kosygin, striding into the ornate Georgyevsky Hall for the signing ceremony, just as the TV cameras began telecasting to the nation. He shook Brandt's hand warmly, nodded to photographers, slapped his colleagues on the back and even said a few words for West German radio. During the signing procedure he stood possessively behind Kosygin's chair, then to everyone's surprise, invited Brandt to spend a few hours with him the next day before flying back to Bonn.

That treaty, however, was merely the curtain-raiser on a complex new relationship in Europe. There remained the difficult question of Berlin guarantees for which Brezhnev would have to negotiate not only with the two Germanys but also the US, Great Britain and France. Moreover, the convoluted problem of inter-German relations had yet to be dealt with and on that issue Brezhnev faced mounting opposition from an increasingly truculent Walter Ulbricht.

To understand the relationship between Ulbricht and Brezhnev it is necessary to appreciate that Ulbricht, thirteen years older than Brezhnev, had always regarded the Soviet Party chief as somewhat of an upstart – one of those junior *apparatchiki* who needed to be put in their places. He never failed to remind his younger Soviet "peers" that he had met and known Lenin personally. After all, Ulbricht had already been a secretary of the German Communist Party's Central Committee when young Leonid Brezhnev left Kamenskoye to study land reclamation in Kursk. Ulbricht's seniority in the Communist world obviously gave him great prestige and influence which he never failed to wield, often roughly, whenever he came to Moscow. That may have been human and understandable, but politically it was not very smart.

Ulbricht was not opposed to *Westpolitik* as such or to the idea of a European security conference. On the contrary, he recognized the conference idea as a perfect vehicle for enhancing the

GDR's international position. East Germany, he knew, would take part in such a conference and participation would mean *de facto* recognition of the GDR by all participants, including the United States should Washington join the talks, which seemed likely. *De facto* recognition would undoubtedly lead to *de jure* recognition from a number of participating European states.

What Ulbricht did object to was Brezhnev's *tactical* approach which raised the spectre of East German isolation within the Communist bloc itself and would force the GDR to abandon its most important demand – formal diplomatic recognition by Bonn. Ulbricht suspected, correctly, that a series of bilateral renunciation-of-force parleys, such as those which Moscow and Warsaw had initiated with Bonn in late 1969, would eventually set a precedent and ultimately compel him to hold so-called intra-German non-aggression talks with Bonn on a level below full diplomatic recognition. For Ulbricht that was tantamount to jettisoning the whole policy edifice he had constructed so carefully since the early 1950s.

As Ulbricht began dragging his feet and digging in his heels in 1970, Brezhnev decided to abandon him. Retirement on "grounds of age" in May 1971 was neatly engineered. Ulbricht's crown prince, Erich Honecker, a more tractable man, became party leader while Ulbricht stayed on as chief of state until his death in 1973.

It was against this background that Brezhnev invited Brandt to the Crimea in September 1971 for consultations. Brandt and Brezhnev cleared the air on a number of issues and exchanged views on European security, Soviet-German relations, intra-German affairs, the Berlin question, and reduction of military forces in Europe. Brezhnev apparently promised to exert more pressure on Honecker and in exchange Brandt agreed to drum up enthusiasm for Brezhnev's European security conference. As Brandt explained the difficulties he was encountering in getting the Soviet-German treaty ratified in the Bundestag, Brezhnev obviously gained some direly needed insight into how convoluted democratic political systems operate. Conversely Brandt and his aides came away from the meeting visibly impressed by Brezhnev's geniality, his total grasp of domestic problems and his willingness to learn about the problems of others.

But beyond that the meeting showed Brezhnev in an entirely new light. It was his debut in the arena of international diplomacy and he demonstrated that he was an able performer.

Moreover, it was a singular display of his immense power. None but his personal aides, including Alexandrov Agentov, and a few foreign ministry specialists assisted him and it was apparent that he felt no requirement to "check back" with anyone. The most surprising aspect was that Brezhnev seemed not the least inhibited by his lack of a government position or title. Before the visit sovietologists had wondered whether Brezhnev might not solve the protocol problem by greeting Brandt as chairman of the Social Democratic Party so as to make the meeting one between two party leaders. In fact, Brezhnev simply dropped considerations of international protocol and accepted Brandt as the "boss" of West Germany and demonstrated in no uncertain manner that he himself was the "boss" of the USSR.

A completely new Leonid Brezhnev presented himself to the world. He was even more effervescent and urbane when he appeared later that month in Belgrade and in Paris in October.

For weeks after the trip to France, treated in Moscow as the most significant event in the world at the time, Soviet news media continued to discuss it effusively as occupying the "center of international attention". Moscow television showed an hour-long documentary about the visit which, in addition to dramatizing the vigorous new Soviet diplomacy, highlighted Brezhnev's role as the nation's leading statesman. Simultaneously the film sought to reassure people that Brezhnev does not play the Khrushchevian clown abroad but acts as a restrained, dignified representative of a major power. He was shown being enthusiastically welcomed by Frenchmen (which had not been the case), chatting genially with President Pompidou, conversing earnestly with workers at a Renault automobile plant, standing alongside his portly wife Viktoria in a reception line, and walking with near-regal dignity and self-confidence down the ornate corridors of the Elysée Palace.

There was, of course, an ulterior purpose. Brezhnev was making yet another bid for the premiership, or at least some suitable substitute.

The first speculation about a new leadership crisis emanated from Western circles in August 1971 when observers began to wonder why neither the Central Committee nor the Supreme Soviet had held their annual summer meetings. The only plausible explanation seemed to be that both bodies were expected to ratify an important decision on which the Politburo had thus far failed to reach agreement. That decision could well be the lingering question of Kosygin's retirement.

Kosygin had definitely slipped a notch in the protocol standings at the Party Congress. When Brezhnev read out the names of the re-elected and newly elected Politburo members, he did not mention Kosygin second – as he had done at the XXIIIrd Party Congress in 1966 – but third, after Podgorny. Soon there were other signs. It was Podgorny who went to Cairo for a crucial meeting with President Sadat. Podgorny and Brezhnev met with the top East European leaders in the Crimea just before the Brandt visit. And instead of Kosygin, Foreign Minister Gromyko went to New Delhi to sign a friendship treaty with India's prime minister Indira Gandhi.

Then a sharp esoteric attack was launched against Kosygin on the front page of *Pravda* on 14 October. In a lead editorial the paper said: ". . . empty assurances and commitments not supported by realities, which certain staff members dispense so generously, merely undermine confidence (in those workers). Could an economic leader, for example, really count upon genuine esteem if he promises year after year to guarantee the introduction of new technology and to improve the working and living conditions of the workers but does practically nothing?"

By the middle of November Western kremlinologists were reporting a full-scale debate in *Pravda* and some of the theoretical party journals over the question of reuniting party and government leadership under one man, presumably Brezhnev. The main protagonists in this between-the-lines and esoterically worded discussion were Pyotr Fedoseyev, director of the Institute of Marxism-Leninism, who appeared to be advocating Brezhnev's assumption of both positions, and Mikhail Suslov, who was arguing strenuously for continued separation of party and government powers.

On or about 19 November, a compromise – to enhance Brezhnev's prestige and power without loss of face to Kosygin –

seems to have been reached or offered by the Brezhnev faction. It was on that day that correspondents in Moscow and some East European capitals received tips that the forthcoming Central Committee plenum and Supreme Soviet session might create a state council, similar to those in Romania and East Germany, whose chairman – Brezhnev – would become the "president" of the USSR. One Yugoslav report even linked this intended reorganization with a "desire to increase the efficiency of administering state and primarily economic affairs". The advantages seemed obvious: Kosygin would not have to step down formally as premier, Brezhnev could assume direct control of the Government, and a Central Committee floor fight over Dmitry Polyansky's future rule could be avoided.

But something must have gone awry, for several days later, on the eve of the 22 November Central Committee plenum, foreign correspondents in Moscow were being told that discussion of a state council had been "premature". When the Central Committee met, everything remained as it had been. To demonstrate his strength – or Kosygin's weakness – Brezhnev took it upon himself to sum up the economic debate at the two-day plenum. But the only personnel change in the top leadership was the promotion of Mikhail Solomentsev, Voronov's successor as prime minister of the RSFSR, to candidate membership in the Politburo.

Brezhnev had obviously suffered yet another reversal in his relentless drive to assume the mantle of both the party and government leadership as Lenin, Stalin and Khrushchev had done before him. But he would have little time to worry or brood about it. Other developments were soon to preoccupy him.

Foreign affairs and Brezhnev's peace offensive had been one of the main issues under discussion at the November Central Committee plenum. During the last two weeks of 1971 virtually the entire leadership – Politburo members, candidates and Central Committee secretaries – toured the country in a determined bid to win support for the new line. They delivered forty-two speeches in almost as many cities.

No doubt there were many critics and skeptics, but the most outspoken, unquestionably, was the Ukraine's Pyotr Shelest.

Shelest had been opposing the Politburo majority on the question of *rapprochement* with Bonn for some time and in October 1971 visited East Berlin as head of a parliamentary delegation to express his obsession with the notion that the treaties with Bonn would cause splits among the Communist countries, especially between the GDR and the USSR. A month later, during an ideological conference he had convened in Kiev, he returned to his theme.

Alone among the touring Politburo members in December, Shelest did not speak in his own home base. Instead, Podgorny rushed to Kiev to give the talk in support of *Westpolitik* while Shelest's role on the platform was reduced to that of a spectator. Eventually, of course, he did his duty and delivered *one* address – in Voroshilovgrad, a provincial backwater with 380,000 population.

Shelest, however, was merely the very bald-headed tip of an iceberg that threatened to capsize Brezhnev's foreign policy. For in the winter and spring of 1972, as he could do little more than watch Willy Brandt fight it out with his own Christian Democrat opposition, Brezhnev embarked on the even riskier course of *rapprochement* with Washington and a summit meeting with Nixon.

As Brezhnev moved relentlessly toward that historic encounter with the President of the United States, he appeared to be a man obsessed, completely oblivious of the ground swell of criticism around him, seemingly blind to the challenge and affronts Nixon was delivering by mining North Vietnam's harbors.

Even Brezhnev's friends and neighbors backed away. The navy chief, Admiral Gorshkov, reportedly suggested sending in mine-sweepers to clear the ports, but Brezhnev told him not to. Grechko spoke of the "growing aggressiveness of imperialism, and primarily American imperialism". Andropov warned ominously that "we certainly have no illusions and are not exaggerating the possibilities of cooperation".

All this is not to say that Brezhnev was not trying other foreign policy approaches as well. On 20 March, for example, at the Soviet Trade Union Congress, he once more offered the carrot of cooperation to China, emboldened no doubt by his new assistant, Konstantin Rusakov.

"Official Chinese representatives tell us," said Brezhnev, "that relations between the USSR and the Chinese Peoples' Republic must be based on the principle of peaceful coexistence. Well, if that is the most Peking can offer to another socialist state, then we are ready to build Soviet-Chinese relations on that basis, too." But Peking was not interested.

Brezhnev's showdown with his critics took place a few days before Nixon's arrival in Moscow. On 19 May the Central Committee met to "approve entirely" Brezhnev's foreign policy report. Presumably it also took cognizance of Shelest's demotion, for on 21 May his appointment as one of the USSR's nine deputy prime ministers was announced. The decisive issue, according to some reports, had been Shelest's refusal to greet Nixon on his scheduled visit to Kiev or shake "a hand bloodied in Vietnam". Within four days Vladimir Shcherbitsky was to be named party leader of the Ukraine. Brezhnev had every reason to be in a jubilant mood.

Only Brezhnev knows how he felt on the afternoon of Monday, 22 May 1972; when Richard Nixon walked into the austere Kremlin office for an unscheduled, private preliminary meeting to a week of summitry. It had been more than twelve years since they had last seen each other in less auspicious circumstances during the "kitchen debate". They had been equals then, they were equals again. Both had grown in stature and both had undoubtedly walked a long political distance since that time when polemics and shouted insults seemed a proper way to settle international affairs.

The summit was everything Brezhnev could have asked for. An entire series of minor and major agreements were signed. They ranged from pacts for cooperative and coordinated research on environmental problems and cancer to the first phase of the strategic arms limitation treaty. A joint declaration of principles was issued. It embraced broad but hopeful pledges that both sides would do "their utmost to avoid military confrontations", would "always exercise restraint in their mutual relations", and would refrain from attempts "to obtain unilateral advantage at the expense of the other". The principle of "peaceful coexistence" was reaffirmed as the sole framework for relations in the nuclear age. Both Brezhnev and Nixon underscored the need for "reciprocal" reductions of armed forces and armaments in Europe and expressed their support for a European conference on security. Nixon even held out prospects for more trade and Soviet access to some advanced US technology.

Perhaps what pleased Brezhnev most was the Cadillac which Nixon gave him to add to his already impressive collection of foreign cars: the Rolls-Royce, a Renault and a Citroen-Maserati.

At one point during the final reception in the Kremlin's Georgyevsky Hall, Nixon talked about some of the words he had learned during his stay in Moscow. "As we made these agreements," the President explained, "I would say 'OK' and he would ask 'What does that mean?' And after I told him, he would say '*khorosho*.' But now when we agree I say '*khorosho*' and Mr Brezhnev says 'OK'." Then, turning to Brezhnev, Nixon asked: "Is that right?" And Brezhnev replied, "OK".

Unfortunately for Leonid Brezhnev, everything was not OK. After the summit came the summer of his discontent. The metereological combination was the familiar one: a long, severe winter with insufficient snow cover which had destroyed much of the winter wheat; a dry-heat wave which swept the central black soil zone and the grain lands north of the Caucasus to destroy much of the spring planting and the potato crop. The result was a failure which *kolkhozniki* and government officials unanimously described as "the most catastrophic in a century".

Brezhnev faced virtually the same dilemma that had confronted Khrushchev in 1963. He arranged to purchase 28 million tons of grain from Western capitalist countries – more than 60 percent of that amount from the United States – at an estimated total cost of $2 billion. The Soviet people were never informed about it, though. Then he stumped the virgin lands in a desperate effort to drive in what, eventually, was a record crop in Kazakhstan that helped somewhat to offset the failure in the Ukraine and the Northern Caucasus. By late fall he could at least report a harvest of almost 168 million tons of grain. Although that was 22 million tons short of the 1972 plan target, it still equaled the average harvest during the previous (1966–70) *pyatiletka*.

But it was not enough to prevent trouble. As early as August 1972 the Soviet press and propaganda mechanism had been cranked up to caution the public to save on bread and potatoes and to warn against hoarding. By March 1973 the situation had deteriorated to a degree where officials were publicly confirming that some basic commodities, including butter and potatoes, were being rationed in some parts of the country, including the industrial cities of Gorky, Volgograd and Astrakhan. Not even under Khrushchev had matters been quite that bad.

The worst news, however, was disclosed at the December 1972 Supreme Soviet meeting. Predictably, the weather and the harvest had taken their toll on the economy as a whole. But the extent to which growth rates had been affected was shocking. In every category with the exception of labor productivity, 1972 was worse even than 1969. Gross industrial product had increased by only 6.5 percent; national income by only 4 percent and agricultural gross product had actually declined by 5 percent.

For the Soviet Union's long-suffering consumers the greatest disappointment was the news that those industries which were expected to raise the standard of living had fallen the furthest behind. The textiles branch registered only fractional increases and shoe production fell off by 4 percent. The supply of television sets, radios, tape recorders and record players improved only marginally and the construction industry, as it had consistently since 1961, once again failed to meet its targets for new housing.

The fervent hopes of the XXIVth Party Congress had been dashed. The great new deal for the consumers which Brezhnev had heralded became just another of many unfulfilled Soviet promises. The targets for the 1971–75 *pyatiletka* were sharply reduced and drastic cutbacks in the 1973 growth plans were imposed. The severest curtailment of all, however, was for the consumer goods sector.

To underscore the shift of emphasis from consumer to producer goods, Vladimir Dolgikh, a hard-nosed metallurgist who is no friend of Brezhnev, was named Central Committee secretary for heavy industry to replace Solomentsev.

This time Brezhnev found it difficult to lay the blame all on Kosygin. After all, whose plan had it been? Scapegoats were nonetheless found. Vladimir Matskevich, the luckless minister of agriculture, was sacked in February 1973. Dmitry Polyansky, who lost his title as first deputy prime minister in the process, was appointed to replace him. For Polyansky, the one-time Khrushchev "golden boy" and erstwhile pretender to Kosygin's premiership, it was the first step down the ladder.

Brezhnev's main concern, however, remained foreign affairs and during the spring of 1973 he seemed obsessed with the idea that improved relations with the United States and West Germany would also solve his domestic economic difficulties. He embarked on what for a Soviet leader could only be a most daring course: Brezhnev made plans to visit both Bonn and Washington.

In April 1973, just a few weeks before his scheduled departure for Bonn, Brezhnev did what he had done just before Nixon's arrival in Moscow. He convened a plenum of the Central Committee to obtain its backing for his foreign policy once more.

In many ways it may have been the most important plenum of recent years, for it was a major step towards finally establishing Brezhnev's dominant position in the Politburo. For the first time since Khrushchev's fall two members were purged from that tightly knit circle of Soviet oligarchs: Shelest and Voronov. But even more surprising, three new men were added to it: Grechko, Andropov and Soviet Foreign Minister Andrei Gromyko.

Those promotions were nothing short of sensational. Grechko's elevation marked the first time since 1957 that a Soviet defense minister had been a member of the Politburo; Gromyko's the first time a foreign minister had belonged to it since 1956, the era of Vyacheslav Molotov. And Andropov's promotion revived a tradition that had been broken with Lavrenti Beria's fall in 1953. One could well ask whether Soviet history had come full circle.

What did those changes mean for Brezhnev? With Grechko and Andropov, two of his personal friends had joined the ranks of the Party's top executive and policy-making body. And with Gromyko, the USSR's foreign minister since 1957, Brezhnev had obviously added an ardent supporter for his *Westpolitik*.

But once again there were signs that Brezhnev had been compelled to compromise. Personal friendship notwithstanding, it is obvious from their public statements that neither Andropov nor Grechko quite share Brezhnev's enthusiasm for *rapprochement* with the West. On the other hand, there may have been an ulterior motive for their promotion. As members of the Politburo they become party to the political decision-making process and share responsibility for it. For them to criticize the adopted policy then becomes difficult.

Shelest's and Voronov's demotions and the addition of two close allies such as Grechko and Andropov obviously gives Brezhnev a more stable majority. But he could not have been happy with the size of the Politburo – the largest since Stalin's death, or the fact that the even number of members, theoretically at least, made it prone to tie votes.

As sovietologists sought to analyze the developments, pondering whether and when other Politburo heads might roll, Brezhnev arrived in Bonn for a political performance that left most observers stunned and convinced that further discussion about his role and power was superfluous.

Until two hours before his plane touched down at Bonn-Cologne airport, West German officials were still arguing the protocol question of whether or not to give Brezhnev a formal gun salute. The field pieces were already in place when Bonn's Foreign Minister Walter Scheel prevailed with his argument, that since Brezhnev was neither head of government nor chief of state a salute would be improper.

Chancellor Brandt solved the problem neatly by welcoming Brezhnev at plane-side as "the first man in the Soviet Union". Brezhnev's behavior during the next five days left no doubt that this is what he really is. Exuding confidence and displaying complete command of nearly every situation, Brezhnev demonstrated that even without the titles his power and authority are virtually unchallenged. Although accompanied by Gromyko, several government ministers and a small army of advisors and experts, not to mention twenty bodyguards, he was acting entirely on his own and told his German hosts in as many words that he had the authorization to do so.

"The policy I am pursuing here," he said on one occasion, "has been unanimously approved by the Central Committee. That means I have 15 million party members, 32 million *Komsomoly* and the 250 million people of the USSR behind me."

Brezhnev seemed to waver only once when Scheel, contending that Moscow might be fulfilling the letter but not the spirit of the four-power agreement on Berlin, told him: "Mr Secretary-General, let's make nails with heads on them and set down in the final communiqué what we both see as the spirit of the agreement. My people expect that." Upon that note Brezhnev retired to his suite in the Petersberg Hotel overlooking the Rhine and, according to reliable sources, put in a call to Moscow over his direct phone line. Presumably he conferred with other Politburo members. During his next session with Scheel he said: "I don't want any troubles in Berlin and you don't either. What we both want is mutual understanding. So that settles Berlin. And what I need now is a drink."

As nearly 800 German and foreign journalists jostled each other for the right to get closer to him, Brezhnev visibly basked in the publicity and obviously enjoyed every moment of his new power and the attention he was getting. The real litmus test of his position, however, was not the exposure he was getting in the West but back home in Moscow. And that was considerable. Most of his visit was covered live by Soviet television and for a week his photographs, name and stories of his activities dominated the official press.

Although the trip to West Germany confirmed Brezhnev's position as the USSR's supreme ruler, it must also be viewed in historical context. Considering the ballast of past strife and enmity that has beleaguered relations between Bonn and Moscow, Brezhnev proved not only daring in undertaking the trip but by accepting the hand of reconciliation which Willy Brandt offered him, went a long way toward influencing the course of history for years to come.

In many respects the visit to the US a month later was even more daring and historically significant. Rushing to the side of an American president weakened and shattered by a massive scandal – the Watergate affair – was risky indeed. But the outcome of the summit meeting – a nuclear non-aggression agreement between the United States and the Soviet Union – was momentous. For all practical purposes it codified the end of a quarter century of cold war between the two superpowers.

The journey to America demonstrated something else as well. Notwithstanding centuries of isolation from the mainstream of

Western culture and more than five decades of tense, mutual distrust, Russians and Americans may have more in common and may sense a closer affinity toward one another than Russians and Europeans or Americans and Europeans. The personal rapport between Brezhnev and Nixon – both essentially self-made men, both tough and pragmatic politicians who have boxed and elbowed their way to the pinnacles of their respective power pyramids – was evident from the minute Brezhnev's helicopter landed on the White House lawn. In the United States, though he saw little of the people or the country, Leonid Brezhnev obviously felt at home and acted accordingly.

"It seems inconceivable," said one Western diplomat with extensive Moscow experience, "that this is the same man whom we wrote off as a faceless *apparatchik*, as a compromise candidate, after Khrushchev's fall. How much further is he going to go?"

That question may well have been asked in Moscow, too. It is not just coincidence that two days after Brezhnev's return from the US *Pravda* published an anonymous and cryptically worded article reminding its readers of the evils of the "cult of personality" and the need for the principle of collectivity in leadership.

A gentle hint to Leonid Brezhnev? Perhaps More gentle, at any rate, than the dispute which broke out between Suslov and Shcherbitsky over Brezhnev's role in foreign policy.

In a speech to the Ukrainian conference of newspaper editors in July 1973 Shcherbitsky went out of his way to praise Brezhnev for his summit performance, describing it as an "event of great international significance importance." Recapitulating Brezhnev's personal role, Shcherbitsky reminded his listeners how "tirelessly and purposefully Leonid Ilyich Brezhnev worked," carrying out "this peace mission with dignity and confidence."

Suslov, on the other hand, addressing a group of Communist dignitaries in the Kremlin three days later, mentioned the "enormous constructive work of the Politburo" in the field of foreign affairs and obliquely mentioned Brezhnev's "personal contribution" in this sphere, pointedly avoiding the adjective "great" which the Central Committee itself had used to describe Brezhnev's role just before he went to the U.S.

A careful reading of the lines revealed other criticism of Brezhnev and his foreign policy in the summer of 1973. His difficulties were due partly to his failure to obtain the trade deals and concessions, such as "most favored nation status" from the US Congress, on which his *Westpolitik* counted. Concurrently positions in the West were hardening: in the US over the issue of Jewish emigration and Kremlin attitudes toward intellectual freedom, in Bonn over Moscow's stance on Berlin.

In August and September there may even have been a concerted effort by Soviet hardliners to scuttle Brezhnev and torpedo his *Westpolitik* with an unusually harsh and hysterical campaign against dissenters such as Alexander Solzhenitsyn and Professor Andrei Sakharov, the outspoken father of the Soviet H-bomb, and a Stalin-style show trial of two prominent dissidents, Pyotr Yakir and Viktor Krasin. The drive, more frenetic than any Brezhnev himself had sanctioned, began when he went on his annual vacation and ended abruptly on his return to Moscow, suggesting that he disapproved of it. Many sovietologists saw it as a deliberate attempt by opponents of his policy to discredit by alienating public opinion abroad. And it was partially successful, providing opponents of disengagement in the West with fresh arguments. To many Western observers the mysterious events in August and September of 1973 seemed remarkably similar to the U-2 spy plane incident which had been used to torpedo Khrushchev's embryonic *Westpolitik* in 1960.

There were domestic troubles, too. Although the economy was performing better and a grain harvest of 186 million tons, 20 million more than in 1972, was expected, the harvest was still 10 million tons short of the planned target. Once again wheat purchases abroad seemed likely and once again Brezhnev toured the country personally to supervise the harvest effort.

Hopping from *oblast* to *oblast*, from *kolkhoz* to *kolkhoz* to support the "battle for grain" in Kazakhstan, Brezhnev certainly exuded confidence. But only the future can tell how justified that air of confidence was.

CHAPTER XVII

Of Friends and Foes

At first sight the Soviet political system strikes most observers as an alien, unfathomable labyrinth that defies comparison with anything in the West. In many ways it is, but there is one possible analogy: New York's Tammany Hall.

At its height, Tammany represented the embodiment of bossism, that is, a system of political control centering around a single powerful figure – the boss – and a complex organization of lesser figures – the machine – linked together by reciprocity in promoting their various interests. Not all the bosses were bad. But all of them were powerful. To obtain some idea of the Soviet system one should imagine a "super-Tammany" with political monopoly exercising virtually unchallenged control of the press, the police, the economy, the military, the judiciary, even the cultural establishment.

Leonid Ilyich Brezhnev is the Soviet "boss" today. He got where he is through patronage, intrigue, manipulation, maneuvering and political influence peddling – practices endemic to all societies and all political structures. But nowhere have they been developed to such a degree as in the Soviet Union today. And no one – Khrushchev excepted perhaps – has proven himself such a master of it as Brezhnev. Since the 1930s he has been a textbook example of how Soviet politicians can win friends and influence people to form the power base that vaults them – and keeps them – in the inner sanctum of the Kremlin.

The heart of his political machine is the Dnieper Mafia. Those men – graduates, like Brezhnev, of the Dneprodzerzhinsk and Dnepropetrovsk metallurgical institutes, former engineers and directors in the Dnieper Bend factories, *apparatchiki* in Dnepropetrovsk and Zaporozhe *oblasts* – whose attention Brezhnev caught when he was younger and who caught Brezhnev's attention when they were young. They are the men who helped him to power, just as he helped them; the men who keep him in power, just as he sustains them. Some are older than Brezhnev, some are younger; some have retired from public life on pensions, others have died. Over the decades the "mafia" has grown as the lesser men in it created their own machines which depend on their power and – ultimately – on Brezhnev's. It has also been extended, beyond the narrow geographical confines of the Dnieper Bend, to include those figures whom Brezhnev met, befriended, enlisted or sponsored at the various stations of his political life: Moldavia, Kazakhstan, the armed forces, the Central Committee apparatus and the Supreme Soviet Presidium.

Brezhnev's political machine is undoubtedly a precision instrument. But its smooth operation is not the only explanation for his durability. Another may well be that, unlike Lenin, Stalin and Khrushchev, he has never chosen an heir.

Unquestionably, Brezhnev's reluctance to name a crown prince is a mark of his political prudence. The history of the Communist Party of the Soviet Union, as he probably realizes, burgeons with cases of successors-designate who ultimately challenged the authority of their patrons. But the absence of an heir apparent also poses enormous problems. With each day that passes, the succession question looms larger and threatens to become more difficult to resolve.

At the end of 1973 Brezhnev was in office for more than nine years and celebrated his sixty-seventh birthday. In an era of steadily rising life expectancy that is hardly tantamount to hoariness and one need merely look a bit further afield to find politicians who would consider Brezhnev a youngster. Nevertheless, the fact remains that he presides over a gerontocracy.

Yet, he is the chief of a party with more than 14 million members of whom more than half are under forty years of age. This younger generation constitutes the disenfranchised and unrepresented majority of the Party whose leaders – in the Central Committee, on the republican and even on the *oblast* levels – are for the most part men in their fifties and sixties.

The generational imbalance has been allowed to grow to such proportions that a normal evolutionary turnover of membership is no longer possible. No one can predict when that imbalance may become the epicenter of conflict within the Party, but the potential grows with each year that the old guard clings to power.

The average age of the Politburo's full members is 63, that of the candidates 59. The youngest member of either group is still Shelepin, now 55. The only new blood infused into the hierarchy since 1968 consists of two Central Committee secretaries: Katushev, now 46, and Vladimir Dolgikh, 49. The Soviet leadership, that is the twenty-five men who comprise the Politburo and the Secretariat, are, as a collective, the oldest in Eastern Europe. Yet it is from this collective that Brezhnev's successor must come. As time passes the choice narrows.

Among Western sovietologists it has been postulated that, upon his accession to power, the party chief of the future would have to be a man who is a full member of the Politburo, of Russian nationality, in his middle to late fifties – as Brezhnev was in 1964 – and a man with relatively broad experience in domestic and foreign affairs, in agriculture and industry, in state or government affairs as well as party matters. Moreover, he would also have to be a leader with a reasonable power base and a career which is recognizably on the ascent. If those criteria are as valid in the Kremlin as Western experts believe them to be, then there are very few Brezhnevs waiting in the wings.

The only man who meets all but one of these standards is Aleksandr Shelepin. He is a Russian, he is young enough and he certainly has the breadth of experience. The major factor against him is that his career has been on the decline steadily since 1965 and that his carefully constructed power base has been decimated over the years. This does not put him totally out of the running, however. Brezhnev's own career and that of his closest Politburo cronies – Kirilenko, Kunayev and Shcherbitsky – attest to that. Weaker and less ambitious men than Shelepin have bounced back from political disgrace and defeat. Until Shelepin loses his seat in the Politburo he must be regarded as in the running and it would be imprudent to simply dismiss him.

No doubt, Brezhnev's own choice – and that of the "mafia"

would be Vladimir Shcherbitsky. He certainly meets most of the presumed qualifications. Born in 1918, he is the right age. He has twice been prime minister of the USSR's second largest republic and now he is its party chief. He has even had some experience abroad, having traveled to the Communist countries and accompanied Kosygin to Turkey in 1966. But his greatest disadvantage, and one that he may be unable to overcome, is his nationality. Shcherbitsky is a Ukrainian and it would be surprising if a Ukrainian became party leader in a country where national rivalries and animosities are playing an ever larger role. But there can be a first time for everything.

The nationality question works to even greater disadvantage for Dinmukhamed Kunayev, a Kazakh by passport although his mother is believed to have been Russian. Though Lenin himself was one quarter Kalmyk, it seems inconceivable that an Asian could become secretary general of the CPSU, at least under present circumstances. Moreover, Kunayev is already sixty-one. But in every other respect he fills the qualifications.

Kirill Mazurov, fifty-nine, is another leader dogged by the nationality issue. He is a Byelorussian. But that is virtually the only mark against this erstwhile World War Two partisan fighter whose ties to the military may be as good, if not better than Brezhnev's. And faced with a decision between a Ukrainian and a White Russian, the great Russian majority of the establishment might opt for the latter. Mazurov, in a word, has always had a lot going for him. Since Polyansky's demotion in February 1973, leaving Mazurov as Kosygin's *only first* deputy premier, he has had even more going.

In a sense Mazurov is even a Dnieper man, for he was born along the river's upper reaches, in a village near Gomel in the southeastern corner of Byelorussia where the republic's frontier meets with those of Russia and the Ukraine. Mazurov's parents were peasants and his education was limited. He completed a technical high school for motor transport and a correspondence course of the Party Higher School. He made his career almost entirely through the Party. He began the war in uniform, but after being wounded was delegated to organize partisan resistance behind the German lines. After the war he climbed rapidly and by 1953 was named prime minister of Byelorussia. In 1956 he became party chief, a post he held until he was called to Moscow as first deputy prime minister in 1965 and elevated to full Politburo membership.

Byelorussia, like the Ukraine, is a member of the United Nations and Mazurov in his capacity as premier and party chief has represented his state in numerous international conferences. In fact, since 1953, he has traveled more and further abroad than most other members of the present Soviet leadership. He has repeatedly been entrusted with strategically important and politically delicate foreign missions, from Afghanistan to North Korea, from Vietnam to the Middle East.

What Mazurov displays in apparent drive, energy and ambition, Viktor Grishin who is fifty-nine, seems to lack. But Grishin at least is a Russian. His career, even by Soviet standards, has been highly unspectacular. Born in Serpukhov, about fifty miles south of Moscow, he attended two vocational high schools in tandem: the Moscow Geodetic Technicum, from which he graduated in 1932 and the Moscow Technicum for Locomotive Traction, which he completed in 1937. His military service was limited to a peacetime stint in the army. By 1942 he was in party work in Serpukhov, initially as the city's second, then its first secretary. In 1950 he arrived in Moscow and began climbing up the ladder of the Moscow City Party committee – traditionally one of the most important political power bases in the USSR. In 1956 he became head of the Soviet trade union council, the post he held until 1967 when he replaced Shelepin's protégé Nikolai Yegorichev as Moscow City Party chief and Shelepin became the trade union leader. Grishin has seen a bit of the world and he is urbane by Soviet standards. But is he a future leader of his country and his party? Except for his spectacular promotion to full Politburo membership at the XXIVth Party Congress, he would not be entitled to a place in the sweepstakes.

Almost the same can be said of the other Russian Politburo member, Fyodor Kulakov, fifty-five, who by-passed the traditional candidate status, jumping right into the inner circle while retaining his Central Committee secretaryship for agriculture. Kulakov's rise through the party hierarchy, including his spectacular demotion at Khrushchev's hands in 1960, has been exclusively as an agricultural expert.

Among the Politburo's candidate members only two men deserve consideration: Mikhail Solomentsev, sixty, the prime minister of the Russian Federation, and Pyotr Demichev, fifty-five, Khrushchev's former chemical tsar who is now the Central Committee secretary for cultural matters. Both are Russians.

Of the two, Solomentsev definitely appears to be the harder-driving. A protégé of Frol Kozlov, he is a heavy industry man who built his party career in the 1950s in Chelyabinsk, a Kozlov fief, and became first secretary of Karaganda *oblast* in Kazakhstan in 1959. Three years later, in 1962, when Kozlov swept the Kazakhstan organization of Brezhnev's men, demoting Kunayev, Solomentsev was named the republic's second secretary. One of Brezhnev's first acts after Khrushchev's fall was to purge Solomentsev who ended up as party chief of Rostov *oblast*. In 1966 Solomentsev made a striking comeback. He was appointed chief of the CPSU Central Committee's heavy industry department and elected a Central Committee secretary. That remained his job until he succeeded Gennady Voronov as prime minister of the RSFSR in July 1971 and became a candidate membership in the Politburo soon after. He is a man Brezhnev would like to keep at a distance, but a man to watch despite his age.

Demichev's name has cropped up over the years whenever the succession question has been discussed. He has had a varied career. Born in Kaluga *oblast*, adjacent to Moscow, he is a graduate of both the Mendeleev Institute of Chemical Technology and the Higher Party School. In other words, he is both technician and *apparatchik*. His party career has centered on Moscow where he was *obkom* chief from 1959 to 1960 and first secretary of the Moscow City Party committee from 1960 to 1963. Then Khrushchev made him head of the Central Committee's bureau for light and chemical industry to spearhead and supervise the chemicalization campaign. He remained in that position until after Khrushchev's fall when the bureau was abolished and he took over the cultural affairs department which he still runs.

Another man whose name comes up repeatedly in any discussion of the succession problem is Konstantin Katushev, the youngest of the present Kremlin team. When and how he first met Brezhnev is difficult to say, but his career since the mid-1960s has been dependent and highly spectacular. A brilliant student and an even more brilliant automobile designer and engineer, Katushev had established a nationwide reputation in automobile circles by the time he was twenty-five. As chief engineer in the Gorky Automobile Plant, he also slid into party work and in 1964 was named first secretary of the Gorky city committee. Coldly efficient and ruthless, he apparently made many enemies in that city of 1.2 million.

In the fall of 1965, when Katushev was nominated as *oblast* first secretary to replace Mikhail Yefremov who had been named a deputy prime minister, local opposition mounted and there were hints of scandal, including talk about favoritism, rising juvenile delinquency and drunkenness in Gorky. Katushev's election was blocked and delayed and in December 1965 Brezhnev personally traveled to Gorky to supervise Katushev's installation as *obkom* secretary. In April 1968 Brezhnev brought Katushev to Moscow as Central Committee secretary for relations with other Communist countries, the position he has filled ever since.

Katushev is, of course, just a member of the Secretariat. His future prospects depend on when and whether he becomes a member of the Politburo. That day does not seem far off, however. Morover, he is a Russian and he is younger than any of his peers.

Ultimately the decision of a successor may depend on who controls the cadres department of the Central Committee apparatus. In fact it is Brezhnev himself, though nominally it is Ivan Kapitonov, fifty-eight, a Central Committee secretary. Brezhnev, who understands the importance of the cadres job, has carefully thwarted Kapitonov's promotion to either candidate or full Politburo status.

One thing, however, is certain. If he is still alive and around when the decision of who succeeds Brezhnev has to be made, Mikhail Suslov will, as so often since 1947, be in on the decision-making process.

Part Six

OF CULTS AND PERSONALITIES

Lenin demonstrated how to run the State.
Stalin demonstrated how not to run the State.
Khrushchev tried to show that anyone can
run the State.
Brezhnev is trying to demonstrate that the
State does not have to be run at all.

Overheard in Moscow 1970

CHAPTER XVIII

The Enigma Unraveled?

Who and what is Leonid Ilyich Brezhnev?

The politician is omnipresent. His portrait is on the wall of nearly every government and party office from Brest-Litovsk to Vladivostok. It is held aloft, icon-like, by thousands of marchers each 1 May and 7 November. It hangs in super-dimensional form from the façades of public buildings on important state occasions and holidays. His name appears in *Pravda, Izvestia* and countless other Soviet newspapers every day. It is mentioned on radio and television several times daily. It appears in headlines and has become a household word around the globe. His speeches are mandatory reading for millions. His books stand on the shelves of all libraries in the USSR.

But Brezhnev, the man, is – or at least until a few years ago, was – largely an enigma, hidden behind a deliberately woven veil of obfuscation. The image he has projected abroad still differs markedly from that which he displays at home where he remains remote from the 250 million he rules. Even those myriad portraits that have flooded the land provide little hint of the human being they represent. All schematically two-dimensional, they depict the face of a man in his mid-forties to early fifties – devoid of wrinkles, the tell-tale streaks of gray in his hair and the heaviness of his jowls retouched so as to obliterate the passage of time.

The press briefing he held for eleven Moscow-based American correspondents on the eve of his departure for the US was precedent-shattering. Only eighteen months earlier, during his first trip to France, Brezhnev had deliberately avoided holding a press conference. When Robert Kaiser, Moscow correspondent of the *Washington Post*, asked a Soviet official why, he was told: "Some people don't like them, you know. You have a multi-millionaire in America: I think his name is Hughes. He doesn't like press conferences either, isn't that right. Not that I want to make comparisons . . ." But the comparison is there. Leonid Brezhnev, on the whole, is a reclusive man. At least he seemed that way until the spring of 1973 when he went to West Germany and the US where his legendary aversion to the press turned into a publicity quest that kept both reporters and bodyguards running breathlessly to keep pace with his demands for exposure and yet more exposure.

Brezhnev is different things to different people. He looks forbidding to some. "Just like my husband," Madame Pompidou allegedly remarked to Brezhnev on their first meeting in Moscow in October 1970. That is because of Brezhnev's fierce-looking bushy eyebrows which have provided numerous opportunities to world cartoonists whenever they wanted to vent their anger at a given Soviet policy. It is easy to make him appear more satanic than the devil himself.

But, as Madame Pompidou added, Brezhnev is no more fierce than her own husband who has the same bushy-browed look. In fact, she found Brezhnev "very charming and polite, especially to the ladies". Brezhnev, who accepted the compliment graciously, ascribed that attribute to his mother's influence on him. Women especially seem to take to him and those who have met him speak of his gentlemanly ways and of the strong impression he makes on them. Clearly, Brezhnev is also attracted to them. During a White House reception when a Broadway chorus sang "There is Nothing Like a Dame", Brezhnev responded with enthusiastic applause and proclaimed loudly: "I agree wholeheartedly. There is nothing better in the world than women." When he first met Chancellor Brandt's attractive Norwegian wife, Rut, he gallantly kissed her hand and showered her with compliments. "You are the first person I am going to invite to Moscow," he said. And after a formal state banquet he settled down on a sofa next to her and announced for the world to hear: "All Moscow will lie at your feet."

Observers who have spent some time with him report that what comes across is "his dimpled smile and almost boyish exuberance". Henry Kissinger allegedly found "common philosophical ground" with him. Occasionally, when his guard is down, Brezhnev even displays disarmingly naïve innocence. Looking up at six-foot-three-inch US Ambassador Jacob D. Beam at a Kremlin reception in October 1969, Brezhnev said: "I guess you really are pretty tall."

He is certainly a hard-working man. Trained in the era of Stalin, who pursued a nocturnal schedule and compelled his aides to emulate him, Brezhnev, even at sixty-six, thinks nothing of putting in a series of sixteen-hour days.

Every weekday morning at 8.45 – unless he is out of town or staying in his country dacha – his Rolls-Royce or a low-slung black ZIL 114 preceded by a KGB Chaika and followed by another security car speeds out of the courtyard of the Stalin-baroque-style apartment house on Kutuzovski Prospekt. Traffic is held up and the convoy turns sharply left onto the avenue and then races down the wide center lane – reserved for emergency vehicles and the cars of the Soviet elite – towards either the Kremlin or the nearby Central Committee building on Staraya Ploshad. Brezhnev has offices in both and push-button intercom connections between them. It would depend on the day of the week to which he would go first. Tuesdays are reserved for Secretariat meetings in the Central Committee headquarters. On Thursdays the Politburo goes into session at 3 p.m. in the Kremlin in a conference room not far from Lenin's old office.

Diplomats and correspondents, like this writer, who lived in the foreigners' compound at 7 Kutuzovski Prospekt, two blocks down the boulevard from *dom Brezhneva* – Brezhnev's house – could set their watches by his rigid morning schedule.

By his own admission, Brezhnev is a man who lets visitors interrupt his work. "When I know there's someone waiting for me outside in the receptionist's office," Brezhnev told *Der Stern*'s Henri Nannen, "I can't concentrate. I feel compelled to talk to whoever is there to visit me and I put whatever I'm working on aside."

That is one reason why Brezhnev rarely quits work before 10.30 p.m. and usually takes a briefcase full of papers and documents home to read. Moreover, he is one of those kind of men who abhor formal schedules. When a conversation or a subject fascinate him, he is inclined to keep on talking and discussing until the early morning hours. He usually eats both lunch and supper at his office or in one of the dining rooms of the Kremlin or the Central Committee building

His office in the Kremlin, adjacent to the Politburo room, is large and austere, devoid of decoration or any hints of personal taste. Wainscoted with silk wallpaper and a crystal chandelier, a portrait of Lenin and of Marx, it is dominated by a huge, modern leather-topped desk. Brezhnev sits facing the door to his receptionist's office. Behind him is what appears to be a glass-fronted, built-in cabinet – a "secret" passageway to a small bedroom, equipped with telephones and TV set, where he can relax in private or take a nap.

The office in the Central Committee building is only slightly more cheerful. Its only decorations are portraits of Marx and Lenin, without whom, Brezhnev says, he cannot work, a wood-inlay picture of Lenin, a yard-high bronze figure group with a revolutionary motif and a scattering of many books and pamphlets.

Brezhnev is a tidy desk man. Important papers are usually filed away in folders which are stacked neatly. There are no nicknacks, no souvenirs: just a looseleaf calendar printed on banknote paper; a lucite holder for small pieces of scratch paper; a small, square-shaped brass clock, card file and pen with dip-in inkwell.

And, of course, there is an ashtray, for Brezhnev is – and has been for decades – a chain smoker: one of those men who lights a new cigarette with the glowing butt of the last one. His trademark is an amber holder and his proudest possession appears to be his cigarette case with built-in timer and lock. When he wants to cut down on his smoking he can set the timer so that the case opens only after a certain period. During the first personal interview he ever gave – to Pierre Durand of the French Communist daily *L'Humanité* in October 1971 – Brezhnev had set the case to open only every forty-five minutes and proclaimed proudly: "Yesterday I managed to limit myself to seventeen cigarettes that way." But to *Der Stern*'s Henri Nannen he admitted, with a mischievous smile, that he keeps a spare pack in his desk drawer "for emergencies". In fact, during his visit to Bonn, Brezhnev was seen fumbling frequently with his case and then, in desperation, borrowing cigarettes from whatever aide was nearest to him. Told that

Brandt had quit smoking entirely and as a result had gained weight noticeably, Brezhnev sighed knowingly and said: "Yes, yes. That's my trouble, too. I sit at my desk all day and if I don't smoke I have to contend with my appetite. 'Go away,' I say, but Comrade Appetite just won't go away."

Brezhnev likes to be known as a family man and, on the whole, he really is. He and Viktoria Petrovna, a motherly looking woman who stays out of the limelight and appeared bewildered when a herd of journalists, photographers and cameramen closed in on her and Patricia Nixon in May 1972, have been married more than forty years. Reputedly her influence on him has been enormous. Even when younger she was probably never a very striking woman physically but she is reported to have come from a bourgeois family and set standards in the Brezhnev household that went far beyond those of his own proletarian upbringing. Her tastes in furnishings, it is said, reflect her background and over the years she has inspired Brezhnev to emulate her. He is reported, for example, to have a fine collection of antique clocks, many of which he has restored himself.

For half of their married life they have lived in the same apartment house – reserved for high-ranking party functionaries. By Moscow standards it is a posh neighborhood. But it is noisy, for Kutuzovski Prospekt, which begins at the Moskva River at the foot of the steel-and-glass Comecon skyscraper and the wedding-cake Ukraina Hotel, is the main road to Smolensk, Minsk and Poland. Truck traffic rumbles along it in a deafening roar from about six in the morning until late in the evening.

The Brezhnevs share their apartment – three bedrooms, a living room, his study and a kitchen – with a great dane whom a bodyguard takes for daily walks on the avenue; a fluffy Siberian husky; and Brezhnev's mother Natasha who, at eighty-six he says proudly, "is still very active on her feet, reads the newspapers, watches television avidly and knits." Until she married in 1972, grand-daughter Viktoria, Galina's child, lived there, too. Now young Viktoria is herself a mother and Brezhnev the proud great-grandfather of a little baby girl named Galina. Shortly before going to the US in June 1973 he and his wife, the baby in a pram before them, posed willingly on a Moscow park bench for Soviet photographers.

Brezhnev's closest personal friend is reported to be a former Dnepropetrovsk circus director. The others are his two neighbors, Yuri Andropov and Nikolai Shchelokov, who drop in unannounced, and his political cronies – the "mafia" men from the Dnieper Bend. "Auntie" Natasha has known some of them since they were kids and fellow students of her "Lonya", as she and his pals call Brezhnev.

When all of them have time, which Brezhnev laments is rarely, then there are cook-ins on Kutuzovski Prospekt with the chief reportedly doing the honors as chef in the kitchen and plenty of heavy drinking in the Russian manner.

It would be an idyllic picture of upper-middle-class Soviet life were it not marred by the problems of so many upper-middle-class *apparatchik* families: the un-Soviet-like airs of the children.

Next to affairs of State and Party, Galina has been Brezhnev's greatest problem. Her penchant for men from the circus and her romantic escapades were the primary reason why her daughter Viktoria lived not with her but with Brezhnev. Galina, her friends and acquaintances in Moscow and at Novosti Press Agency, where she works, would be the first to say, is bright, talented and in her own plump way attractive. But motherhood is not her thing.

By comparison her brother Yuri, 40, is a paragon of good behavior. A metallurgical engineer like his father, he has worked for many years for V/C Promsyrioimport, a subsidiary of the ministry of foreign trade, which specializes in importing raw materials. He is now its managing director. His wife Ludmilla is two years younger than he and they have two sons, Leonid who is 16, and Andrei, 11. Yuri has seen a bit of the world. He and his family spent three years in Stockholm where he was attached to the Soviet trade mission. He has been on numerous business trips abroad, including visits to Austria, England, Japan and France. On a recent visit to Paris, in January 1972, he made news on his own by going to the Crazy Horse Saloon, the French capital's best-known and most expensive strip-tease club, and allegedly paying the head waiter a $100 tip. Some West German newspapers reported the episode, saying that Yuri had been in the company of five strip-tease girls and been uproariously drunk. Yuri does drink, but his behavior that evening was proper and there were no girls at all: only four other Soviet trade officials. Brezhnev is neither a prude nor a teetotaller but the embarrassing headlines and the publicity about Yuri's extracurricular activities in Paris must have produced quite a row at home.

Brezhnev's paternal anger might be understandable, but is it justified? The issue is not only one of like father like son but the fact that Yuri – like the offspring of all high-ranking *apparatchiki* – was raised in an environment that affronts puritan Communist sensibilities. The fact is that Brezhnev arrogates privileges for himself which the average Soviet citizen would never dream of and which violate the pronounced standards of Communist frugality. But it has always been that way. Even in Lenin's time membership of the Communist Party was equivalent to a meal ticket and a party card was appropriately called a "bread card". Leonid Brezhnev has been a member of the elite since 1931 and now he is at its apex. Government dachas and limousines for his private use, servants, Black Sea vacation villas and, above all, the right to buy in special Central Committee and Kremlin stores where premium Soviet-made and the finest imported merchandise is available at cost and below – these have been his privileges for nearly two decades. He takes them for granted. Though he also denies them. To questions about his reputed elegance he told one reporter in Bonn: "That's not true. I don't even own a decent winter coat. Not only that, for our parade on 7 November my wife sewed a Persian fur collar on my old coat so I wouldn't freeze."

If Brezhnev even has a salary, then it is probably not more than 1,000 rubles ($1,350) per month – less than what he was earning as a lieutenant general – which is approximately eight times the average monthly wage (122 rubles) of a skilled industrial or white collar worker. But salary is not the issue, for like all other members of the Politburo and the Secretariat, Brezhnev is entitled to an "open account" at the State Bank from which he may draw and spend as much as he wishes, for anything he pleases.

Naturally he has a flat-roofed, California-style bungalow with fireplace, swimming pool and patio in the Politburo compound at Kolchuga, a village about eighteen miles west of the center of Moscow. A restricted area, it is surrounded, like most of the dachas of the elite, by a ten-foot-high wooden fence and a small army of grim-looking uniformed police and security men who guard the access roads. By American or West European standards it would not be regarded as luxurious – at the most upper-middle class. But by Soviet criteria it is opulent. So, incidentally, is Brezhnev's Kutuzovski Avenue apartment. Not that five-room apartments are all that uncommon in Moscow. But most of those that do exist are inhabited by five *families* – one family to each room, all five sharing the single kitchen and bath. In fact, more than 30 percent of Moscow's population still lives in such "communal apartments".

His fleet of automobiles is legendary but in addition to those he has a whole park of Kremlin and Central Committee limousines, including foreign-made ones, from which to choose. And what was it he told Willy Brandt? Oh yes, he has another, bigger yacht than the one on which they cruised off Oreanda.

The fact that a Kremlin physician measures the water temperature before Brezhnev takes a dip in the Black Sea may seem like official solicitude for the leader's health, but whatever the motivation, by now Brezhnev no doubt considers it the most natural thing in the world.

The fact is that Communism in the Soviet Union has given birth to a new upper class which enjoys and guards its privileges just as jealously as the old one. It is very much an hierarchical system in which each step up the ladder brings with it greater and additional perquisites.

It is inconceivable that Brezhnev has any notion of the crowded communal flats, the persistent shortages, the endless queues, the shoddy workmanship, the battles with bureaucracy, the collectivized vacation resorts and medical care or the drabness bordering on poverty which are the bane of most of his 250 million subjects.

As one iconoclastic but idealistic Soviet journalist once told me: "The men in the Politburo as well as the *apparatchiki* on several power echelons below them are more isolated from the people of this country than were any of the tsars and *boyars*. Even at the local level officials are entitled to enormous perquisites and haven't the faintest notion how the rest of the country really lives."

What does Brezhnev do with his privileges? He is neither an intellectual nor culturally inclined – despite Viktoria's reputed efforts over the years to broaden his interests. There was an audible sigh when he told a French interviewer that his visits to the Bolshoi Theater are official. "I see Swan Lake a good ten times a year," he said. Brezhnev prefers cowboy movies.

Though a full-time politician for nearly forty years, Brezhnev still has an engineer's heart and he likes technical things. The intricate push-button and telephone panel sunk into the top of his Kremlin office desk, heatable swimming pools, automatically operated sliding doors – those are the things he shows visitors with pride.

He is unquestionably a car enthusiast. Brezhnev would, if he could, drive himself about Moscow. But protocol and security precautions prohibit it most of the time. Thus he makes up for it when he goes to the countryside. He loves the technique and the mechanics of driving. As he told *L'Humanité*'s Durand: "When I am driving I relax, I recuperate from all the cares and I have the impression that nothing can go wrong." Well, almost nothing. When the Bonn Government presented him with a $12,000 Mercedes-450 sports coupé Brezhnev settled behind the wheel, slammed the door shut and, leaving his bewildered bodyguards aghast, sped down the serpentine road from the Petersberg Hotel to the Rhine at top speed, hit a pothole and tore open the oil pan. But then, he had not liked the car's color – silver gray – in the first place and officials of the company promptly agreed to replace it – in steel blue.

Brezhnev is a man's man with male tastes – all of them. Soccer is his favorite sport. Rumor has it that in 1970 Moscow television purchased the rights for live showing of the world soccer championships in Mexico at Brezhnev's behest. And no doubt he groaned with the rest of the country when Uruguay eliminated the Soviet team on a fluke goal. In Moscow games have been held up for as long as twenty minutes so that Brezhnev, late and preoccupied with state or party affairs, can watch the kick-off from his private box.

Brezhnev is more than a sedentary spectator, however: he participates. He has boasted that before World War Two he won a parachutist's diploma and lamented that he no longer has time to jump. The security regulations may also preclude it, even if his physicians were to approve. In the summer he bicycles and he is an enthusiastic swimmer. In the winter, like almost all Russians, he ice skates and goes cross-country skiing – presumably in the lovely woods around his Kolchuga dacha.

But the sport about which he is most enthusiastic, and on which he will speak endlessly when someone gets him started, is hunting. He claims to have shot everything from hares around Moscow to bears in Kazakhstan. His favorite area is at Savidovo, on the so-called Moscow Sea – an artificial reservoir created by the construction of the Moscow-Volga canal, about eighty miles northeast of Moscow. There the Politburo maintains a private 140-square-mile game preserve with hunting lodges – within sight of a special vacation encampment reserved for foreign diplomats and correspondents. One day there, Brezhnev has never failed to boast to visitors, he shot six boars. For all his talk about what he has shot, however, Brezhnev also claims to be a conservationist. Prodded by a friendly foreign visitor, he will launch into lengthy dissertations about the need to protect wild life and the environment and what has already been accomplished.

Although there have been persistent rumors about Brezhnev's health, he insists it is perfect and most of the time he looks it. If he has had a heart attack, he denies it and has stated emphatically that the only medicine he has ever taken were sleeping pills: he suffers from insomnia.

"You know," he told Durand, "when one has worked all day long, the problems that face you during the day continue to spin in your head at night. And there are problems in a country as big as ours. When the people in the south are demanding summer clothing we have to supply fur-lined boots to the north. There are the little and the big things. Industry and agriculture. There are ups and downs. All of them reach us and we have to occupy ourselves with them and find solutions. Foreign policy too requires a lot of work. We want peace in the world, but it seems that everyone does not always agree with us."

One cannot help speculating about whether sometimes Leonid Brezhnev lies awake at night wondering how history will judge him and his stewardship, especially compared with that of Khrushchev.

They have much in common. Khrushchev was a man of limited formal education; Brezhnev's has been narrowly technical. Both found their teacher in the Communist Party. The Party provided both of them with a view of the world that confirmed their own experience. Its simple tenets are to be found in the speeches of both men: capitalism is a system of exploitation whose days are numbered; Communism represents the wave of the future because it is a superior social and economic system that frees the masses from exploitation and promotes the well-being and happiness of all mankind; the Communist Party, which led the working class of old Russia to victory, provides a pattern of organization and leadership which alone can guarantee the triumph of Communism on a world scale. For Khrushchev these propositions were sacred and unassailable, Are they also for Brezhnev?

As one of Stalin's lieutenants, Khrushchev was chained to a jealous master who demanded unquestioning obedience and obsequiousness from all who served him. Brezhnev, too, served Stalin obediently and then Khrushchev who was equally jealous and also demanded obedience and servility. The evidence to hand shows that Khrushchev chafed under the restrictions imposed by Stalin, but at the same time no one could match him in fulsome tributes to his mentor and no one was more zealous in defending Stalin's course. Brezhnev in turn chafed under Khrushchev, yet few could match him in tributes to his mentor and few were more zealous in defending Khrushchev's course.

Khrushchev's administrative assignments under Stalin were largely confined to the party apparatus. Though his responsibilities mounted they were largely party-centered. The same can be said of Brezhnev under Khrushchev. Both had experience, before they came to power, which was narrowly provincial, Khrushchev albeit more than Brezhnev.

As the power and prestige of both men grew, the range of their interests broadened and they began to place their own personal stamps on foreign as well as domestic policies. There, however, the similarities cease.

Khrushchev had vision. He believed in ideas and in the

development of ideas. True, his style was characterized by opportunism. But he was also bold, willing to experiment and to strike out in new directions, though he did not always calculate the costs and the consequences. Leonid Brezhnev, no matter how charming or personable he may have turned out to be once he emerged from the shadow of Khrushchev's personality, has no vision. He is not absorbed by ideas, theories or dialectics.

Khrushchev's visions may not always have been realistic or practicable, but he undeniably had a sense of historical purpose and stimulated articulate ideas about the Soviet Union's road to the future. Brezhnev not only scrapped almost the entire edifice of Khrushchev's vision but has turned out to be unconcerned or unable to suggest any new concept of social development. The old Marxist-Leninist tenets and dogmas have been kept alive, to be sure, but he has presented no statement of purpose or any concept about the future of Communism in the USSR itself.

Leonid Brezhnev is a conservative. His only aim, thus far, has been to preserve the *status quo*.

There was never more obvious proof of this than his role in the Czechoslovak crisis of 1968. The suppression of the "Prague Spring" and the Invasion undoubtedly represent the darkest epoch in Brezhnev's career. He was simply incapable of dealing peacefully and constructively with the challenge posed by Alexander Dubcek's "Communism with a human face."

It was not his only failure.

Brezhnev began his term as party leader by reshaping Soviet agricultural policy. His reforms have brought tangible improvements to the peasants, but few to the consumers. As the 1972 harvest fiasco revealed, Soviet agriculture is not crisis-proof. For all the money and effort he has poured into the farm sector, it remains crippled by under-mechanization, excessive bureaucracy and general managerial bungling. Brezhnev's Soviet Union has passed the threshold from want to sufficiency, but it is still decades removed from affluence.

Economic reform is dead – a victim of internecine party-government strife and the legacy of Stalin. With it the only hopes for genuine economic progress have also been buried. In desperation, Brezhnev resorted at first to draconian measures, but then turned quickly to the carrot of more consumer goods. Both these approaches failed, too, for they were in essence stop-gaps that did not meet the real nature of the economic dilemma, namely that the system provides no incentives and stifles initiative. As a consequence the state of the economy ranges between hapless and chaotic, leaving the Soviet Union even further behind in the race to catch up with the United States, Western Europe or Japan than it was when Khrushchev fell.

The technological gap *vis-à-vis* the industrialized nations of the West has widened. Brezhnev's only remedy thus far has been to purchase more technology abroad, failing to appreciate that by the time it is operable or applied, it is already out of date.

For all his efforts to cement the cracks, the Communist world seems even less whole today than it did in 1964. Above all, what was politely called the Sino-Soviet rift in Khrushchev's day turned into open warfare on the border under Brezhnev. The confrontation has continued and it has placed Brezhnev in a position of weakness in suing for peace and understanding with the West. He could have fared worse, for the West did not exact a price. But someone else may yet present a bill: the restive people of Eastern Europe and the Soviet Union's own minorities may recognize in China the tail with which to wag the Soviet dog.

Brezhnev has never been really anti-Semitic, as far as we know. On the contrary, the record shows that as long ago as his childhood in Kamenskoye he was at least equivocal, and there have been hints that he may be philo-Semitic – at least by Russian standards. But this does not alter the fact that he has pursued a policy at home and abroad which, whatever its motivations, has alienated world Jewry from the Soviet Union.

When history finally assesses him, his achievements will appear primarily in the field of foreign affairs. In that area Brezhnev comes closest to what might be called vision.

Having established the principle of Soviet hegemony over the East European empire through the invasion of Czechoslovakia, Brezhnev now appears set on improving relations with the West.

To call it a "grand design" might be overstating the case. But there is clearly a long-term line.

Stated in the simplest terms, it calls for reducing his military obligation and pressures in Europe and the West in order to concentrate on what has become Russia's foreign-policy concern Number One – China. Moreover, he hopes through trade and improved relations to gain access to Western money, know-how and industrial potential.

In this sphere he tends to think many years ahead. During his trips to Bonn and Washington in 1973 he frequently reiterated his concept that long-term trade agreements and co-operative ventures are the best possible guarantees for long-term peaceful co-existence.

After years of cold war Brezhnev has obtained American acquiescence to the principle of strategic parity and West Germany's recognition of the postwar European *status quo*. Willy Brandt – and to a lesser degree Richard Nixon – helped him in both. The full story of his own role in achieving a ceasefire in Indochina – undoubtedly one of the keys to the changed world situation of the 1970s – has yet to be told.

He has placed a more mature, more self-assured Soviet Union on the international stage. He is not the type of man who would bang his shoe on the desk at the United Nations. But he has also created a situation in which shoe-banging is no longer necessary for the Soviet Union to gain attention. He has come closer to fulfilling an ancient dream of Russian and Soviet leaders: Moscow is now a power which no other nation can ignore.

That is, in itself, a major accomplishment. But it is not enough.

History will also record Brezhnev's greatest transgression: placing the ghost of Stalin in the niche left by Khrushchev's fall.

Khrushchev, whatever his motivations, at least held out the *hope* of a society in which citizens might breathe more freely, officials could exercise initiative without fearing the consequences, the bond between Party and people might be strengthened and the authority of the regime might, some day, be based on legality and confidence, rather than fear.

Brezhnev destroyed that hope. On 21 June 1970, almost nine years after the body had been removed from the

Lenin Mausoleum, a ten-foot bust of Stalin was unveiled over the dead dictator's grave by the Kremlin wall. One year after that Khrushchev died. *His* body was relegated to an obscure corner of Novodevichy cemetery. Both acts were symbolic.

Culturally, intellectually and in terms of human freedom, the USSR has regressed under Brezhnev's rule. The limited freedom of discussion which prevailed until Khrushchev's fall has virtually disappeared. Much of the secrecy of the Stalin era has been restored. This was bound to engender protest and dissent to which Brezhnev's only response has been repression.

Under Khrushchev the labor camp gates opened and the prisons emptied. Brezhnev is no Stalin, of course, and instead of terror he has relied largely on the threat of terror. But under him a tentative thaw has turned to a new freeze. The prisons have begun to fill again and the camp gates are once more being slammed shut on desperate thousands whose only crime has been to speak their own minds. Brezhnev has but one prescription for the Soviet Union's intellectual malaise: more vigilance against foreign influences and more ideological discipline. The Soviet Union he will leave behind him will be an infinitely sadder country than the one he found upon becoming its ruler.

The day after Khrushchev fell an American visitor to Moscow reported that his Intourist guide's eyes were red from many hours of crying. Khrushchev, she explained to him, had been responsible for the release of her family from a Stalin-era prison camp in the mid-1950s.

But who will cry when Leonid Ilyich Brezhnev passes from the political stage?

Bibliography and Sources

General works:

Adams, Arthur E., *Bolsheviks in the Ukraine*, Yale University Press, New Haven, Conn., 1963

Alliluyeva, Svetlana, *Twenty Letters to a Friend*, Hutchinson, London, 1967; Harper and Row, New York, 1967

Armstrong, John A., *The Soviet Bureaucratic Elite*, Stevens & Son, London, 1959; Frederick A. Praeger, New York, 1959

Avtorkhanov, Abdurakhman, *Stalin and the Soviet Communist Party*, Frederick A. Praeger, New York, 1959; Stevens & Son, London, 1960

Bialer, Seweryn, (Ed.) *Stalin and His Generals*, Pegasus, New York, 1969; Souvenir Press, London, 1970

Brezhnev, Leonid I., *Following Lenin's Course*, Moscow, 1970, 1972

Brzezinski, Zbigniew, *The Soviet Bloc*, Harvard University Press, Cambridge, 1967

Carr, Edward H., *The Bolshevik Revolution* 3 Vols., Macmillan, London and New York, 1952

Cash, Anthony, *The Russian Revolution*, Ernest Benn, London, 1967

Conolly, Violet, *Beyond the Urals*, Oxford University Press, London and New York, 1967

Conquest, Robert, *Russia After Khrushchev*, Pall Mall Press, London, 1965; Frederick A. Praeger, New York, 1965

Conquest, Robert, *Power and Policy in the USSR*, Harper & Row, New York, 1967

Conquest, Robert, *The Great Terror*, Macmillan, London, 1968; Rev. Ed. Macmillan, New York, 1973

Deutscher, Isaac, *Stalin*, Oxford University Press, London and New York, 1967; Penguin Books, London, 1970

Dornberg, John, *The Other Germany*, Doubleday, New York, 1968

Dornberg, John, *The New Tsars: Russia Under Stalin's Heirs*, Doubleday, New York, 1972

Fainsod, Merle, *How Russia is Ruled*, Rev. Ed. Harvard University Press, Cambridge, 1967

Fis, Teodor, *Mein Kommandeur General Svoboda*, Europa Verlag, Vienna, 1969

Frankland, Mark, *Khrushchev*, Penguin Books, London, 1966; Stein & Day, New York, 1967

Gray, Ian, *The First Fifty Years*, Hodder and Stoughton, London, 1967

Grechko, Andrei A., *Battle for the Caucasus*, Moscow, 1970; Central Books, London, 1971

Grechko, Andrei A., *Through the Carpathians*, Moscow, 1971

Grushevoi, Konstantin S., *Back in the Forty-first Year*, Moscow, 1972

Kellen, Konrad, *Khrushchev, A Political Portrait*, Thames & Hudson, London, 1961; Frederick A. Praeger, New York, 1961

Khrushchev, Nikita S., *Khrushchev Remembers*, André Deutsch, London, 1971; Little, Brown, Boston, 1971

Kohler, Foy D., *Understanding the Russians*, Harper & Row, New York, 1970

Kostiuk, Hryhory, *Stalinist Rule in the Ukraine*, Stevens and Son, London, 1960; Frederick A. Praeger, New York, 1960

Kravchenko, Viktor, *I Chose Freedom*, Robert Hale, London, 1961

Leonhard, Wolfgang, *The Kremlin Without Stalin*, Oxford University Press, London, 1962; Frederick A. Praeger, New York, 1962

Leonhard, Wolfgang, *Nikita Sergejewitsch Chruschtschow*, C. J. Bucher Verlag, Zurich, 1965

Lewytzkij, Borys, *Die Rote Inquisition*, Societaets Verlag, Frankfurt, 1967

Macduffie, Marshall, *The Red Carpet*, Cassell, London, 1955; W. W. Norton, New York, 1955

Manning, Clarence A., *Ukraine Under the Soviets*, Bookman Associates, New York, 1953

Manstein, Erich von, *Verlorene Siege*, Athenaeum Verlag, Bonn, 1955; *Lost Victories*, translated by A. G. Powell, Methuen, London, 1958

Medvedev, Roy A., *Let History Judge*, Macmillan, London, 1972; Alfred A. Knopf, New York, 1972

Page, Michael, *The Day Khrushchev Fell*, Hawthorn, New York, 1965

Pethybridge, R. W., *A History of Postwar Russia*, Allen and Unwin, London, 1966; New American Library, New York, 1966

Pidhainy, S. O. (Ed.) *The Black Deeds of the Kremlin, A White Book*, Vol. I, The Basilian Press, Toronto, 1953; Vol. II, Globe Press, Detroit, 1955

Pirker, Theo (Ed.), *Die Moskauer Schauprozesse, 1936–39*, Deutscher Taschenbuchverlag, Munich, 1963

Pistrak, Lazar, *The Grand Tactician*, Thames & Hudson, London, 1961; Frederick A. Praeger, New York, 1961

Schapiro, Leonard, *The Communist Party of the Soviet Union*, Eyre & Spottiswoode, London, 1959; Random House, New York, 1971

Schwartz, Harry, *The Red Phoenix*, Frederick A. Praeger, New York, 1961

Shawcross, William, *Dubcek*, Weidenfeld & Nicolson, London, 1970; Simon & Shcuster, New York, 1971

Shtemenko, Sergei M., *The Soviet General Staff at War*, Moscow, 1969; Central Books, London, 1971

Shub, Anatole, *An Empire Loses Hope*, W. W. Norton, New York, 1970; Jonathan Cape, London, 1971

Sullivant, Robert S., *Soviet Politics and the Ukraine*, Columbia University Press, New York, 1962

Tatu, Michael, *Power in the Kremlin*, Collins, London, 1969; Viking Press, New York, 1969

Tigrid, Pavel, *Why Dubcek Fell*, Macdonald, London, 1971

Vladimirov, Leonid, *The Russian Space Bluff*, Tom Stacey, London, 1971

Weit, Erwin, *Ostblock Intern*, Hoffman und Campe, Hamburg, 1970; *Eyewitness: The Autobiography of Gomulka's Interpreter*, translated by Mary Schofield, Macmillan, New York, 1972; André Deutsch, London, 1973

Reference Books

The Large Soviet Encyclopedia, 3rd Edition, Moscow, Vols. I–IX.

Prominent Personalities in the USSR, Pub. Institute for the Study of the USSR, Munich, Eds: Edward L. Crowley, Andrew I. Lebed, Dr. Heinrich E. Schulz, Scarecrow Press, Metuchen, N.J., 1968

The Small Soviet Encyclopedia, 3rd Edition, Moscow

Das Sowjetische Establishment, Michael Morozow, Seewald Verlag, Stuttgart, 1971

Sowjetische Kurzbiographien, Borys Lewytzkij and Kurt Mueller, Verlag fuer Literatur und Zeigeschehen, Hannover, 1964

Yearbooks of the Large Soviet Encyclopedia, 1959–1970, Moscow

Newspapers and Magazines

Current Digest of the Soviet Press, Vol. 1949–1972
Current History, Vol. 1952–1965
Foreign Affairs, Vol. 1922–1972
Harpers Magazine, April 1965
Izvestia, Moscow, Vol. 1950–1956
Kazakhstanskaya Pravda, Alma Ata, Vol. 1954–1956
New Times, Moscow, Vol. 1970–1972
New Leader, Vol. 1956–1957
Newsweek, Vol. 1964–1970
New York Times, Vol. 1921–1972
Ost-Europa, 1953–1970
Ost-Probleme, Vol. 1952–1953
Pravda, Moscow, Vol. 1931–1941; 1946–1972

Problems of Communism, Vol. 1953–1972
The Reporter, Vol. 1956–1964
Slavic Review, Vol. 1970
Soviet Studies, Vol. 1967
Der Spiegel, Vol. 1970–1972
Time, Vol. 1964, 1968
The Ukrainian Quarterly, Vol. 1944–1972

As well as:

Dagens Nyheter
Frankfurter Allgemeine Zeitung
L'Humanité
Neue Zuercher Zeitung
Sueddeutsche Zeitung
Washington Post

Glossary of Abbreviations
and Important Terms

ALLY: a party official who has struck a political association with another, usually more powerful figure and who is generally loyal to him and can be expected to support him and his policies, but not to the degree a client would.

apparatchik: full time Communist Party worker, government bureaucrat, who makes his career within the Party, sometimes the government apparatus.

CENTRAL COMMITTEE: (CC) highest organ of the Party between Party Congresses which elect its members. Present size, constituted at the XXIVth Party Congress in April 1971: 241 full (voting) and 155 alternate (sometimes referred to as candidate) members who do not have a vote. Occasionally likened to a party parliament, it is composed of top professional party functionaries, government officials, provincial and republican *apparatchiks* as well as a scattering of "worker", "peasant" and "intellectual" representatives who are elected more for show than for any real political weight they carry. All the constitutent republic party organizations also have central committees. At the province, district and city level they are referred to simply as "party committees". The CC elects a Political Bureau (Politburo) and a Secretariat of which the first secretary or secretary-general is *de facto* chief of the Party. By party statute the CC is required to convene in plenary session at least twice yearly. Each of the secretaries (at present there are 10, of which 7 are also full or candidate members of the Politburo) is responsible for a special area of work: heavy industry, agriculture, relations with other Communist Parties, ideology etc. The CC has a vast, full-time administrative apparatus whose department heads rank just below party secretaries in protocol and power.

CHEKA: term for the secret police under its first post-revolutionary chief and organizer, Felix Dzerzhinsky.

CLIENT: a party official whose career has been wholly or almost entirely dependent on the fortunes and patronage of a more powerful functionary and therefore can be expected to be fully loyal to him.

CONFEDERATE: see ally. The association is usually not as close and as interdependent.

COUNCIL OF MINISTERS: the Government of the USSR, headed by a chairman (the prime minister or premier) a number of first deputy and deputy chairmen (prime ministers). Comprises all the ministries, state committees and ministerial-level government departments including the classical departments such as foreign affairs, interior, justice etc. as well as dozens of technical ministries concerned with running the economy of the USSR. The 15 republics of the USSR also have councils of ministers.

CPSU: abbreviation for Communist Party of the Soviet Union.

CPU: abbreviation for Communist Party of the Ukraine

DISTRICT: used in this text to denote a *rayon*, a geographical-political area subordinate, administratively, to a city or *oblast* (province). Comparable, when part of a city administration, to a borough, when part of an *oblast*, to a county. District party committees are the lowest echelon of party administration.

ESOTERICAL: used in this text to describe publications and writing couched in terms usually understandable only to senior party officials and Western experts who specialize in reading between the lines of party literature to search for hidden meanings and debates.

INTER-GERMAN (ZWISCHENDEUTSCHE): used by the East Germans who contend that there are two Germanys divided by a border.

INTRA-GERMAN (INNER-DEUTSCHE): used by the West Germans since it implies that there is only one German state, artificially divided by a "demarcation line".

KGB: Russian abbreviation for Committee for State Security, present term for the secret police. The Committee, like the committees for science and technology, radio and television etc. is equal in status to a ministry.

kolkhoz: collective farm.

kolkhoznik: collective farmer or member of a collective farm.

Komsomol: The Young Communist League, presently comprising 32 million members. Membership is usually from age 14 to 26, though professional organizers and officials are often older.

METAL EATERS: Western expression for the heavy industry, steel, military-industrial interests in the Soviet economy.

milits: militia, actually the uniformed police, presently organized under the ministry of interior. During part of the Khrushchev era it was decentralized, under the control of the republican governments and subordinated to the ministry for public order which was renamed ministry of interior in 1968.

MVD: Russian initials for ministry of interior. Presently in charge of the uniformed police, it was, under Stalin, a term for the secret police.

NKVD: Russian initials for People's Commissariat of Internal Affairs, term for ministry of interior and secret police under Stalin.

obkom: Russian abbreviation for *oblast* committee, expression for the party committee of a province.

oblast: Russian term for a geographical, political, administrative area, alternately referred to in the text as a province. *Oblasts* vary in size, population and importance but Dnepropetrovsk, with more than 12,000 square miles and presently more than three million population, comprising the cities of Dnepropetrovsk, Dneprodzerzhinsk, Nikopol and Krivoy Rog is typical of the more than 100 *oblasts* in the USSR. *Oblasts* and their party and government apparatuses are subordinate to the republican governments and party organizations.

OGPU: Russian abbreviation, former term for the secret police.

PARTY CONGRESS: theoretically the supreme body of the Party, a conclave of delegates, theoretically elected at the grass roots level by local and republican Party Congresses, which in turn elects the central committee and chief party organs. Twenty-four Party Congresses have been held since 1898 when the first congress of the All-Russian Social Democratic Labor Party was held in Minsk. Until 1971, in theory, Party Congresses took place every four years, although Stalin had let 13 years pass between the XVIIIth Congress in 1939 and the XIXth in 1952. In 1971 at the XXIVth Party Congress, the statutes were altered so that congresses would be held every five years to coincide with the introduction of each new five-year plan.

POLITBURO: Russian term for political bureau of the Central Committee: chief executive body of the Party in which full (voting) and candidate (non-voting) members sit in fashion not unlike that of cabinet in Western parliamentary democracies. Full members have equal vote and voice. The CPSU Politburo, presently with 16 members, meets at least once weekly in the Kremlin. Formally it has no chief or chairman, although increasingly Brezhnev is being referred to as head of the Politburo. Republican party administrations also have politburos. *Oblast* party organizations have similar bodies, referred to as the *oblast* party bureau

PRESIDIUM: Term used in place of Politburo from October 1952 to April 1966. Also denotes chief executive body of the Supreme Soviet, the USSR's parliament. The chairman of the Presidium of the Supreme Soviet is the USSR's "president" or chief of state.

PROVINCE: as used in the text, synonymous with *oblast*, a political, geographical, administrative subdivision of the USSR such as Dnepropetrovsk.

pyatiletka: Russian for five-year economic plan period.

rayon: russified French term synonymous with district.

REPUBLIC: political, geographical administrative term for the 15 largest, theoretically independent and autonomous constituent subdivisions of the USSR. Described as Soviet Socialist Republics, the largest of these is the Russian Federation, sometimes referred to as the Russian Republic or Russian Federation. Two of them, the Ukrainian SSR and the Byelorussian SSR are independent members of the United Nations. Also used for the Autonomous Soviet Socialist Republics, ethnic and national subdivisions of the SSRs, usually located on their peripheries.

RSFSR: abbreviation for Russian Soviet Federative Socialist Republic, that is, the Russian Republic.

SECRETARY: senior executive official of the Central Committee, a republic central committee, province or *oblast* party committee, district or *rayon* or city party committee. The first secretary is always the chief of the party organization at the respective level, interchangeably referred to in the text as "party chief". There is only one secretary-general in the USSR, Brezhnev.

soviet: Russian term for council. The Supreme Soviet, or Supreme Council is the parliament of the USSR. Each republic also has a Supreme Soviet. Also used as an adjectival term referring to the USSR, its leaders, government, economy, culture, policies etc.

sovkhoz: abbreviated term for state farm, which differs from a *kolkhoz* in that instead of members it employs farm laborers on a wage basis.

sovnarkhoz: abbreviated term for regional economic council, an economic-administrative establishment of the Khrushchev era.

YOUNG PIONEERS: Communist children's organization in the USSR. Members are 10 to 14 years old.

Index